Critical Studies in Gender, Sexuality, and Culture

Series Editors

Danielle Egan
St. Lawrence University
Canton, New York, USA

Patricia Clough
Queens College and The Graduate Center
City University of New York
New York, New York, USA

Highlighting the work taking place at the crossroads of sociology, sexuality studies, gender studies, cultural studies, and performance studies, this series offers a platform for scholars pushing the boundaries of gender and sexuality studies substantively, theoretically, and stylistically. The authors draw on insights from diverse scholarship and research in popular culture, ethnography, history, cinema, religion, performance, new media studies, and technoscience studies to render visible the complex manner in which gender and sexuality intersect and can, at times, create tensions and fissures between one another. Encouraging breadth in terms of both scope and theme, the series editors seek works that explore the multifaceted domain of gender and sexuality in a manner that challenges the taken-for-granted. On one hand, the series foregrounds the pleasure, pain, politics, and aesthetics at the nexus of sexual practice and gendered expression. On the other, it explores new sites for the expression of gender and sexuality, the new geographies of intimacy being constituted at both the local and global scales.

More information about this series at
http://www.springer.com/series/14939

Hosu Kim

Birth Mothers and Transnational Adoption Practice in South Korea

Virtual Mothering

Hosu Kim
City University of New York
College of Staten Island,
Staten Island, NY, USA

Critical Studies in Gender, Sexuality, and Culture
ISBN 978-1-137-53851-2 (hardcover)   ISBN 978-1-137-53852-9 (eBook)
ISBN 978-1-349-71151-2 (softcover)
DOI 10.1057/978-1-137-53852-9

Library of Congress Control Number: 2016949416

© The Editor(s) (if applicable) and The Author(s) 2016, First softcover printing 2018
This work is subject to copyright. All rights are solely and exclusively licensed by the Publisher, whether the whole or part of the material is concerned, specifically the rights of translation, reprinting, reuse of illustrations, recitation, broadcasting, reproduction on microfilms or in any other physical way, and transmission or information storage and retrieval, electronic adaptation, computer software, or by similar or dissimilar methodology now known or hereafter developed.
The use of general descriptive names, registered names, trademarks, service marks, etc. in this publication does not imply, even in the absence of a specific statement, that such names are exempt from the relevant protective laws and regulations and therefore free for general use.
The publisher, the authors and the editors are safe to assume that the advice and information in this book are believed to be true and accurate at the date of publication. Neither the publisher nor the authors or the editors give a warranty, express or implied, with respect to the material contained herein or for any errors or omissions that may have been made.

Cover illustration: © Jane Jin Kaisen

Printed on acid-free paper

This Palgrave Macmillan imprint is published by Springer Nature
The registered company is Nature America Inc. New York

Acknowledgments

Writing this book has made me realize how my life has been so nourished and enriched by the attentive and generous supports of friends and family. During this book's long gestation period, my feelings of fear, self-doubt, and despair sometimes arrested my passions and paralyzed my conviction about this project. At those moments, the care, support, and belief in me that I received from friends and family, and from various communities of which I have been a part, were vital sources of energy that sustained my journey. It is my great pleasure to finally write an acknowledgment recognizing the immense care that I have received from others over the past 15 years, from the conception to the delivery of this book.

Foremost, this book would not have been possible without the birth mothers' willingness to re-visit painful memories of separations from their children, and their trust in the project. When I was collecting their oral histories, birth mothers shared not only their life stories, but always made sure to feed me. Shin Young Eun and "Jaewon" showed me the personal journals they kept at the time of adoption. After depositing their adoption stories in me, they often suggested that we go to a *zzimjil bang* (public sauna) together. Though I wasn't able to follow up on their invitations, I really appreciated their openness and warmth. Looking back, what drove me not to give up on this book was the promise I made with, Jang Yeon Ja, a birth mother, in 2005. At the end of the interview, she asked what I would do with her stories. I told her, "Your life stories will become part of my doctoral dissertation research, it will probably be in a book on birth mothers." She responded, "Please finish your degree—then, you will be the first person I know with a PhD." Until this time, my promise with her was only half fulfilled. So, this book is the other half of my promise. I hope my book will help to bring some justice to the 60-year-long silent history of Korean birth mothers.

There is a long list of people I wish to acknowledge. To start, I wish to express my gratitude to my dissertation committee: Patricia Ticineto Clough, Hester Eisenstein, and Barbara Katz Rothman. As my former dissertation advisor and mentor, Patricia guides and inspires me with her own unconventional path as a sociologist; learning from Patricia has been an amazing joy and ecstasy. Her provocatively transdisciplinary endeavors—encompassing psychoanalysis, science/technology studies, and performance studies—have shaped my intellectual foundation and trajectories, and her embrace and encouragement of experimental writing has freed me, to a certain extent, from a canonical mastery of the American academic language, and helped me to engage in more fundamental questions of language and power. Finally, her sharp critique of sociological methods and her enthusiasm for new frames of analysis have allowed me to explore performance-based hermeneutics and praxis-oriented knowledge production. Early in my graduate studies, I experienced a difficult adjustment and took a one-year leave of absence, moving back to Korea. During that period, when I doubted my capacity to continue graduate school, Barbara Katz Rothman (later to serve on my dissertation committee) mailed me postcards of the Brooklyn Botanical Garden and of the Brooklyn Bridge that helped me to hold onto my aspirations, and I finally moved back and continued the program. And, finally, thanks to Hester Eisenstein, a bona fide feminist scholar, who generously helped me to secure multiple research assistantships and provided me with much-needed opportunities to work as a graduate student; she also guided me with her keen power analysis of how mainstream feminism had appropriated women's lives in the Global South.

This book would not have been possible without two friends, Grace M. Cho and Rose M. Kim, whom I met at the Graduate Center, CUNY. Grace, you taught me the ropes of academia, an institution for which I had a difficult time developing a sense of affinity and of belongingness. You have been a rock for me, particularly in times of difficulties. Our 15-year-long friendship has produced two co-authored articles. Collaborating with you always extends my purview of research and bolsters my development as a rigorous scholar. Grace, I really thank you for your loyal friendship and the care that you have given me, as I was writing this book. Now, it is my turn.

My dear friend, Rose, whom I secretly regard as a mentor, has provided me an exceptional quality of support and care. Her perky, eccentric, artistic temperament, which I attribute to her writerly craze, allowed me to have a sense of freedom and pure joy in her companionship. She read multiple drafts of this book at various stages; during the final stage of writing this book, she visited my home twice to offer much-needed support and to help edit this book. She took on tensions and nervousness I was feeling, so that I could work calmly; with her presence, the final stage of writing and preparing the manuscript moved along swiftly. Her incredible ability to share and to give will remain with me for a long time.

This book reflects the cherished lessons and visions that I have gleaned from my encounters with Nodutdol, a progressive community organization, based in New York City. During my 15-year-long involvement with this multi-generational, Korean diasporic community for peace and justice, I have been inspired by its incisive political analysis, and empowered by its bold vision for social justice. Though my writing has encroached on and taken over my time at Nodutdol over the past few years, the sense of camaraderie I received from Nodutdol is vital to my life, and helped to carry this book forward. I would like to thank Seung Hye Suh for her visionary leadership of the organization in its initial stages; Hyun Lee, Yulsan Liem, Juyeon Rhee, and J.T. Takagi, for their unwavering commitment to racial and economic justice and their selflessness; Sukjong Hong, for her extraordinary creativity at turning artful the spaces and culture of the organization; Kisuk Yom, for her love and generosity, shown through almost a hundred free meals and drinks during my graduate school years. Furthermore, my gratitude goes to Young Choe, Injoo Hwang, Sharon Chung, and Betsy Yoon. The inspiration and support I received from friends only prove my words too brief; please know your fierce and firm dedication to peace and social justice work always impress me as a sound understanding of life's priorities, and humble me.

Through my involvement in community activism, I gained experience as a performance artist, by participating in *Still Present Pasts* (2005–2010), a multi-media exhibit on memories and legacies of the Korean War. Ramsay Liem, in collaboration with activists, artists, and scholars, opened up and realized the radical possibilities of oral history as a crucial site for re-engaging memory and re-staging history. Through my participation, I was given the opportunity to ruminate on the Korean War and its living legacy. His innovative endeavors of bridging oral history with art, and his conviction in the peace movement set an exemplary example for me, as

I developed an oral history collection with birth mothers, and sought to analyze the performative narratives within the context of the unending, ongoing Korean War.

I am greatly indebted to scholars, activists, and social workers in the South Korean transnational adoption community. From the early stages of this project, Tobias Hübinette and Eleana Kim, both of whose analyses have been crucial to this book's formation, were invaluable. I thank Tobias for his prompt responses and helpful information in response to my numerous email questions; and, Eleana for her generous reading of my work at various stages, and her supportive critiques of the manuscript. For her help in developing the oral history collection of birth mothers, I thank Jane Jeong Trenka, an adoptee activist, who helped to recruit birth mother participants, and who traveled with me, several times, to introduce them to me. And, to Reverend Kim Do Hyun, thank you for offering organizational support in producing transcriptions of the oral history interviews. My gratitude goes to the anonymous volunteers, as well as to Choi Hee Sun, for the transcriptions. During the data collection process in Korea, I appreciated the help of Yu Yŏng Im, the director of *Durebang*, U Sun Tŏk from *Haessal Sahoepokchihoe* (Sunlit Sisters' Center), and Jang Bo Kyung and Shin Hee Suk from Esther's Place.

In addition, many adoptees, young and old, whom I met over the course of this project's development, expressed great enthusiasm and appreciation for my research and generously shared their personal experiences as adopted people. I appreciate Daniëlle Van Oostrom, Kim Park Nelson, and Deann Borshay Liem for their friendship and for their support of my work. Their enthusiastic responses and empathic curiosity about the senders' perspective became a rich soil for this project to grow.

At various stages of writing this book, my writing group offered me timely and practical advice, helping me to move forward on the book, despite my tendency to hold on to a project. I thank Rafael de la Dehesa for his insightful mind, deftly capturing the underlying organization of my writing and helping me to clarify my thesis. Jean Halley's affectively cued up advice and firm belief for my project has always enlivened my passion, so that I could go another round. And, Francesca Degiuli helped me to engage questions from audiences unfamiliar with transnational adoption and/or Korea.

My thanks extend to my colleagues/friends at the Department of Sociology and Anthropology at the College of Staten Island, CUNY. At times when I was engaged in intense writing, many volunteered to cover my service work duties and other responsibilities so that I was able to secure time for writing. For their support, I thank Jay Arena, Leigh Binford, Roz Bologh, Grace M. Cho, Ismale García Colón, Kate Crehan, Rafael de la Dehesa, Ozlem Goner, Jean Halley, Saddia Toor, Don Selby, and Tom Volscho. Particularly, I thank Jeff Bussolini for intellectually stimulating conversations on the X 10 bus rides to Staten Island. And thanks to my friend, Ananya Mukherjea, who taught me how compassion and empathy are integral ingredients in our lives. I feel very fortunate to be part of an academic department in which a mutual sense of respect, collegiality, and trust is practiced, thus creating a supportive, nurturing learning and teaching community.

There are a few more individual scholars and friends that I need to mention for their support. I thank Laura Fantone and Ji Young Yoo for their companionship and encouragement. Sung Hee Yook has been a special friend that I have cherished throughout graduate school and even after she moved back to Korea. During my 2008–2009 visiting professorship at Drake University, Joseph Schneider provided mentorship, which was indispensible to my existence. Jung Joon Lee, my friend and newest neighbor, has been refreshing company during my retreats from long bouts of solitary writing. Throughout many different stages of writing this book, I have received editorial support from Erin Heiser, David Hong, and Betsy Yoon. I appreciate their deeply engaged editing services.

I appreciate the permission to reprint two previously published works: an earlier version of Chapter 3 was published as "The Biopolitics of Transnational Adoption in South Korea: Preemption and the Governance of Single Birthmothers" in *Body and Society*; and, Chapter 4 was published as "Television Mothers" in *Cultural Studies ⇔ Critical Methodologies*. Also, a preliminary analysis of Chapter 5 appeared as "A Flickering Motherhood: Korean Birthmothers' Internet Community" in *Scholars and Feminist Online*. Furthermore, my participation in CUNY's Faculty Fellowship Publication Program and the PSC-CUNY grants I received assisted the development of my oral history collection and secured more time for writing. In addition, I would like to thank the audiences and organizers for my presentations at the University of California, Los Angeles, the University of Toronto, Wagner College, and Scripps College.

Finally, to my family in South Korea: I am greatly indebted to my parents, my mother, Jung Ok Im, and my father, Kim Jung Bok. My mother's prescience and unwavering support for my education enabled me to survive as an academic. The final completion of this project is indebted to her respect for my perseverance and her firm belief in my abilities. For my father, who worked overseas as a merchant marine for 15 years to provide for his family, I have a great appreciation of and respect for his dedication and sense of responsibility. And to my two sisters, Kim Su Ri and Kim Hae Ri, I feel and have felt so close to you in my heart despite the long lapse of time and space apart. Su Ri, your postcard was a saving grace in my fight against loneliness and homesickness during my time in Illinois. My sister, Hae Ri, you provided an amazing quality of care through listening, especially during your visit to Des Moines, solely to stand by me. With your assurance and laughter—not at—but to—my melancholic narrative of work and life, I was able to regain my equilibrium and to keep writing. And, in closing, I wish to acknowledge my family here in the US. I thank my study buddy, Shamee, for her magical ability to support my work, mostly by sleeping behind my work station. My partner, Kim Yeong Ran, has been an energizer and a tranquilizer during the process of writing this book. Yeong Ran was extremely patient and supportive of me as I worked on the book. At almost all steps of writing the book, from its conceptualization to the reading of multiple drafts to reviewing the final manuscript, she read, critiqued, and gave me the supports I needed. Additionally, she dragged me out of my paranoid, desk-bound state, and helped me to forget about the agonies of writing and to enjoy life in the moment. Without her well-balanced temperament, love, and care, this book might not have been feasible.

Contents

1 Introduction: From Invisible Mothers to
   Virtual Mothering ... 1

Part I Unbecoming Mothers: A History of Gendered
        Violence ... 33

2 Secure the Nation, Secure the Family ... 35

3 Maternity Homes, the Birthplace of the
   Virtual Mother ... 79

Part II Reconnection: Virtual Mothering ... 113

4 Television Mothers: Birth Mothers Lost and
   Found in the Search-and-Reunion Narrative ... 115

5 Performing Virtual Mothering and Forging
   Virtual Kinship ... 145

| 6 | "I Am a Mother, but Not a Mother": The Paradox of Virtual Mothering | 189 |

References 225

Index 235

List of Figures

Fig. 2.1 Shin Young Eun's journal entry (courtesy of Shin Young Eun) — 35

Fig. 4.1 A photo taken at the reunion between Cho Soon Ok and her daughter (courtesy of Nina de Bruijin) — 128

CHAPTER 1

Introduction: From Invisible Mothers to Virtual Mothering

In 1994, a few months before I left South Korea to attend graduate school in the US, my mother told me that she wished that some Americans would adopt me, and support me, as if I were their own daughter, during my stay. I was puzzled by her seemingly outrageous wish, and asked, "How can I be adopted when you're still alive?" She said, "That doesn't matter; there have been cases." While my memories of that day have become fuzzy, I recall her saying, "You can tell them I am dead." I was devastated by her motherly death wish, driven by the hope of her daughter being adopted by unknown Americans.

After moving to the US, I soon realized my mother's wild wish had some validity, and that it seemed to be rooted in the significant, yet buried, history of transnational adoption in South Korea. I noticed its effects during my random encounters with Americans in the Midwestern town where I lived. After finding out about my Korean heritage, many inevitably mentioned their acquaintance with Korean orphans who were adopted by Americans. Though these comments were meant to be friendly, my gut response was embarrassment and annoyance. I did not know why they were telling me these stories, over and over again, nor could I guess what the proper response should be. Should I thank them for adopting my fellow Koreans? Or should I apologize for Korea's inability to raise children domestically?

© The Editor(s) (if applicable) and The Author(s) 2016
H. Kim, *Birth Mothers and Transnational Adoption Practice in South Korea*, DOI 10.1057/978-1-137-53852-9_1

Transnational adoption binds two parties: the receiver of a child and the giver of that child. In South Korea, which has a 60-year-long history of transnational adoption, it also binds two nations: South Korea and the US. These two nations, and, thus, all their citizens, not just those engaged in adoption, share a relationship—a relationship that is caring, but hierarchical; generous, but embarrassing; loving, but violent. My mother's wild wishes, like those of so many South Koreans of her generations, suggest that the US, as the largest receiving nation of Korean adoptees, has a powerful reputation as a prosperous, benevolent country, extending its help to all who might be deserving of its support. And, as a result, many Americans, even nonadopters, must tend to view Korea as a once impoverished, war-ravaged nation with needy orphans, and feel good about self-identifying with their fellow Americans' good deeds.

This book was sparked by my perspective as part of the Korean diaspora. Today South Korea is known as the largest and longest provider of children placed into transnational adoption, a practice that has gone on for the past 60 years, though now in decline to a few hundred a year. Not an adoptee, birth mother, or an adopter myself, I still felt an affinity with "the givers," and began to wonder whether the mothers of Korean adoptees were really all dead, as evoked in the powerful figure of "the orphan." I thought to myself, "*Their mothers might still be living, behind the face of death,*" as my mother had been so willing to do, in her expectation that random strangers in the US might provide me with care, support, and opportunities. Who were these women, I wondered. Under what circumstances had they felt compelled to give up their child to unknown foreigners? Why were so few people interested in them?

Born out of puzzlement and curiosity, this book is about South Korean birth mothers involved in transnational adoption. Although the total number of birth mothers is unclear, South Korean birth mothers constitute the largest group from any single nation. As of 2014, 165,944 Korean-born adoptees have been displaced and are currently living in 14 different countries, primarily in North America and Western Europe.[1] The figure is estimated to account for 20 % of all displaced children who are placed in families engaged in transnational adoption.[2] As the first academic work to focus on birth mothers who have relinquished babies to transnational adoption, this book draws on my 15 years of research on Korean birth mothers and tells a history that is long overdue.

This book begins with the critical observation that two divergent figures of birth mother have come to dominate the cultural imaginary in

South Korea from the 1990s onward. The first figure is of an elderly, sacrificing mother who awaits her adopted child's eventual return in order to reclaim her motherhood; the second figure is of an unmarried, sexually irresponsible woman who has no viable option except to relinquish the child to adoption. This book observes how these two figures have been separately produced and exclusively managed, so as to assign poverty as the root cause of South Korea's past involvement in transnational adoption, and to blame irresponsible female sexuality, as represented in single motherhood, for its ongoing involvement. With a critical awareness of the structural forces underlying South Korea's involvement in transnational adoption, this book examines how these two birth-mother figures have been orchestrated to maintain the nation's dissonant adoption politics and practices: for while South Korea's past involvement in transnational adoption is remembered as part of a traumatic national past, its continuing practice today is rationalized as a necessity.

It is important to underscore that the emergence and manipulation of these two maternal figures occurred amid rapidly shifting demographic, cultural, and political terrains in South Korea in the post-1990s. During this time, the number of Korean children being placed into transnational adoption was sharply declining; however, at the same time, the number of adult adoptees living overseas "returning" to Korea to search for their families began steadily rising. These returning adoptees, under the aegis of South Korea's neoliberal ethnic nationalism, were considered as part of the community of overseas Koreans. Their stories of searching for cultural and familial roots became a topic of growing popular interest in media, discussed in the news, and depicted in television dramas and reality shows, and in films.

After the mid-1990s, South Korea's adoption discourse recast the stories of returning adoptees as success stories of resilient Koreans who had overcome their unfortunate past and achieved glorious success. Corresponding to the adoption narrative, a collective memory of transnational adoption tended to cluster around the figure of an older, maternal birth mother, who was portrayed as a victim of personal misfortunes, primarily poverty, in combination with her husband's death, and/or illnesses, thus requiring her to give up her child to adoption. In this way, the figure of the sacrificing birth mother erased—and continues to erase—South Korea's ongoing involvement in transnational adoption by framing it as ancient history. This collective memory of birth mothers and transnational adoption, while recognizing birth mothers for the first time, simultaneously enforced—and continues to enforce—a collective amnesia about other birth mothers whose stories and lives fall outside the clean-cut narrative of poverty and/or catastrophic circumstances.

While information about the existence and experiences of birth mothers is seriously limited in the South Korean discourse on transnational adoption, the experiences of birth mothers is even less acknowledged in the adoption discourse in North America and Western Europe. In particular, prior to the mid-1990s, far too often, the dominant representations depicted adopted children as orphans, and focused on the humanitarian motivations and efforts of adoptive parents to provide better lives for these poverty-stricken children. Highlighting developmental outcomes (e.g., physical growth and intelligence test results) as scientific proof of the adopted child's well-being, the dominant transnational adoption discourse, long spearheaded by the behavioral sciences, especially psychology and social work, hollowed out the children's lives before adoption, treating their past as irrelevant to their present lives. As a consequence, birth mothers have remained treated, at best, as a symbol of a remote, unknown, and unfortunate past, and, at worst, are assumed to be literally dead.

The lack of scholarly attention to birth mothers involved in the transnational adoption practice has persisted, even as a critical adoption scholarship has emerged over the past 15 to 20 years.[3] Arising from various disciplines, from anthropology to literary criticism, this critical scholarship uncovers the structural forces circumscribing the development of transnational adoption, a practice largely embedded in the history of Western colonialism and military violence, and their ongoing influence in the sending regions.[4] By pointing out the global power asymmetry between the involved nations, it challenges the all-too-prevalent benevolent salvation narrative. In addition, by illuminating the adoptees' experiences, these critical scholars address the dilemmas and complexities of racial and ethnic identity formation among transnational adoptees, thus contributing to a reconsideration of assumptions about identity, kinship, and belongingness, and helping to develop a new theoretical terrain beyond one of traditional, blood-related kinship. This emergent adoption scholarship provides a theoretical framework of critical, geopolitical, feminist engagement, as well as rich field research, based on the experiences of adoptees; furthermore, it presents postcolonial and neoliberal critiques of transnational adoption, thus illuminating the void of in-depth, empirical research on the life experiences of birth mothers.

Engaging these two terrains—the emergent, but limited, visibility of birth mothers in South Korea, and the persistently absent recognition of birth mothers in the transnational adoption discourse—this book aims to flesh out the birth mothers' shadowy existence and life experiences, with a critical analysis of the structural forces at work from the 1970s to the 2000s. This book examines four sites to study birth mothers: (1) maternity homes; (2) television search-and-reunion shows; (3) a birth mothers' Internet forum; and (4) an oral history collection.

The concept of *virtual mothering* has been coined to refer to the performative, ephemeral, fragmented, and technologically enacted qualities of mothering that birth mothers engage in beyond the domain of the normative family. This book examines virtual mothering as a two-part process: first, there is a severing from the child; and then, a reconnection to the child, whether this connection is imagined or real. At the register of their virtual mothering, this book observes the multilayered violence implicated in adoption circumstances and the volatile vestiges of losses and trauma after the adoption placement. Via a critical and creative engagement with the existence and experiences of birth mothers, this book analyzes the global and local contexts for geopolitical, economic, cultural, and familial imperatives in the history and practice of transnational adoption in South Korea.

1.1　The Ungraspable Community: Birth Mothers in South Korea

To establish the parameters of the Korean birth mothers who are the purview of this study, let me first address the term *birth mother*. The birth mother has many different names, such as biological mother, blood mother, natural mother, origin mother, genetic mother, real mother, and first mother.[5] In the US, the term acquired a political connotation of self-validation and self-identity in the mid-1970s, as a group of birth mothers organized themselves in opposition to the secrecy and silence surrounding closed adoptions;[6] eventually, the self-advocacy group Concerned United Birthparents (CUB) was established in 1976.[7] Largely constituted by birth mothers who had given up their children during the post-WWII period into the 1960s, CUB characterized the adoption experience as "surrender[ing] [the baby] …without options and without compensations for our loss," and gave voice to the traumatic, long-term consequences of adoption losses on birth mothers.[8] The birth mothers' activism supported the rights of single motherhood, which had gained increasing social acceptance in the US during the 1970s, and led to more mothers keeping their babies. This cultural and demographic shift led to a scarcity of white babies available for adoption, thus creating an environment where birth mothers could negotiate terms and procedures that were more favorable to themselves.

The term, birth mother, once associated with the shame and secrecy of an out-of-wedlock birth, was re-signified into a self-determined, free-willed—if not altruistic—mother, planning her own pregnancy. For example, Myrl Coulter defines birth mother as "a woman who gives birth to a child she then gives up for adoption. .. or pregnant women planning to give their children up for adoption."[9] Coulter's definition suggests that the birth mother's decision to give up her child is based on her free will, illustrating the relative leverage of birth mothers in the US.

However, in South Korea, while several terms denote a birth mother, all are still shrouded with the shame and guilt of child abandonment. For example, the term, *saengmo*, refers to a biological mother who gives birth to a child whom she does not raise and has no legal responsibility over.[10] Following a recent revision to the *Special Adoption Law* which went into effect in 2012, another term, *ch'insaengmo*, appears in legal texts to refer to a birth mother in the adoption context. Finally, the most popular word to refer to birth mothers is *mihonmo*, or, not-yet-married women, reflecting the overwhelming association of single mothers with adoption throughout the history of the practice. A misnomer, *mihonmo* is automatically understood to indicate *birth mother* in South Korea. While *saengmo* and *mihonmo* may be used interchangeably to refer to a birth mother involved in transnational adoption, these terms are neither definitive nor self-evident to even birth mothers themselves; at best, these terms may be described as amorphous, not fully sealed, and obscure.

It is important to understand that during the 60-year-long practice of transnational adoption in South Korea the relinquishment of a child to adoption did not *always* require the informed consent of the birth mother. Instead, either the child's father or grandparents or relatives, or another legal guardian with custody over the child, could decide and finalize the child's adoption, without the direct agreement of the birth mother. The law only stipulated that, if someone were relinquishing a child's custody on behalf of the child's parents, he or she must provide legal proof of the child's custody, or documentation of unusual circumstances (e.g., a dead or missing parent). However, liberal interpretations of "unusual circumstances" by adoption agencies created inevitable loopholes, so that some birth mothers were excluded from making an informed, adoption decision, and thus never knew of their child's fate.

Another reason why the category of birth mothers remains obscure is attributable to the fact that the adoptable children supplied by orphanages until the early 1980s, almost 30 years well into the emergence of transnational adoption, were not all actually orphans, or parentless; specifically, some of these children were lost or missing, or had come from poor or dissolved families.[11] Thus, the 30-year period during which children were processed for adoption through orphanages included a significant number of children whose parents did not know or approve of their child being placed into transnational adoption; in some cases, it was possibly against the explicit wishes of the birth mother.

Even when a birth mother makes the conscious decision to relinquish her child, and clearly expresses a preference for adoption, whether domestic or transnational, the category of birth mother still holds a great degree of ambiguity. First, the mother's act of relinquishment does not guarantee the child's adoption. Analyzing adoption trends in the 1990s, South Korean social work scholar Lee Bong Ju points out that the actual adoption rate ranged from only 10 to 17 % of all the children available for adoption.[12] Although the exact figure is disputable, Lee's finding indicates an inevitable discrepancy between the number of children available for adoption and the number of children who are actually placed into families.[13] Such a gap between the initiation and the completion of adoption creates a precarious condition, whereby birth mothers are not entitled to know the final outcome of their adoption decision, nor to ascertain whether their preference for a domestic or transnational adoption has been fulfilled.

The elusive, ambiguous boundary of the population of birth mothers who are involved in transnational adoption has long been maintained by the systematic lack of legal protection for birth mothers, and the government's lax oversight of the relinquishment process; furthermore, the broad criteria for adoptable children give adoption agencies a great deal of self-discretion in claiming custody of a child.[14] In the absence of adequate governmental, legal, and administrative supervision and enforcement, adoption agencies follow demand-driven principles, soliciting and prioritizing, foremost, the interests of adoptive parents, and facilitating the process to clearly favor their interests, even before those of the birth mother, birth families, and child. Various factors—the lack of governmental protection and supervision; the principles of market rationality, that is, speed and efficiency; and, foremost, the finality of transactions in the humanitarian adoption market economy—all conspire to extinguish the birth mother's right to essential information about her child's fate, as well as her right to overturn any of her decisions.

These structural ambiguities potentially open up all mothers who "abandoned" their children, that is, in the sense that they did not raise their children, to be vulnerable or included in the category of birth mother. The population of such mothers potentially includes divorced women, poor mothers, single mothers, women involved with married men, and mothers who ran away from home and left behind their children because of domestic abuses or other reasons.[15] Under patriarchal family practices and by law in South Korea, the mother, by leaving behind her child, is seen as no longer having any rights to knowledge about her child's whereabouts. This closure of information on her child's life creates the possibility in which the boundary of birth mothers could include not only birth mothers who surrender their children to adoption, but all mothers who are not able or willing to raise their children, or who lack access to them. Numerous women exist in such a liminal space, in which they could be birth mothers, yet may not know, for sure, whether they are.

1.2 THE SOCIAL DEATH OF BIRTH MOTHERS: A VITAL MECHANISM OF TRANSNATIONAL ADOPTION PRACTICE

The birth mother has no legal rights; in fact, she is not even legally existent. Once the baby is transferred over to the adoption agency, the birth mother loses custody and no longer has any responsibility to, or rights over, the child. The birth mothers' legal erasure is a critical step for the child to be considered adoptable by prospective adoptive parents; and, the erasure is sealed when a new birth certificate is issued to the adopted child, completing the transfer of legal custody to the adoptive parents. As shown in the legal adoption process, the powerful ideology of biological kinship dictates that the adoptive family fill in as the "as-if" genealogical relation, and thus organizes adoptive parenthood, in terms of an exclusive, proprietary right over a child's custody, thereby necessitating the birth mother's legal erasure.

This legal erasure, or nonexistence, as Christine W. Gailey argues, renders the population of birth mothers as legally dead, and produces a general lack of social recognition.[16] Postcolonial feminist scholar Jodi

Kim argues that the birth mothers' lack of visibility "functions to cover over—even as it is intricately linked to—the material conditions of possibility for the making of the social orphan and transnational adoptee."[17] By drawing upon Orlando Patterson's concept of social death,[18] Kim notes the abject material conditions that often compel birth mothers to give up their children, and thus describes them as the "socially dead."[19] In her critique of transnational adoption practice, Kim points out how racialized, working-class, poor birth mothers in the Global South are disproportionately devalued and delimited to a woman's capacity to bear a life, while their opportunities to parent that life are severely curtailed.[20] A "profound natal alienation," Kim argues, stems from such abject life circumstances and functions as the necessary condition for creating a surplus of children for transnational adoption.[21]

To consider the birth mothers in South Korea via the framework of social death, I draw upon Lisa M. Cacho's astute measurement of social death in the differential valuations of human life in racialized, sexualized, and state-sanctioned violence.[22] Describing the violent mechanism of social death over a vulnerable, unprotected population, for example, incarcerated and undocumented immigrants, Cacho points out that its feedback loop is composed of two constituents, "rightlessness and misrecognition."[23] That "rightlessness" excludes the population from a right to demand rights, and works together with a system of "misrecognition" that renders them "dead-to-others."[24] Applying Cacho's analysis to the social death of birth mothers elaborates how the legal nonexistence of birth mothers, as reflected in their lack of "the right to ask for rights" pertaining to the child, and in their misrecognition, is managed by their abstract existence, thus making them appear "dead-to-others."

The misrecognition of birth mothers and their rightlessness is useful for maintaining the status quo in the transnational adoption practice. The omission of birth mothers from the child's post-adoption life serves to appease the adoptive parents' prevalent fears or anxieties that the birth mother might one day show up to reclaim the child.[25] As Christine W. Gailey states, the legal erasure of birth mothers, "has a certain appeal to adopters in search of clear-cut, exclusive rights to a child."[26] In analyzing an adoptive mothers' online blog, Ann Anagnost observes that adoptive mothers feel a certain comfort over the lost connection to the birth parent, while simultaneously acknowledging the mournful aspect of such a loss.[27]

Furthermore, the omission of birth mothers from the adoption narrative fails to focus attention on the sending regions, and thereby naturalizes abject life conditions that often stem from a long colonial history of US military intervention and economic and cultural dominance. Obscuring the long history of Western economic, political, and military domination, and its implications in the production of orphans in sending regions, creates an epistemological condition that reproduces what David Eng has incisively referred to as "generalized narratives of salvation—from poverty, disease, and the barbarism of the third world—often attached to narratives of transnational adoption."[28] Such salvation narratives smooth over complex, contradictory realities, and frame the transnational adoption market as a decontextualized, depoliticized humanitarian activity, performed by conscientious private citizens, taking part in global family formations, to the benefit of all involved parties.

Additionally, the social death of birth mothers in South Korea has served to bolster and advance South Korea's national development agenda in its quest to become a leading global economy. First, under the influence of Cold War capitalism, and then under subsequent neoliberal regimes, South Korea's national development agenda has relied heavily on the imaginary of a national family. By making the population in need—that is, birth mothers and their children—legally unrecognizable and socially dead via a population management technique, South Korean state regimes have continuously upheld the imaginary of the patriarchal national family, thus rationalizing its persistent, inexcusable lack of a comprehensive social welfare policy to help single mothers and/or other nonnormative families. The social death of birth mothers serves the state's interests as it obscures the multitudes of interpersonal and institutionalized gendered violence that occur in the state's promotion of transnational adoption as the best, even natural, solution for dealing with excess children from single, working-class, poor mothers in crisis; thereby, it obviates any need to allocate national expenditures toward children or families that exist beyond the patriarchal national family framework.

1.3 Virtual Mothering for a Frame of Recognition

How shall we recognize a population of birth mothers so elusive and socially dead? What frames can bring light to their existence and experiences, without asserting a universal, normative ideology of motherhood?

In order to engage the birth mothers' living existence and life experiences, I conceptualize the population of birth mothers as "virtual" in two primary senses: virtue and capacity.

In the *Oxford English Dictionary*, the first definition of "virtual" is "senses relating to a particular quality, or virtues."[29] The primary meaning of "virtue," in the same dictionary is "a moral quality regarded as good or desirable in a person; a particular form of moral excellence; *applied to qualities conventionally regarded as vices or negative qualities, especially, with reference to certain circumstances in which such qualities may be beneficial*" (my italics). My claim that virtual birth mothers possess "moral excellence," despite not having raised their own children, an act that is commonly seen as morally bankrupt, might suggest an appalling paradox. However, as the definition states, virtue does not always refer to qualities that we view as good, but, at times, to "vices or negative qualities, … [yet] beneficial" in certain circumstances.

By characterizing the birth mothers' relinquishment of the child as a virtuous act, my frame of analysis focuses on the specific circumstances or events under which the birth mothers' relinquishment of the child might be regarded as beneficial, good, or even necessary. In framing the population of virtual birth mothers as being virtuous, I propose to uncover the social death of birth mothers in light of their roles and values in the biopolitics of the transnational adoption practice. By what means is the relinquishment of a child turned into a virtuous maternal act that secures not only the future well-being of her child, but, more importantly, the future of a greater "social good"?

I employ the second definition of virtual, "producing or capable of producing (a particular result)," to attend to the bodily potential of birth mothers, a population excluded from normative frameworks of recognition. Characterizing the birth mothers' marginality in terms of being "simultaneously real but not real," Barbara Yngvesson suggests the birth mother's existence is powerfully evocative, as instantiated "in [how] her existence or even her death may pull the adopted child 'back' to seek some trace of her or may pull the birth mother 'forward' to seek information about the child."[30] Her observation, based on the contemporary cultural phenomenon of "motherland trips" by transnational adoptees in search of their birth mothers, highlights the population of birth mothers in another light of becoming, that is, becoming a birth mother through the potentiality to reconnect with the adopted, bygone child.[31]

In framing the birth mothers' virtual existence as immanently effective and/or powerful, I do not wish to suggest that all birth mothers will manifest as fully, volitional subjects in the future. Rather, my rendition of the birth mothers' virtual existence engages the body as a constellation of affective forces, never fully actualized, but full of potentialities in the realm of the virtual. Conceptualizing the body as virtual, Brian Massumi emphasizes the unactualized and incipient qualities of a body, operating at the substratum of individual consciousness, and prioritizes its potentialities, emergencies, and tendencies as the body's most central qualities.[32] Following Massumi's postulation, I understand the body not as a discrete, self-contained human being, and instead see the intensity of affects, caused by various forces of bodily encounters, including sensations, unconscious desires, traumas, and pre-discursive events, as vital to invoking bodily transformations.[33]

Yet, the affect that propels the bodily capacity to transform is not exclusive to human bodies. In *The Affective Turn*, Patricia Clough argues that affect also needs to be considered within the domain of technology, since technological interventions and mediations, as they put it, "[allow] us "both to 'see' affect and to produce affective bodily capacities beyond the body's organic-physiological constraints."[34] Their insight, locating affect in the realm of the technological, informs a new configuration of body and technology; and, their symbiotic articulations of becoming have inspired me to prioritize the becoming—or emergence—of birth mothers, and to conceptualize the process as not just being derived from birth mothers, but as occurring in and between organic birth mothers' bodies and technological bodies. Theorizing the population of birth mothers in terms of the virtual allows me to configure the body as an assemblage of discourses, affect, technology, as something more than a human body, and to emphasize its emergent and performative nature. In framing the population of birth mothers as being virtual in the sense of a capacity to affect and be affected, I underscore the significance of intense sensations, especially grief, but, more importantly, the unacknowledged grievances resonating in the collective body of the birth-mother population.

Furthermore, my frame of analysis calibrates discourses, affects, and actions of mothering. To specify a scholarly orientation on mothering, I draw upon Evelyn Nakano Glenn's (1994) working definition of mothering, which is "a historically and culturally variable relationship 'in which one individual nurtures and cares for another.'"[35] Mothering, according to Glenn, "occurs within specific social contexts that vary in terms of material and cultural resources and constraints."[36] Taking a critical stance toward universal notions of mothering based on gender roles, Glenn's definition of mothering underscores the actions and relationships of nurturance and care. By extending Glenn's insight of social contexts to the realm of technology, I define mothering not only as a historically and culturally variable relationship but also as a technologically enacted and mediated relationship of care and nurturance. Combining the dual functions of virtual—as both its moral quality for a greater good and its bodily affectivity—with a definition of mothering as historically, culturally specific and technologically enacted parental actions of nurturance and care, I develop my frame of analysis, called *virtual mothering*.

By framing the population of birth mothers as virtual mothers, I engage with virtual mothering as a phenomenon that occurs in a two-part process: (1) by their severance from the child and (2) by their belated reconnection with the child whether imagined or real. In contrast to the traditional notion of mothering, the framework of virtual mothering underscores the process of becoming birth mothers, a process that is performative, ephemeral, fragmented, and technologically enacted. Virtual mothering emanates from incipient and unactivated qualities of mothering that are rendered legible—that is, sensed and/or felt—when joined with a particular set of discourses, practices, and technology.

My framework of virtual mothering does not presuppose the subjectivity of birth mothers. I do not wish to impose a naturalistic, predetermined understanding of mothering onto birth mothers, based simply on the fact that they gave birth to a child. Nor do I presume that all mothers either should be, or are, willing to raise their children, even given enough resources or support. Virtual mothering is utterly distinct from the individual identity of any birth mother as a particular, coherent subject, and instead focuses on practices of mothering. The patterns and characteristics of mothering that emerge in my analysis are not meant to represent the whole population of birth mothers, and their life experiences in South Korea. They do, however, reveal the historical contingencies and the geopolitical, cultural, material, and technological contexts that have shaped, and continue to shape, transnational adoption practice. In short, while I explore common structural paths that lead birth mothers to relinquish their child, I do so without imposing any normative sense of motherhood upon them. Virtual mothering, through its refractions, holds together the ungraspable community of South Korean birth mothers who have been involved in transnational adoption for over 60 years.

By focusing on birth mothers, this book helps to fill the scholarly void of birth mothers' perspectives in the transnational adoption scholarship. Fleshing out the existence of birth mothers, who are bodily alive, but socially and legally dead, unsettles the dominant salvation narrative. Examining their life experiences, fraught with multiple layers of gendered violence and exploitations, opens up a scholarly conversation on the dilemmas and politics of a global, so-called "humanitarian practice" that is deeply entrenched in a long history of colonialism, military interventions, and resulting global inequalities.

This book offers a critical analysis of how the South Korean state has appropriated the birth mothers' reproductive labor to serve a national security and economic development agenda (whether under aegis of the Cold War, or today's global, neoliberal, capitalist state), and offers a rich case study for scholarship on biopolitics; gender and nationalism; as well as, reproduction and globalization. By engaging a conceptual framework not exclusively predicated on human subjectivity or identity, but rather emphasizing how a birth mother's unclaimed motherhood becomes intelligible through the multiple intersections and circulations of technologies, institutions, and human subjectivity, this book builds a non-identity-based politics, and promotes affective frameworks of transformative knowledge and engagement.

1.4 Methods for Virtual Mothering

Central to my analysis of virtual mothering is a thorough investigation of the processes by which one becomes a birth mother. I see this process as occurring through two discrete modalities: the first happens at the birth mother's disconnection from the child and any maternal responsibilities, while the second occurs when she reconnects with the adopted child and/or affects of adoption loss, whether this connection occurs through the actual physical presence of the mother–child connection or as an imaginary ideal. Examining the production of birth mothers at these two points captures processes that are not normally considered in relation to one another. These two contrasting moments also reveal South Korea's contradictory posture toward transnational adoption. By considering these two contrasting modalities of becoming birth mothers, this book examines the shifting valuations and divergent meanings and practices of mothering in South Korea.

Analyzing the birth mother's exit from—and re-entry into—mothering in terms of virtual mothering, I contend that the initial disconnection cannot be understood simply as a volitional act by an individual birth mother, just as a reconnection cannot be explained by her desires or actions only. To understand the constellation of forces that produce these social relations, I employ a discursive-material-affective configuration as my methodology.[37] First, by casting virtual mothering as a discursive formation, I trace South Korea's shifting national agenda between the 1970s and the 2000s, decades during which the military developmental state was replaced by the current neoliberal global state.

By focusing on the discourses surrounding national security, the normative family, and motherhood, I examine the selective visibility of birth mothers in the post-1990s' popular media, and observe how the birth mothers' severance from, as well as their re-attachment to, their own mothering is rendered in nationalistic terms through the lens of a naturalized motherhood. Through a critical analysis of nationalism and gender politics, I delineate the ways in which birth mothers, once viewed as impoverished mothers or single mothers who had to give up their children for adoption, are revalorized into self-sacrificing mothers, who paradoxically renounced their mothering in the service of better mothering.

Set against this nationalistic, naturalizing discourse of motherhood, I analyze the birth mothers' personal narratives regarding their separation from, and reconnection with, their children, as well as their general discourse on adoption. Challenging the commonsense understanding that abstract poverty or the hope for a better life are major factors in the adoption decision, the birth mothers' discursive performances provide concrete details, fleshing out the poverty and violence they have suffered. Their narratives describe domestic and/or sexual violence, economic exploitation, and legal discrimination against single mothers; they tell of reuniting with the adopted child. The narratives in this book powerfully reveal the structural impediments that constrain the reproductive rights of working-class, single mothers and other mothers existing outside the normative patriarchal family, as well as illuminate the birth mothers' ambivalence about adoption, and their paradoxical engagement with motherhood. My analysis of virtual mothering, thereby, encompasses both the public and personal discourses of emergent birth mothers.

Secondly, I investigate virtual mothering as a material configuration that consists of material conditions, material practices, and technological engagements that occur in the process of becoming a birth mother. After examining the birth mothers' accounts of how they separated from their child, I then conduct a historical analysis of the material conditions in which these women lived, thereby contextualizing individual adoption stories within historical contingencies and structural conditions that include economic travails, domestic violence, patriarchal family law, an ill-equipped social welfare system, and the structure of adoption agencies.

To analyze emergent mothering after the adoption placement, my methodological framework involves a site-specific analysis that considers the material practices and technologies of four sites that produce virtual mothering. The four sites are (1) maternity homes; (2) television search-and-reunion shows; (3) a birth mothers' Internet forum; and, (4) an oral history collection. In my analysis of the operational logics and central governing technologies of each site, I attend to a given site's particular spatiotemporality, and observe how it shapes the specific patterns and dimensions of virtual mothering that emerge there. In so doing, I emphasize the nonhuman, material, and technological permutations that activate virtual mothering, and illustrate the emergences of birth mothers who are dispersed across, circulated through, and confined to the virtual time-space of technologies, whether mediated, mediatized, or regularized. I argue that birth mothers do not share the same axis of time and space as virtual mothering, and thereby, once again, affirm that birth mothers are not automatically virtual mothers. Rather, the interaction and mediation of materiality with the technological yields various forms of virtual mothering.

The third constituent of my methodological framework is an affect-driven analysis. Thus, I utilize the concept of affect, which denotes the body's capacity to affect and to be affected. In order to do so, I follow a strand of affect theories that treats affect as "an entire, vital, and modulating field of myriad becomings across human and non-human."[38] Understanding affect as a force of immanence and emergence shapes the temporal grid of my analysis, so that virtual mothering exists only within the present progressive tense, becoming activated through certain interactions. Since affect is not fully actualized, it exists as open-ended energy for the future, from and within present bodies. I frame virtual mothering as an iterative enactment of mothering that is ephemeral and spontaneous, a conjoined performance of maternal qualities. Virtual mothering exists as a transient, but powerful, evocative quality, rather than as a fixed state.

Through this analysis, I search for affects to illuminate how birth mothers' lives have been and continue to be affected by the adoption, thus rendering their experiences and existences intelligible as a felt quality. These affects include intense emotions (e.g., shame, guilt, sadness, anger, or a sense of injustice), whether articulated in words or envisioned in dreams and fantasy; as bodily responses that are nondiscursive expressions (e.g., facial expressions, gestures, the pitch/tenor of one's voice, sighs, and tears); and as images (adoptee photos) that resonate with, or trigger, a vitality. Through a close examination of these words, episodes, and events, all of which convey affect, I flesh out the birth mothers' voids and abstractions as being affectively dense and full in the register of virtual mothering.

Affective analysis does not just analyze affective configurations, it also considers how such affectivities produce and promote a politics of empathy. In this vein, I consider writing as a genre of affective analysis, and employ varying degrees of experimentation in narrative construction and argument development, as well as in the writing itself, so as to render the existence and experience of birth mothers as more fully alive and tangible in the sensitivity of "here and now."

As stated above, I understand virtual mothering as the process of becoming a birth mother. It begins with the severance from—and then the reattachment to—mothering, as structured by discursive-material-affective configurations. How do I formulate the relationships among these three elements and between my observations and my analysis? In what ways do my methodological choices maintain theoretical consistency with virtual mothering? Here, I draw upon Karen Barad, a feminist philosopher of science and technology, who argues that a relationship between a phenomenon—the object of inquiry—and its apparatus for observation—the means of inquiry—is inseparable and mutually constitutive.[39] By extending physicist Neils Bohr's observation of how an apparatus intersects with what is being observed, Barad brings forth a new epistemological framework that challenges a clear demarcation between the object/subject, knower/known, and discourse/materiality, and that recognizes the relationships between these frameworks as vessels that resonate with each other.[40] Here, Barad elaborates on Bohr's *apparatus*:

> Apparatuses are not mere static arrangements in the world, but rather apparatuses are dynamic (re)configurings of the world, specific agential practices/intra-actions/performances through which specific exclusionary boundaries are enacted. Apparatuses have no inherent "outside" boundary.

> This indeterminacy of the "outside" boundary represents the impossibility of the closure—the ongoing intra-activity in the iterative reconfiguring of the apparatus of bodily production. Apparatuses are open-ended practices. Importantly, apparatuses are themselves phenomena.[41]

Underscoring the apparatus' constant modulations to calibrate what is being observed, Barad emphasizes the dynamic quality, especially the interactive and intra-active constituents of phenomena. The co-evolving quality during the process of observation stems from the open-endedness, interconnectivity, and adaptability of bodies and apparatuses. Barad's argument privileges the analytical hierarchy of becoming and movement over fixed or given positions. Her notion of apparatus powerfully resonates with my theoretical rendition of the body as a state of becoming, and as an open-ended boundary, and provides the framework within which I define the relationship between my methods and the phenomenon of virtual mothering.

Drawing upon Barad's notion of apparatus, my methodology—a discursive, material, affective configuration—emphasizes two interlacing features: reflective engagement and performance engagement. Recognizing the apparatus' inseparable and co-evolving relationship to the phenomenon being examined, my analysis reflects on how dynamism and variability of measurements reverberate with the variegated shapes and textures of virtual mothering; and, furthermore, attends to how they play a constitutive role in the production of virtual mothering itself. By developing such a self-reflexive lens, I describe my methodology for approaching virtual mothering as an apparatus of discursive formations and material configurations, both of which produce and examine affective qualities registering as vibrant matter, and for unacknowledged and unactualized mothering in virtual mothering that is always already coming into being. Thus, I, like Barad, argue that my apparatus for virtual mothering is itself a phenomenon of virtual mothering.

Central to my approach of mutual entailment between my methodology and virtual mothering is a self-reflective engagement. I define my role as an analyst and as a cultivator of new terrains for exploration as performances. In my efforts, I further multiply the contact zones for analysis by employing interdisciplinary approaches, ranging from conventional social scientific methods (e.g., interpretive analysis, ethnography, interviews, and content analysis) to methods applicable to other areas of study, such as historical analysis, literary criticism, cultural studies, visual studies, performance studies, and trauma studies. Perched on multifarious facets and an in-betweenness of methodologies across disciplines, I carve out multiple angles from which one can encounter the emergence of virtual mothering.

My performative engagement commits to what Dwight Conquergood calls an engaged knowledge production.[42] He emphasizes the praxis of performance-based research as a radical research tool and exemplifies it as "an ethnography of the eyes and heart that reimagines participant observation as co-performative witnessing."[43] Conquergood's engagement in performance-based research and his commitment to a radical knowledge production helps refine my performative engagement to a performative ethnography. By traveling across all these sites where birth mothers enact virtual mothering, I co-perform alongside the birth mothers and co-produce their virtual mothering. Through this performance-based ethnography, I aim to explore a relationship between recognizing and becoming, and to produce affective and transformative knowledge.

1.5   My Involvement in Virtual Mothering

Several years after my initial encounters with adoption that I described at the opening of the book, I began my formal research with a visit to *Ae Ran Won*, a maternity home, in 2002. A maternity home is a social-service, residential facility for unmarried, pregnant women. Since that first visit, I have made more than a dozen trips to South Korea, staying on average a month, during which time I conducted research and carried out data collection. The majority of the data presented and analyzed in this book were collected during two separate time periods: 2005 and 2010–2012.

In 2005, I collected data through two main channels. First, in June 2005, I searched for online communities of Korean birth mothers by using a keyword search of "adoption" and "mother." I found three online communities for birth mothers, and decided to focus my research on an independently established community of about 200 birth mothers. To gain full access to the website, I introduced myself as a researcher, with the user name "lake71ny," and joined the community on June 23rd, 2005. Then in August 2005, I was given the opportunity to serve as a translator between an adoptee and her birth mother on a live search-and-reunion TV show. Throughout my involvement in, and analysis of, these two sites, I met five birth mothers, and conducted life history interviews with them. These interviews helped me to develop a critical understanding of maternity homes and their institutional promotion of adoption. In turn, the life histories and my understanding of maternity homes informed the second phase of my data collection.

In 2010, I resumed my data collection, adding maternity homes and an oral history collection of birth mothers to my sites of analysis.[44] This process did not begin deliberately—rather, the beginning of my second phase of data collection started with a promise that I had made to Jang Yeon Ja, a birth mother, in 2005. After three or four hours of telling me her life story, she urged me to finish my dissertation. In summer 2008, I went back, just to tell her that her contribution to my dissertation research had been vital, and to thank her in person. She then updated me about her life, telling me how she had gotten involved in advocacy work for transnational adoptees and single mothers. Meeting her, once again, and listening to her passion for adoptee justice work compelled me to resume what I had left undone in the first phase of my data collection.

From July 2010 to January 2012, I investigated maternity homes and collected oral histories from 16 birth mothers, whose ages ranged from 21 to 70, at the time of the interview. My data on maternity homes include personal recollections from my field notes; interviews with three agency directors, three veteran staff members, and four former maternity home residents; and, Korean academic literature on maternity homes, single motherhood, and birth mothers. At the outset of collecting the oral histories, I recruited potential narrators, by contacting key individuals who were active in adoptee circles or working with birth mothers. Through Jang Yeon Ja's dedication and network of birth mothers, I was able to meet with six birth mothers whose children were surrendered to adoption during the 1970s and the 1980s. In addition, I contacted Jane Jeong Trenka, a Korea-born adoptee, essayist, and activist, who has lived in Korea since 2004, and is a founding member of Truth and Reconciliation for the Adoptee Community in Korea (TRACK), an adoptee organization. She offered not only organizational and personal support, and access to networks, but also her insightful critique of how adoption procedures violated universal human rights.

Since I wanted to cover a wide age range of birth mothers corresponding to the long history of transnational adoption practice in South Korea, I reached out to the moderator of an online community for birth mothers, and exchanged several email correspondences with her. In addition, I made several visits to various advocacy organizations, such as *Haessal Sahoepokchihoe* (Sunlit Sisters' Center) and *Durebang* to find former US camptown sex workers, who comprise the first generation of South Korean birth mothers.

In addition to my role as an analyst and cultivator for these sites, I also performed as a translator of Korean and English, at various stages of, and on numerous occasions throughout, my research. As shown in Chapter 4, Television Mothers, my translations did on occasion take place in official settings, but most of my translation work took place in unofficial, private settings. On those occasions, I translated letters to—and from—adoptive parents.[45] My translation work was not limited to handling mechanical aspects of language, but also included providing cultural background and references; thus, I was often required to become an informant for the birth mothers I was interviewing. In addition to my translation work for birth mothers, translation was consistently a major part of the data collection and analysis process, ranging from reading and interpreting Korean or English texts, to then writing up analyses about them in English. All my interviews were conducted in Korean, except for one with a Dutch adoptee, and the vast majority of my archival and discursive analysis were based on Korean texts.

Translation can occur in many forms, and have many goals. In my translations, I sought to express the intent of the original. "The task of the translator," Walter Benjamin beautifully articulated, "consists in finding that intended effect [*intention*] upon the language into which he is translating which produces in it the echo of the original."[46] Thus, my translations are not word-for-word. In fact, a word-for-word translation, from Korean syntax to English syntax, can often lead to distorted meanings. Thus, I approached my work of translation with Benjamin's metaphor of a re-assemblage of a fragmented vessel: "… a translation, instead of resembling the meaning of the original, must lovingly and in detail incorporate the original's mode of signification, thus making both the original and the translation recognizable as fragments of a greater language, just as fragments are part of a vessel."[47] As a result, my translations, at times, intentionally retain words and phrases that do not conform to the grammatical conventions of English. Via this translation method, I acknowledge the impossibility of a transparent transfer of meaning from one language to another, and further recognize the impossibility of representation as a method, and encourage instead a politics of critical analysis.

My task of translation did not end with the compilation and translation of the data, but, rather, extended to writing a final analysis. It was at this stage that I found my ability to translate from English to Korean, and from Korean to English, to be as debilitating, as it was helpful. My bilingual and bicultural background equipped me with the tools to perform the much-needed role of a translator for all parties involved, thereby justifying my intrusions in the field. However, without then translating everything back into English, these translations could not fulfill their potential effectiveness. As a PhD with aspirations for a successful academic career, my fear of writing in English is unspeakable. My fear and shame of writing is mutated with, but also masqueraded in, the critical reflection of my own subject location. I have resisted donning the uncritical role of a "Third World" researcher, who is granted authority to speak for, and about, her own natives, due to her ability to speak the language. Instead, I made and honor a silent pact, connecting my work to the flight and freight of shame that birth mothers carry for giving up their children to adoption. Thus, I write about shame, with shame.

1.6   Other Sites for Mothering: Sites for Other Mothering

My analysis of virtual mothering spans four sites: (1) maternity homes, (2) television search-and-reunion shows, (3) a birth mothers' Internet forum, and (4) an oral history collection. These sites make visible the development of South Korea's transnational adoption practice in the decades following the 1970s. While the television search-and-reunion shows and oral history collection illuminate the circumstances of older birth mother populations, that is, working-class, single mothers, whose children were adopted during the 1970s and 1980s, the maternity homes and online community are populated by a younger cohort, those who became birth mothers during the 1990s and the 2000s. Not only do the television shows and oral history collection convey critical details about the historical development of adoption since its wartime origins, but both sites also attend to the public discourse, as well as to personal accounts, of adoption. South Korea's nationalistic and patriarchal rendition of adoption practice, as seen in maternity homes and on television shows, stands in striking contrast to the birth mothers' accounts and perspectives, as provided in their online community and in their oral histories.

I engage all these sites in terms of *heterotopia*, a term that Michel Foucault designated to refer to sites imbued with a particular set of relations, connected to all other sites: they designate, mirror, reflect, but simultaneously suspect, neutralize, or invert.[48] To detail the ways in which these sites alter the convention of mothering, let me reflect upon Foucault's example of the mirror as a heterotopia. Foucault writes:

> [But] it is also a heterotopia in so far as the mirror does exist in reality, where it exerts a sort of counteraction on the position that I occupy. From the standpoint of the mirror I discover my absence from the place where I am since I see myself over there. Starting from this gaze that is, as it were, directed toward me, from the ground of this virtual space that is on the other side of the glass, I come back toward myself; I begin again to direct my eyes toward myself and to reconstitute myself there where I am. The mirror functions as a heterotopia in this respect: it makes this place that I occupy at the moment when I look at myself in the glass at once absolutely real, connected with all the space that surrounds it, and absolutely unreal, since in order to be perceived it has to pass through this virtual point which is over there.[49]

In juxtaposing Foucault's analogy of the mirror to the various sites for virtual mothering, one sees how these sites function as a mirror through which one can recognize a form of "other" mothering, in the absence of normative mothering. While reflecting social orders that enforce a set of normative conventions about motherhood and mothering, these sites recognize birth mothers as mothers of some sort, thus carving themselves into "other" sites for mothering. Occurring beyond the domain of the normative patriarchal family configuration, such mothering, observed across these sites, does not follow the normative patriarchal notion of motherhood, and, instead, features other kinds of mothering, or *other mothering*. Hence, I argue these four sites are heterotopic, reflecting, reinforcing, and resembling a set of relations that curbs mothering among birth mothers, yet also refracting and inverting such forces. These sites for virtual mothering, therefore, function as counter-sites against normative motherhood, and open up the possibility for other types of mothering.

Yet the very peculiar way in which other mothering is rendered legible is noteworthy: it involves "passing through a virtual point which is over there." Recasting these sites of mothering by emphasizing their heterotopic qualities aptly captures the interconnectedness, as well as discontinuities, between the birth mother "over here" and the virtual mothering enacted at a virtual point "over there." The relationship between a birth mother and virtual mothering is mutually interdependent and reinforcing; connected, but simultaneously severed; challenging, and disconnected.

Framing these sites as heterotopic elucidates the paradox of virtual mothering, making clear how a mother's disconnection from mothering compels her engagement in a virtual mode of mothering, while simultaneously, her reconnection with mothering paradoxically affirms her disconnection from mothering.

I argue that each of these four sites functions as nonnormative sites for mothering, rendered absolutely real, but simultaneously absolutely unreal. The unreality stems from the fact that, for mothering to be recognized, the birth mother's existence must pass through a virtual point, which is "over there," where they cannot exist with their mothering. For example, maternity homes promise virtual mothering via its operative logic, whereby single, pregnant women experience an "over there" mothering, as they prepare to relinquish their child to adoption, in the name of a better mothering. Television search-and-reunion shows, meanwhile, materialize the birth mother's absent mothering into good mothering, where virtual mothering "over there" emerges along, and within, its particular narrative and frame of circuitry. Similarly, against an everlasting imaginary of good motherhood, the birth mothers' online community fleshes out their tensions over a desire to both connect with and disconnect from the child. In the Internet café, virtual mothering emerges "over there," as birth mothers deposit their ambivalent traces of losses onto an infinite traffic of information: in cyberspace, where they cannot possibly exist, they are immanent and seething. In providing their oral histories, the birth mothers' mothering is enacted "over there", where they no longer can go back to relive or recover their moments of separation from the child, life experiences, and reunion. Upon reuniting with the child "over here," they realize the impossibility of recovering the bygone losses of mothering.

Yet the birth mothers and their mothering, as I have said before, must not be understood as a mere reflection of inherent maternal qualities of any mother who gives birth to a child. Instead, I want to draw attention to how a felt or sensed quality of mothering mirrors the condition of possibility, in which the existence of both birth mothers and their mothering are not mutually compatible in the same axis of time-space. Unlike normative time, which is continuous, contingent, and under the domain of the patriarchal family, virtual mothering is enacted "over there" at virtual points across these four sites, operating along multiple axes of spatio-temporality. Existing virtually, these heterotopic sites produce a mothering, which is unlike traditional mothering; I call it *virtual mothering*.

This book is organized into two parts. Part I, Unbecoming Mothers: A History of Gendered Violence, encompasses the first two chapters and identifies the structural path along which birth mothers have been separated from their child and their mothering; Part II, Reconnection: Virtual Mothering, the last three chapters, analyzes how birth mothers, who once had their motherhood revoked, became reengaged with their mothering via intermediated technologies.

Chapter 2, "Secure the Nation, Secure the Family," establishes the historical, geopolitical, and socioeconomic context behind the peak in South Korea's participation in transnational adoption during the 1970s to the 1980s. By highlighting the influence of private, foreign-aid organizations in postwar Korea, this chapter presents a critical analysis of South Korean state policy during this period, especially focusing on how the lack of public welfare and the promulgation of a national family planning policy negatively impacted *kijich'on* (US military camptown) mothers; single mothers; and poor, working-class mothers. Juxtaposing the birth mothers' stories with the structural impediments in place at the time of the adoption makes clear that the birth mothers' involvement in transnational adoption practice has served to securitize the national economy and to prop up the ideology of a self-reliant, patriarchal family. This chapter concludes that transnational adoption has served as the state's de facto family planning policy, by removing "excess" population that did not fall within the purview of the national patriarchal family.

Chapter 3, "Maternity Homes, the Birthplace of the Virtual Mother," focuses on social governance and the emergence of virtual mothering via maternity homes since the 1980s. Considering the disproportionate, consistent rate of unmarried mothers in transnational adoption, this chapter examines maternity homes, a key organization of social governance over the population of single mothers and their excess children. In conjunction with various institutions, including the law, healthcare, the family, state welfare, and adoption agencies, the maternity home operates along its own regulatory reproductive cycle. Through this cycle, which is one of containment, classification, and circulation, adoption plans for children are initiated, facilitated, and completed. Simultaneously, the cycle produces the subjectivity of a self-sacrificing birth mother who, by choosing adoption, is making the best and most rational decision possible for her child; through this process, the birth mother emerges as a virtual mother.

Part II, Reconnection: Virtual Mothering, begins with Chapter 4, "Television Mothers: Korean Birth Mothers Lost and Found in the Search-

and-Reunion Narrative," which examines the cultural phenomenon of returning adoptees and their televised searches for, and potential reunion with, their birth families. Drawing upon my own role as a translator for such a show, I offer a critical, discursive analysis of such search-and-reunion shows and provide rich, ethnographic details about their production. By employing deconstructive and creative intervention into the search-and-reunion narrative, this chapter highlights the naturalized, developmental, and affective configuration of birth mothers. It further offers a critique of the nationalistic appropriation of motherhood at work in South Korea's popular adoption narrative and its insidious implications for South Korea's ethnic nationalism and its neoliberal globalization agenda.

Chapter 5, "Performing Virtual Mothering, Forging Virtual Kinships," examines a Korean birth mothers' Internet forum called *A Sad Love Story of Mothers Who Sent Their Children Away*. It frames the birth mothers' postings and the baby photographs they upload as an animated "show-and-tell" performance, thereby illuminating the losses the birth mothers experience as a result of transnational adoption, and their ambivalent desires and efforts, both to remember and share memories of their bygone child, while, simultaneously wishing to forget. These affective trails left online by birth mothers denote ephemeral acts of virtual mothering. With a critical awareness of the social stigma against birth mothers and the collaborative aspect of mothering on the Internet, this chapter features the Internet forum as a counterpublic, wherein birth mothers provide support and care for one another, forging a sense of solidarity and building a site of resistance.

Chapter 6, "'I Am a Mother, but Not a Mother': The Paradox of Virtual Mothering," examines a birth mothers' oral history collection as a knowledge-producing performance. The performative narratives detail their involvement in adoption, their lives afterward, and their own experiences of reunion with the bygone child as a lived paradox. Engaging with the performative vision of paradox as a heuristic lens of the birth mothers' life experiences, this chapter uncovers the profound sense of alienation that exists about the adoption decision and processes, and the long-term effects of transnational adoption on birth mothers' lives, and birth mothers' reflections about reuniting with their child. Thereby, this chapter bears witness to the impossibility of recovering losses involved in transnational adoption practice, and poses a counterhistory for both the all-too-prevalent narratives of salvation and/or an odyssey home.

Notes

1. The Ministry of Health and Welfare, Current State of Domestic and International Adoption (*kungnaeo ibyang hyonhwang*). Seoul: Korea, Ministry of Health and Welfare 2014.
2. Peter Selman, "Intercountry Adoption in the 21st Century: An Examination of the Rise and Fall of Countries of Origin" In *Proceedings of the First International Korean Adoption Studies Research Symposium*, ed. Kim Park Nelson, Eleana Kim, and Lene Myong Peterson, (Seoul: International Korean Adoptee Associations 2007), 55.
3. See Ann Anagnost, "Scenes of Misrecognition: Maternal Citizenship in the Age of Transnational Adoption," *Positions* 8, no. 2 (2000): 389-421; Sara Dorow: *Transnational Adoption: A Cultural Economy of Race, Gender, & Kinship* (New York: New York University Press, 2006); Christine W. Gailey, "Race, Class, and Gender in Intercountry Adoption in the USA," in *Intercountry Adoption: Developments, Trends, and Perspectives*, ed. Peter Selman (London: Skyline House Press, 2000), 295–314; Tobias Hübinette, "Comforting an Orphaned Nation: Representations of International Adoption and Adopted Koreans in Korean Popular Culture" (Ph.D. diss., Stockholm University, 2005); Eleana Kim, *Adopted Territory: Transnational Korean Adoptees and the Politics of Belonging* (Durham: Duke University Press, 2010); Arissa Oh, "A New Kind of Missionary Work: Christians, Christian Americanists, and the Adoption of Korean GI Babies, 1955–1961," *Women's Studies Quarterly* 33, no. 3 (2005): 161–188; Soojin Pate, *From Orphan to Adoptee: U.S. Empire and Genealogies of Korean Adoption* (Minneapolis: University of Minnesota Press, 2014); Barbara Yngvesson, *Belonging in an Adopted World* (Chicago: University of Chicago Press, 2010).
4. See Laura Briggs, *Somebody's Children: The Politics of Transracial and Transnational Adoption* (Durham: Duke University Press, 2012); David Eng, *The Feeling of Kinship: Queer Liberalism and the Racialization of Intimacy* (Durham: Duke University Press, 2010); Christina Klein, *Cold War Orientalism* (Berkeley: University of California Press, 2003), and Pate, *From Orphan to Adoptee*.
5. These variances of the term indicate the speaker's perspective on motherhood and adoption. For example, the phrase *first mother* is often used in the birth mothers' community in the US.

6. According to Katarina Wegar, closed adoptions refer to a sealed-record practice of adoption that keeps information about the birth parents in a secret file (Katarina Wegar, *Adoption, Identity, and Kinship: The Debate over Sealed Birth Records* [New Haven, CT: Yale University, 1997]).
7. In the mid-1970s, CUB, composed largely of birth mothers who until then had lived with the secrecy of adoption, fought against the social stigma and culture of silence around adoption; they demanded an open access to all adoptee records, and argued for the right to search for and meet adoptees.
8. Rickie Solinger, *Beggars and Choosers: How the Politics of Choice Shapes Adoption, Abortion, and Welfare in the United Sates*, (New York: Hill and Wang Publishing Company, 2001), 105.
9. Myrl Coutler, "Birth Mother," in *Encyclopedia of Motherhood*, ed. Andrea O'Reilly (Thousand Oaks: Sage Publications, Inc., 2010), 129.
10. *Ch'inmo* is a slightly different term, yet often conflated with *saengmo*. *Ch'inmo* refers to a legal mother.
11. Many children had living parents who were suffering economic hardships, or other forms of personal crisis, and who had placed the child is in the orphanage as a temporary measure in a larger family survival strategy. However, once the child is in the orphanage's care, the orphanage director acquires parental custody over the child. Many such children were placed into the transnational adoption by an orphanage director. Birth parents would be unaware of the adoption unless they came back to retrieve their children.
12. Bong Ju Lee, "Recent Trends in Child Welfare and Adoption in Korea: Challenges and Future Directions," in *International Korean Adoption: A Fifty-Year History of Policy and Practice*, ed. Kathleen Ja Sook Berquist, M. Elizabeth Vonk, Dong Soo Kim, and Marvin D. Feit (Binghamton: The Haworth Press, 2007), 195.
13. Children older than five years or who have not been adopted within three years of their arrival are removed from the pool of available children and are sent to group homes or affiliated orphanages.
14. There have been a few cases of missing children adopted only two weeks after the child was reported missing. In Hübinette, "Comforting an Orphaned Nation."

15. South Korea's patriarchal marriage law did not grant custody of a child to a divorced woman, unless the father was willing to agree to such an arrangement. In 1972, *Kyunghyang Daily News* reported that agencies customarily required only the father's consent in the relinquishment process. Given the primacy of the father's decisions, it was not uncommon for divorced women or mothers otherwise separated from their children to learn of their child's adoption after the fact.
16. Christine W. Gailey. "Race, Class, and Gender in Intercountry Adoption in the USA," 305.
17. Jodi Kim, "An 'Orphan' with Two Mothers: Transnational and Transracial Adoption, the Cold War, and Contemporary Asian American Cultural Politics," *American Quarterly* 61, no. 4 (2009): 867.
18. Orlando Patterson, *Slavery and Social Death* (Cambridge, MA: Harvard University Press, 1982).
19. Jodi Kim, "An 'Orphan' with Two Mothers," 868.
20. Ibid., 857.
21. Ibid., 867.
22. Lisa M. Cacho, *Social Death: Racialized Rightlessness and the Criminalization of the Unprotected* (New York: New York University Press, 2012), 4.
23. Ibid., 8.
24. Ibid.
25. Kristi Brian, *Reframing Transnational Adoption: Adopted Koreans, White Parents, and the Politics of Kinship* (Philadelphia: Temple University Press, 2012).
26. Christine W. Gailey, *Blue Ribbon Babies and Labors of Love: Race, Class, and Gender in U.S. Adoption Practice.* (Austin: University of Texas Press, 2010), 107.
27. Ann Anagnost, "Scenes of Misrecognition," 401.
28. Eng, *The Feeling of Kinship*, 102.
29. *Oxford Dictionaries,* 'virtual,' accessed June 20, 2015. (http://www.oxforddictionaries.com/definition/english/virtual)
30. Yngvesson, *Belonging in an Adopted World*, 13.
31. Ibid.
32. Brian Massumi, *Parables for the Virtual: Movement, Affect, Sensation.* (Durham: Duke University Press, 2002).

33. To contemplate such dynamisms and the configuration that affects circulate and forge between bodies—both human and technological—it is important to understand the body in terms of Gilles Deleuze and Felix Guattari's concept of "assemblage" by which they postulate a radical configuration of the body, its boundaries, and its becoming from an epistemological perspective. Describing assemblage as the process in which heterogeneous elements (signs, feelings, desires, nonconscious bodies, etc.) are randomly arranged, organized, and joined together, Deleuze and Guattari do not privilege the human body over an inorganic entity; instead, they conceptualize the body in such a way so as to focus on its permeability, its openness to join other bodies, and its adaptability. Through this process, the boundaries of bodies encounter various forces, are disintegrated, and then forged into new boundaries, and articulated into new bodies. By attending to the articulations of the body, they emphasize its dynamism—in other words, the body is not a fixed or given entity, but is instead always in formation. Along this radical postulation of the body is fashioned a mode of inquiry that privileges the process of movement over the location of the body. (Gilles Deleuze and Felix Guattari, *A Thousand Plateaus: Capitalism and Schizophrenia* [Minneapolis: University of Minnesota Press, 1987]).
34. Patricia T. Clough, Introduction to *The Affective Turn: Theorizing the Social*, ed. Patricia T. Clough and Jean Halley (Durham: Duke University Press, 2007), 2.
35. Alison M. Jaggar, *Feminist Politics and Human Nature* (Totowa: Rowman and Allanheld, 1983), 256, quoted in Evelyn Nakano Glenn, "Social Contruction of Mothering," in *Mothering: Ideology, Experience, and Agency*, ed. Evelyn Nakano Glenn, Grace Chang, and Linda Rennie Forcey (New York: Routledge, 1994), 3.
36. Ibid.
37. The phrase "discursive-material-affective" draws upon Karen Barad's conjunctive term "material-discursive," and denotes the techno-scientific aspects of materiality, as used by Barad in her work "Posthumanist Performativity: Toward an Understanding of How Matter Comes to Matter," *Signs: Journal of Women in Culture and Society* 28, no. 3 (2003): 801–831.

38. Gregory J. Seigworth and Melissa Gregg, Introduction to *The Affect Theory Reader*, ed. Melissa Gregg and Gregory J. Seigworth (Durham: Duke University Press, 2010), 6.
39. Karen Barad, "Posthumanist Performativity," 814.
40. Ibid., 815.
41. Ibid., 816.
42. Dwight Conquergood, "Performance Studies: Interventions and Radical Research," *Theater & Drama Review* 46, no. 2 (2002): 145–156.
43. Ibid., 149.
44. I use pseudonyms for the birth mothers throughout the book, but the adoption agency workers who are named in the interviews with the birth mothers remain unchanged. Second, stylistically, I follow the format of Korean names, with the last name first and the first name second.
45. Sometimes, they were already in possession of a translated copy of the letters, as adoption agencies sometimes offered translation services for birth mothers. In those cases, the birth mothers still wanted my translation, to confirm the accuracy of the adoption service's translation.
46. Walter Benjamin, *Illuminations: Essays and Reflections*, trans. Harry Zohn (New York: Schocken Books, 1969), 76.
47. Ibid., 78.
48. Michel Foucault, "Of Other Spaces," trans. Jay Miskowiec, *Diacritics* 16, no. 1 (1986): 24.
49. Ibid.

PART I

Unbecoming Mothers: A History of Gendered Violence

CHAPTER 2

Secure the Nation, Secure the Family

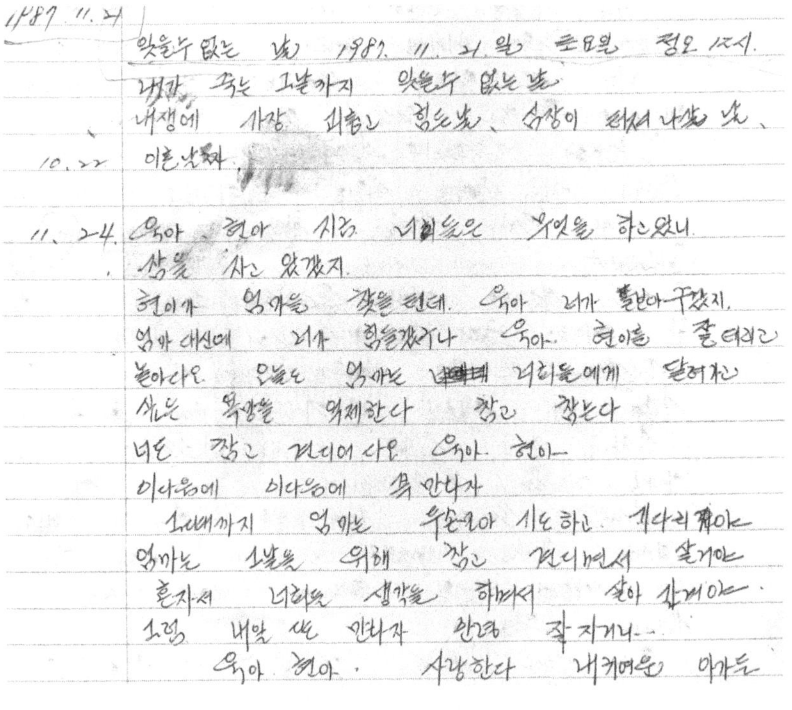

Fig. 2.1 Shin Young Eun's journal entry (courtesy of Shin Young Eun)

November 21st, 1987
　　Unforgettable day. 1987 November 21, a Saturday afternoon. The day I won't forget until my death; the most painful and heart-wrenching day of my life. The day that my heart was torn asunder.
November 24th, 1987
　　Dear Ook and Hyun. What are you doing? You must be sleeping right now. Hyun, you must be wondering where I am. Ook, you must take care of Hyun. I know it must be difficult. Please take care of your brother since I am not there. I tried to stop myself from going to see you again today. I will endure. I hope you two can be patient. We will find each other someday. Until then, I will pray and wait for you. I will survive my days with endurance and persistence. I will always be thinking of you as I go through life by myself. I will see you tomorrow. I love you both, my dear children.

Shin Young Eun wrote these journal entries after she gave up her two children for adoption in 1987.[1] Her two boys were among the almost 8000 Korean children who were separated from their birth country and families that year and placed in adoptive families in the US and Western Europe.[2] When I probed her for the details on why she gave up the children, she said, "There was no other option, but to give them up." She added, "People might wonder under what circumstances a mother could possibly abandon her children. Probably they would not know. Yes, there is a situation like that. If you haven't experienced it, you absolutely would not be able to understand it; but, there truly is." The first part of this book, Chapters 2 and 3, offers insight into the seemingly incomprehensible circumstances that drive numerous mothers, such as Shin Young Eun, to choose transnational adoption.

The 1970s and the 1980s are a critical period in South Korea's transnational adoption history.[3] During these two decades, there was an alarming growth in the number of children being sent abroad every year, from slightly more than 1000 in the late 1960s to its peak of over 8800 in 1985. In sum, the children sent abroad during this time constitute more than two-thirds of South Korea's total overseas adoption placements. This explosive growth in transnational adoption corresponds with the nation's rapid economic growth, following its postwar devastation. Some critics began to argue that the country's impressive economic development was partly explained by its steady reliance on the transnational adoption practice as a de facto surrogate child welfare system for children in need.

Rather than simply assuming that poverty leads a birth mother to choose adoption, this chapter considers how South Korea's inadequate social welfare policy has structurally influenced the rise of adoption. What explains South Korea's persistent dearth of a social welfare system? How has it been rationalized and justified? To understand the lack of a comprehensive social welfare system, it is crucial to understand the historical and political contexts of the Korean War (1950–1953). Thus, this chapter begins by highlighting the unresolved state of the Korean War. With a war that has lingered for more than 60 years, the South Korean state set national security as its top priority, rendering all other social policy needs as secondary; furthermore; it has operated an exceptional mode of governance that, at times, assailed the basic life necessities of its own people.

In highlighting South Korea's lack of a comprehensive social welfare policy as the result of a deliberate security state policy, this chapter examines two major institutions, child welfare and the national family planning policy, which were both heavily influenced by foreign aid programs. South Korea's heavy reliance on foreign aid in its postwar recovery, as well as the participation of foreign aid organizations in orphan relief efforts, formed the practical and affective basis for a humanitarian market of excess Korean children.

South Korea's family planning policy, which was initiated under the aegis of foreign aid organizations, provides the ideological mechanism by which some children and some families were rendered excess population, unworthy of protection or care. In the promotion of a self-reliant family as the cornerstone of national security, family planning policy regulated women's reproduction and rationalized South Korea's limited public welfare policy. Basing the well-being of the family on patriarchal protection and authority, the state's family planning policy left numerous children and their mothers who lived outside the normative patriarchal family with little means to receive any public assistance when in crisis. The child welfare initiatives via transnational adoption and the family welfare policy via family planning, both originated in the convergence of the US's Cold War–era geopolitical and economic interests and South Korea's national security interests, thus paving the way to institutionalize what began as an emergency orphan relief program to develop into a permanent institution for child welfare.[4]

With a critical assessment of South Korea's national security agenda, and its geopolitical and ideological state apparatus, this chapter engages the birth mothers' accounts of their separation from their child. These stories, collected from mothers of mixed-race children, single mothers, widows, divorcées, working-class mothers, and poor mothers, provide details about the life struggles of those beyond the purview of the ideal, normative, self-reliant family. The birth mothers' accounts describe a prevalence of domestic violence, spousal neglect, and economic hardship, fraught with interpersonal, gendered violence, and multiple exploitations. Furthermore, the birth mother's separation from the child is fraught with institutionalized gendered violence, such as the economic marginalization of women; the absence of legal recognition for single motherhood; the lack of custody rights for divorcées; and the unavailability of public relief for battered women. Their life stories poignantly convey the concrete effects of gendered violence at both the interpersonal and institutional levels, illustrating how a family crisis can escalate into a family's disintegration, due to a dearth of public provisions.[5]

A critical analysis of the development of transnational adoption illuminates how South Korea has pursued this practice as its de facto policy for removing excess children existing beyond the normative, self-reliant, patriarchal family. Originally the practice began as a way to deal with mixed-race children. Then, it was applied to children from poor families and/or those from single mothers, widows, and divorcées; twined children or children with special needs were also targeted. This practice continues today, although the number of adoptees has dropped to a few hundred as of 2015. Drawing connections between the birth mothers' surrender of their children and South Korea's national family planning policy, this chapter ends with a rumination on the roles of birth mothers in relation to the building of the national family and national security. I argue that, by pursuing adoption, Korean birth mothers joined millions of Korean women who performed a virtuous maternal citizenship by self-regulating their own reproduction. By surrendering a child born out of wedlock, or into dire poverty, they participated in a national security policy that linked the idea of a self-reliant family with the nation's economic development. Through their participation, birth mothers upheld the state's ideology about the family and the nation, and thus became virtual—or, in a sense, virtuous—mothers.

2.1 The Unresolved War: A Permanent Condition for Emergency Relief

The practice of transnational adoption in South Korea can be traced back to the Korean War, and the war orphan crisis that followed.[6] How did a postwar emergency relief program turn into a permanent child welfare institution? What were the particular historical, geopolitical, socioeconomic, and psychological conditions that have facilitated South Korea's ongoing involvement in transnational adoption, even after its rapid economic progress? To consider these questions, I examine the Korean War, not just as an originating event but also as a crucial political mechanism that justified the nation's long-term engagement in transnational adoption. Any analysis that considers the Korean War as a political mechanism must first acknowledge that the war has not yet come to a definitive end, for although the fighting ceased with an armistice, there has not been a peace treaty. According to Charles Armstrong, the armistice signifies "a partial resolution to a conflict, a halfway house between war and peace."[7]

Korea's unresolved war, in which there is neither war nor peace, is a perfect example of Giorgio Agamben's "state of exception."[8] The state of exception, according to Agamben, is the condition of rule in modern democratic states that provides a necessary alibi to justify executive rule in a moment of crisis.[9] The unresolved nature of the Korean War, as Korean sociologist Kim Dong-choon succinctly put it, is characterized by the "present progressive tense," which indicates continuing action, something going on now; thus, the Korean War can be seen as a more than 60-year-long state of exception, establishing the conditions for a government whose primary imperative is national security.[10]

South Korea's modern political history can largely be divided into two phases: (1) the developmental state formation period from 1960 to the 1980s; and (2) the neoliberal state formation period, following the Asian financial crisis in 1997. In the years directly following the Korean War, South Korea experienced great political turmoil that aggravated its war-stricken poverty; its GNP was then one of the lowest in the world. In 1961, Park Chung-hee, a former army official for imperial Japan, executed a military coup d'état and seized the office of the president; his regime lasted until his assassination in 1979, only to be continued by another military junta led by Chun Doo-hwan (1981–1987).

During the period of developmental state formation, the national security paradigm persistently defined two national priorities, and operationalized its security agenda along these axes: (1) the nation's defense; and (2) the national economy. In its drive for a strong military and a robust economy, the South Korean government continuously acted, as Jae-Jung Suh (2010) describes, as "a state that *suspends* democracy in the name of defending democracy and that *denies* its citizens their existence as such in the name of protecting their rights" (my italics).[11] Suh's observation illuminates the operational logic of a South Korean security state regime that sanctioned a curtailment of civil liberties and that neglected basic governmental support for its population, in the name of national security and in the promotion of democracy. Thus, in this way, South Korea's national security agenda was developed at the price of undermining the security of its own people.

Within the context of the security state regime, South Korea's inadequate social welfare policy was justified and enforced as a necessary condition for national security. To put it another way, the nation's perpetual lack of a social welfare system is not the natural outcome of scarcity, but rather a deliberate policy advanced by the security state. Thus, the development of the transnational adoption practice must be contextualized within South Korea's national security paradigm.

However, an inadequate social welfare system does not sufficiently explain how the transnational adoption practice developed from an emergency orphan relief program into a permanent child welfare institution. To answer that question requires an inquiry into the procedures and mechanisms that the transnational adoption practice continuously developed in South Korea during the 1970s and the 1980s. So, first, I turn to examine the patterns and directives set by the foreign aid organizations during the postwar recovery period that paved the way, and then eventually built a child welfare system centered on transnational adoption.

2.2 Foreign Aid-Based Welfare: The Development of the Transnational Adoption Practice

During the Korean War and its aftermath, foreign aid flooded into South Korea from both the US government and foreign humanitarian agencies, which were predominantly American Christian organizations; a smaller number of organizations originated from the UK, Italy, Switzerland, and Canada.[12] Meanwhile, Christian missionary organizations that had been in South Korea before the war significantly expanded their relief operations. During the 1960s, donor countries expanded to include Germany, Australia, France, Belgium, Sweden, Austria, and the Netherlands. These organizations either established a Korean branch office or directly provided emergency relief, which ranged from the distribution of food (grains), old clothing, medicine, and other amenities (e.g., toothpaste, soap, toilet paper, school supplies) to the construction of orphanages, hospitals, and other service facilities. In postwar South Korea, organized relief efforts from these foreign aid organizations were the only social services available to those who suffered from abject poverty and widespread disease.[13]

The South Korean government continued to rely heavily on foreign aid to meet the country's social service needs up to the mid-1970s; as a result, such organizations came to play a strong social service role. From 1960 to 1974, the total annual worth of donations from foreign organizations—both material and financial—constituted a substantial share of South Korea's yearly social welfare budget, ranging from 43.9 to 216 %.[14] Their total annual donations up to the mid-1970s were more or less equal to the annual expenditures of South Korea's Ministry of Health and Welfare.

The nation's heavy budgetary and administrative reliance on foreign aid agencies meant that these external interests shaped the direction and development of South Korea's welfare system, as is the case with its child welfare institutions. Reflecting the Western welfare model, which addresses social problems through institutional means, a large share of aid was devoted to the establishment and maintenance of orphanages.[15] The total number of orphanages and children in institutional care more than doubled from 7338 children in 101 orphanages in 1949, right before the Korean War, to 30,000 children at 280 orphanages in 1952, a year before the armistice was signed.[16] This figure continued to grow and reached 50,000 to 60,000 children at 615 orphanages in 1961. The contributions of foreign organizations to these orphanages increased two-fold from 1958 to comprise 52.5 % of the orphanages' budgets in 1968.[17]

The development of transnational adoption originated in the sustainable donor program implemented by foreign aid organizations. The Christian Children's Fund (CCF) expanded its successful "sponsorship adoption" program for orphaned children in China to include Korean children; later, similar organizations, such as World Vision, Foster Parents' Plan, and the Oriental Missionary Society, followed suit.[18] Sponsorship adoption was a personalized donor program in which a donor would be matched with a child, and communicated with him or her through the exchange of letters and photos. This sponsored adoption program, as Arissa Oh observes, "allowed Americans back home [to] 'adopt' Korean children from a distance."[19] Consequently, sponsored adoption became one of the most popular fundraising methods used by these organizations. As sponsorship adoption grew, there was an increasing number of donors who wished to actually adopt their sponsored child. Humanitarian aid organizations adapted to this demand and began to promote transnational adoption. Thus, what began originally as a fundraising strategy—that is, sponsored adoption—was transformed into a catalyst for facilitating transnational adoption.

Many foreign aid organizations participated in the early development of South Korean adoption practices in various capacities and for varying lengths of time. For example, the Church World Service, which established the Korea Church World Service in South Korea in 1949, was not originally an adoption agency; but, it began developing orphan adoption programs in 1955.[20] International Social Services–USA started to become involved in foster care and international adoption in 1957.[21] In contrast to these organizations that came to Korea with no explicit focus on adoption work, other foreign aid organizations began with the specific mission of child rescue, particularly of mixed-race children. For example, the then-named Holt Adoption Placement, which developed into the adoption agency with the greatest number of transnational adoption cases, was established in 1960, with the explicit purpose of providing child welfare, foreign adoption, and medical services. The Christian Reform Korean Mission, founded and supported by the Christian Reformed Church of Michigan, ran the Christian Adoption Program of Korea (CAPOK) to promote domestic adoption during the 1960s.[22] Finally, the Pearl S. Buck Foundation opened its Korean branch in 1965 with the mission of promoting interracial adoption.

The direct and indirect operation of foreign aid organizations in international adoption was streamlined in 1967 when a new adoption law mandated that every international adoption should be carried out by a Korean government–licensed agency.[23] After this law was instituted, transnational adoption practice came to be carried out exclusively by four government-licensed adoption agencies: Holt International (formerly Holt Adoption Placement), Korea Social Service, the Social Welfare Society, and Eastern Children's Welfare Society (formerly the Missionary Society). Two of these adoption agencies, Holt International and Korea Social Service, were run by foreign aid organizations. The Social Welfare Society, the oldest, Korean-run adoption organization, was established with foreign aid in 1956. The Eastern Children's Welfare Society was Korean-run, but had its origins in the Christian Crusader, an American Christian evangelical ministry.[24] In other words, even those agencies that were Korean-run were funded and were operated directly, or indirectly, by foreign aid organizations.

In the mid-1970s, foreign aid organizations began to incrementally withdraw their 20-year-long support of material and human resources from Korea, by either leaving the country or by diverting their primary objective to missionary or educational activities, which had initially been their original objectives.[25] These changes were spurred by the downturns in the US economy, combined with the nation's defeat in the Vietnam War; South Korea's improved economic conditions; and, a demand for relief work in other regions. In response, the South Korean government expressed its concern and described the withdrawal as premature, citing the fact that its national defense expenditures comprised almost half of South Korea's national annual budget, and, therefore, that it lacked adequate funding to develop a social welfare system. Rather than developing a comprehensive social welfare program to replace child welfare institutions once supported by foreign aid organizations, the Korean government instead encouraged big corporations to carry out charity work and conducted national donation drives for the poor. In 1972, the government allocated 0.75 % of its national budget to social welfare.

The withdrawal of foreign aid had acute implications on the welfare of children, especially children at orphanages since they had been the main target of foreign aid work. To fill the gap of social services, the government's solution was to consign the care of these children to a collection of adoption agencies and other private child welfare facilities. By consigning the financial and administrative care of these children to adoption agencies, these institutions became surrogate child welfare facilities, in charge of maintaining the orphanages. The effect of this policy was to render indistinguishable children in orphanages and children in foster care, intended for adoption. Inevitably, the lack of a governmental child welfare policy caused the orphanages to work more closely with adoption agencies, which were for-profit organizations intended to promote transnational adoption.

The decades-long postwar recovery efforts of foreign aid organizations paved the affective terrain of the humanitarian market for children in need. Not only did these foreign aid organizations initiate the transnational adoption practice in Korea, but they also left behind the image of a benevolent West, which was conflated with the US, due to its ongoing military occupation and predominant role in supplying foreign aid. Soojin Pate argues that American soldiers were mobilized to participate in massive relief efforts during, and subsequent to, the war. She eloquently captures the implications of such relief efforts: "These charitable acts of humanitarianism worked to rehabilitate the image of an imposing US imperial power by not only erasing state violence but also by propping up American soldiers as rescuer rather than colonizer, relief worker rather than occupier."[26]

Extending her observations to the affective ramifications of relief efforts, in general, I argue that humanitarian efforts by the US military and other Western nongovernmental organizations (NGOs) helped to narrativize the imagery of the US and the West into benevolent saviors and protectors. Thus, in South Korea, this image of the US became woven into the cultural fabric of the "American Dream," which associates the personal narrative of development and prosperity with the US or western European countries, like the US. These trends operated as an affective engine to further the development of transnational adoption in South Korea.

While foreign aid left an image of the US and the West that was associated with prosperity, fairness, and generosity, the vast majority of US citizens, affiliated with Christianity, visualized Korea through the powerful photographs of Korean War orphans that many foreign aid organizations persistently used in fundraising drives, even into the 1970s. The images of Korean War orphans not only mobilized donors who once supported children through sponsorship adoption, but they also continued to pull in donors, and helped to transform them into prospective, adoptive parents. In the humanitarian market tides for transnational adoption, the imagery of the wretched orphan is coupled and completed by a benevolent US. Given all these factors, it is not coincidental that the withdrawal of foreign aid, more or less, corresponded to a consistent increase in transnational adoption from South Korea. As a result, the average number of adoptees hovered around 500 to 600 annually in the 1960s; multiplied to well over a thousand in 1970; rose to 5000 in 1975; and, then, hit 8800 in 1985.

The presence of relief efforts by Christian-based, private humanitarian organizations for nearly 20 years after the war left a profound imprint on the development of South Korea's child welfare policy, and laid the groundwork for the development of transnational adoption as a practice in which 'God's love,' could be realized. This Christian perspective meshed easily with the US's Cold-War lens through which adoption was viewed as a way of saving children from communism. In her analysis of US geopolitics in Asia during the Cold War, Christina Klein points out NGOs played a significant role in asserting US influence in Asia.[27] Organizations such as the Christian Children's Fund and Pearl S. Buck's Welcome House issued advertisements that described these war-torn or poverty-stricken Asian countries as a dangerous environment in which communists could be born and flourish, thereby providing the crucial link between the relief efforts of private US citizens and their political participation in the US foreign policy of containing and integrating Asian countries.[28]

From this perspective, an American, by bringing Asian children into his or her home, was able to contribute to defending Asia's democracy and fighting off communism. Through this nationalistic rendition, the private humanitarian action of saving children became a patriotic political act during the Cold War. Embedded in the geopolitical, religious, and economic rise of what the US has called "the free world" is transnational adoption from South Korea, a practice aligned with the US's Cold-War politics that has helped to secure US global hegemony.

Mixed-Race Children: Excess Children from US Camptowns

The South Korean government's interest in the transnational adoption practice developed with a growing concern over the increasing number of mixed-race war orphans during the war. In response to the situation, then President Syngman Rhee identified international adoption as the best solution for such children, arguing that they would suffer discrimination in the future.[29] The Rhee government's special "concern" and "arrangement" for mixed-race children converged well with the foreign aid organizations' priority to provide adoption for mixed-race children. Shortly after the ceasefire in 1953, with a 1954 presidential order, the Child Placement Service (*Adongyangbohoe*) was established with humanitarian funds from abroad for the specific purpose of facilitating the adoption of mixed-race children to the US and other Western countries.[30] In 1956, Bertha Holt, the wife of Harry Holt, who later became a key figure in the establishment of the transnational adoption practice, met with President Rhee and the first lady to discuss transporting mixed-race children out of country and secured the assistance of the Ministry of Health and Social Welfare.[31] With the government's recommendation, South Korean newspapers published promotional articles and advertisements to recruit mixed-race children for adoption.[32] Therefore, from the start, both South Korean government officials and foreign aid organizations designated mixed-race children as the population that needed to be adopted first; thus, until 1962, mixed-race children constituted the vast majority of children sent abroad for adoption.

The problem of mixed-race children, however, did not end with postwar emergency relief programs. Between 1955 and 2005, the estimated number of mixed-race children born in South Korea totaled about 11,000.[33] The background of their births is largely attributed to the US military presence in South Korea, and the development of camptowns, called *kijich'on*, in Korean villages which are adjacent to military bases and that provide services, especially prostitution for soldiers. Since 1945, when the US military occupation was established in southern Korea, informal sexual exchanges with Americans came into being as a means of survival for Koreans, and proliferated during the Korean War. By 1954, there were an estimated 350,000 prostitutes in Korea, 60 % of who serviced American military forces.[34] During the 1960s, military prostitution developed into a major institution, in response to the ongoing presence of US troops, and there were an average of 50,000 to 60,000 sex workers stationed throughout US bases in Korea.[35] Although the South Korean government had outlawed prostitution, camptowns were left alone and came to be a special district wherein the Law Against Morally Depraved Behaviors (*yullakhaengwi pangjibŏp*) was suspended.[36]

For a long time, *kijich'on* women have been treated as social pariahs in Korean society, even as the government sanctioned them and depended on their labor. For example, during the 1960s and 1970s, *kijich'on* women were, at times, mobilized to participate in government-initiated projects, such as the camptown purification movement (1971–1976), and even praised for their sexual labor as a patriotic service needed to maintain the morale of US servicemen and to earn US dollars, thereby bolstering both the nation's economic and military security.[37] However, as illustrated in derogatory names, such as *yanggongju*, which means "yankee whore," they were believed to be morally corrupt and sexually deviant based on their "abnormal" occupation of mixing their flesh with foreign soldiers for money, and viewed as the lowest class of sex workers. By association, mixed-race children were treated as social outcasts, subject to ridicule and disdain, and excluded from educational and occupational opportunities throughout their lives.[38] As a result, adoption became the norm for mixed-race children in military camptowns, as affirmed by the striking fact that only 25 % of *kijich'on* mothers raised their children themselves.[39] The experiences of Grandmother Kang and Im Soon Ja, which are detailed in the next section, shed light on the pressures faced by *kijich'on* mothers. Both—despite their desire and ability to raise their children—decided on adoption for their children.

Kijich'on Mothers—Give for Life

In the 1970s, the proportion of mixed-race children rapidly decreased; they were estimated to constitute fewer than 10 % of the total number of children involved in transnational adoption, a significant reduction from

36.5 % in the 1960s.[40] To include the experiences of *kijich'on* birth mothers, in 2010, I visited *Durebang*, a shelter organization for former military sex workers, in Uijeongbu, a city north of Seoul that has the largest presence of US military bases in South Korea. There, I learned and confirmed the prevalence of adoption in camptowns. In the following year, during my second visit to *Haessal Sahoepokchihoe* (Sunlit Sisters' Center), a Christian advocacy organization for former military sex workers, I was able to meet with two birth mothers, Grandmother Kang, who did not wish to share her full name, and Im Soon Ja. We met on two separate Tuesdays after their weekly communal lunch. Both women worked and lived in a camptown, where the vast majority of local villagers earned their living by running or engaging in small businesses, such as bars, restaurants, dry cleaners, stores, and sex services that targeted US military personnel as their main clientele. Both Grandmother Kang and Im Soon Ja had lived in several different camptowns their entire adult lives and were now settled in Anjeong-ri in Pyeongtaek, which was occupied by the US Air Force base, Camp Humphreys, known as K-6, since the Korean War.

Grandmother Kang is herself a war orphan. Born in 1937 in a town that is now part of North Korea, she was separated from her family while fleeing south during the Korean War. She ended up living with her brother and sister-in-law, but she did not get along with them and finally left the house at 16. She then found work at a *kijich'on* and never left. When she was 23, and eight months pregnant, her client and lover, the father of her baby—a US serviceman—returned home to his wife and three children. After waiting for almost a year to hear back from the baby's father, she inquired about his whereabouts at a family counseling center on the US base. There, she was discouraged from trying to contact him, and told, "If you send [the child] there, you will ruin three children's lives."[41] So, she raised her child alone until he turned 14.

> Soon after my son was born, I was approached by someone associated with the Pearl S. Buck Foundation, an adoption agency. She encouraged me to register with the agency, which would allow me to receive a regular allowance for my child through some kind of sponsorship. There, I was asked whether I was interested in placing my child for adoption ... I said, "No." A few years later, someone visited me, this time, not from the Pearl S. Buck Foundation, but from Holt. So I said, "No, I am not going to send my child away. I will raise him. I was a war orphan myself when I was 13. I cannot make my child an orphan."... The Holt representative persuaded me to

register my child with them in order to receive some aid. So I was deceived again and registered my child. But I was still undecided.... As Seungho [her child] grew older... he said that he wanted to go to the US and asked me to go with him. I told him, "I cannot go with you." He said, "I will go first and you can come later." After that, I would occasionally ask him if he really wanted to go to America. When he began middle school, his response changed. He said, "Yes, I want to go to America, but if *umma* [mother in Korean] does not want me to go, it is okay to not send me to the US." Some time later, I asked him what his dream was. He told me he wanted to become a doctor...and as soon as he said that, I realized that I had to send him to the US ... So I consulted with Yoo Ju Yeol, a Holt staff member. I asked him, "What should I do? My child wants to go to America." Yoo told me, "Of course, you should send him." He must be really happy to have gotten my son. A new law had just been passed restricting adoption to children younger than 15, and so his adoption was pushed through quickly.[42] (Grandmother Kang, whose 14-year-old son was sent to the US in 1974)

Meanwhile, Im Soon Ja, who was born in 1948, lost her mother at a young age. Her father remarried, soon after his wife's death. When she was nine, Soon Ja was sent to a wealthy household as an adopted daughter, and lived there, working as a housemaid. At 13, on her way back from a water well, she fell and destroyed some buckets. She felt too afraid to go back to her adopted home, and ran away. While searching for a new place to work, she met an elderly woman who introduced her to a family, where she worked as domestic help. When she was 16, she ran away, again and fell in with someone who eventually sold her to a bar owner in Songtan, *kijich'on*.

... when he [my child] was three [in American age], five in Korean... it was 1978, I think. At that time, a woman from Holt came around. [They] said, "Isn't it difficult to raise a mixed-race child? For [the child's] future, [it would be better] to give [up the child for adoption]." They had been coming after me for several years.... they came to Songtan when he was one. They had somehow figured out that I had a mixed-race child and asked me to give him up for adoption. I said, "No". Then I moved to Kunsan, and they came to Kunsan, too. Then I moved back to Oori and they showed up again. [I asked, "The same person?"] No, she came from the company, Holt Agency. For future. Overseas, better. Because the child is mixed, if he lived here, he would have no future.

Looking back, it was good that I gave him up.... I have no regrets. As time passed, the only thing that I feel about the adoption is that it was very good that I sent him away. I could not imagine keeping him in such a wretched life, without his father.⁴³ (Im Soon Ja, whose five-year-old, black-Korean biracial child was adopted to the US in 1978)

Both accounts capture the experience of birth mothers of mixed-race children living in US camptowns. They both became pregnant while in a contract marriage arrangement.⁴⁴ They raised their children by themselves, without any assistance from the babies' fathers who returned to the US after completing their terms of duty. In such situations, *kijich'on* mothers, as shown in Grandmother Kang's account, are not entitled to any legal protection or practical assistance from the US military. The lack of access to the enforcement of child support from the baby's father is underwritten in the Status of Forces Agreement (SOFA) between the US and South Korea that protects the privacy rights of American soldiers.⁴⁵ Thus, US military officials are under no obligation to help or cooperate with Korean women trying to locate their child's fathers.

Grandmother Kang and Im Soon Ja did not identify poverty as the principal cause for giving up their child to adoption.⁴⁶ After all, during the 1960s and the 1970s when they were raising their children, their earnings were probably comparatively better than the average pay of factory or domestic workers, the jobs held by the majority of women working at the time. As both women indicated, they really wanted to raise their children on their own. However, the decision to relinquish their child to adoption occurred primarily out of concern for their child's future, which was reinforced and underscored by the repeated efforts of adoption agency workers to recruit the children for adoption.

What is most revelatory about the *kijich'on* birth mothers' adoption accounts is that, although neither Grandmother Kang nor Im Soon Ja initially considered adoption, persistent solicitations from adoption agency workers catalyzed their decision to relinquish their children. The adoption agencies mentioned by the two women, Holt Adoption Placement and Pearl S. Buck Foundation, both came to South Korea as foreign aid organizations. The adoption agencies' active recruitment of mixed-race children for adoption was not isolated to the case of Grandmother Kang and Im Soon Ja, but were part of a larger regulatory mechanism established over time wherein the South Korean government targeted mixed-race children as a specific group of children to be adopted first; it was a deliberate, routine policy for adoption agency workers to visit camptowns, and to actively solicit *kijich'on* mothers to give up their mixed-race children.

Hyun Sook Han, one of the most influential social workers in the development of transnational adoption in South Korea, writes in her memoir, "The social worker's job was to visit different sites—mostly near the military bases—that were known to have high numbers of mixed-race children living with their birth mothers and ask the mothers if they wanted to place their children for adoption."[47] During the 1960s, Han would go to Pyeongtaek—where Grandmother Kang and Im Soon Ja now live—and meet with a local ob-gyn, who would provide Han with medical information about pregnancies, deliveries, and abortions in the area. Han placed hundreds of mixed-race children into foster care for eventual adoption over a period of about 12 to 18 months.[48]

Juxtaposing Grandmother Kang's and Im Soon Ja's experiences with the larger historical context and processes of adoption, especially the targeting of mixed-race children, exposes how transnational adoption operated as a population removal policy that was essentially institutionalized violence against the sex workers' motherhood, and racism against their mixed-race children. The South Korean government manipulated what was originally considered to be a general relief effort, that is, the adoption of war orphans in the aftermath of the Korean War, to resolve the "social problem" of mixed-race children; further, it continued this policy to ensure that the mixed-race population remained sparse, thus shaping a normalized pattern of reproductive behavior among *kijich'on* mothers. As Eleana Kim states, this policy of eliminating mixed-race children served to promote the imaginary of South Korea as an uncontaminated and racially homogeneous group, underscoring the ideology of a nation of one people (*ilmin-jui*), as well as to further defend itself against the North Korean communists' accusations that it was dependent on US military forces.[49]

Mixed-race children in South Korea have been visible for almost 70 years since the US military occupation government was installed in 1945. According to South Korea's official national security rhetoric, the US military presence remains a geopolitical necessity. By extension, this rhetoric implicitly condones militarized prostitution as necessary for South Korea's national security: both US military personnel and local *kijich'on* women were viewed as necessary conditions for national security. Beneath the South Korean government's systematic population removal policy lay the nationalistic view of mixed-race children as collateral, biological excess, or waste, from the sexual labor of militarized prostitutes that needed to be removed via transnational adoption.[50] This policy lays bare the intentional, institutional neglect of the *kijich'on* women's motherhood.

2.3 Family Planning Policy[51]—Economic Development—National Security

Just as foreign aid organizations largely influenced the development of transnational adoption as a major area of child welfare, other foreign aid organizations greatly influenced the nation's reproductive policy, or population control policy in South Korea. Soon after World War II, when global geopolitics were realigning along Cold War politics, Malthusian researchers and US military advisory reports identified the population growth rate in undeveloped regions as presenting the utmost threat to global peace and progress. In 1958, the Draper Committee, a presidential committee under President Dwight Eisenhower, made a policy recommendation to launch official programs to address overpopulation in "Third World" countries.[52]

However, in an era of worldwide decolonization, the US did not want to be seen as directly interfering in the countries of interest, so did not immediately implement an official policy on this matter. Instead, the US government worked with NGOs, such as the World Council of Churches and the Population Council, established by John D. Rockefeller III, to spearhead population control activities in Asia.[53] Then, in 1961, the Population Council established a Korean branch office, promising organizational support for family planning programs in South Korea. That same year, George Cadbury, executive director of the International Planned Parenthood Federation (IPPF), launched the Planned Parenthood Federation of Korea (PPFK), which later developed into a hybrid governmental agency–civil service organization that supervised foreign aid, and trained personnel; it became the central agency for the implementation and promotion of national and regional campaigns for population control over the next 35 years.[54] Throughout the 1960s, 80 % of its annual budget came from foreign aid.[55]

The concern about overpopulation in postcolonial countries in Asia meshed with the US's Cold-War era hegemony that linked anti-communism with economic development.[56] A 1961 speech by US President John F. Kennedy encapsulated the US government's Cold-War narrative: "World peace in the Cold War is achieved not by an arms race but by economic development of the free capitalist regions."[57] Washington's emphasis on economic development as a defense strategy against communism was echoed by Rhew Dahl Yeong, the PPFK president in 1968:

> … (T)here is no other best measure to fight off communism than family planning…. The best way to win over communism is not fighting with arms

but living better. I believe that population management enabled quality education for children, enriched the national economy and eventually contributed to our national power.[58]

Aligned with the US's view that economic development was the best weapon to defeat communism, Rhew Dahl Yeong saw family planning as integral to national development, and to the nation's future. In other words, participating in national family planning not only facilitated economic development for the nation but also promoted national defense. Throughout the national family planning policy period, from 1961 to 1996, the role of the family and its reproduction in South Korea remained closely aligned to national economic development and to the national security agenda. The national family planning policy, which was a central part of a five-year national economic development plan, was initiated by President Park Chung-hee (1961–1979) in 1962.[59] By July 1962, within six months after the family planning program was launched, 182 regional and local health clinics (*pokŏnso*) were established, completing the necessary infrastructure for launching nationwide family planning campaigns.[60] In 1964, the government began outreach programs with family planning agents to introduce the idea and practice of contraception and mobilized mobile vans equipped to perform IUD insertion and vasectomies that had been provided by the IPPF and the Swedish Development Agency.[61]

Furthermore, the government employed invasively specific, family planning objectives that became more intense over time. From 1966 to 1970, the PPFK promoted the "3.3.35 campaign," which set goals for the desirable number of children, the frequency of childbirth, and the age of reproductive termination in each family: families were to aim for three children in three-year intervals until the age of 35. Beginning in the 1970s, the slogan changed to "do not discriminate between a girl or boy and just raise two children well" (*atŭl ttal kupyŏl malko tulman naha chal kilŭcha*), which changed to a milder version of the one-child policy in China in the 1980s: "If you give birth to even one child, the peninsula will overflow" (*hanassikman nahato samch'ŏnlinŭn ch'omanwŏn*). Reflecting its aggressive policy planning and implementation, South Korea's family planning policy was a leader in population control among developing countries, and achieved a drastic fertility reduction, from 6.1 TFR (total fertility rate) in 1960 to 1.6 TFR in 1996. The South Korean government's focused and consistent engagement in family planning from the 1960s to the 1990s stands in glaring contrast to its persistent lack of a social welfare policy during that time; and, that lack was directly responsible for the rise of transnational adoption from South Korea.

In what ways was the family planning policy implicated in the circumstances under which many working-class women surrendered their children to transnational adoption? Drawing upon the feminist critique of South Korea's family planning policy, I wish to highlight how the policy operated as a key mechanism that rationalized South Korea's deliberate lack of social welfare programs and structured the economic marginalization of women, thereby reinforcing normative patriarchal family dynamics and formation, all of which were key material conditions promoting adoption.

In her book *Militarized Modernity*, Seungsook Moon argues that the South Korean family planning policy was a nationalistic appropriation of women's reproductive rights and sexuality, confining the woman's role in the nation-state to that of being a wife and a mother.[62] Moon crystalized the implications of the family planning policy: "[Women's] subjectivity as full-time, permanent workers is overshadowed by the normative feminine subjectivity of the nonproductive housewife."[63] In other words, the family planning policy primarily recognized women in their role as reproducers of the nation, thus providing the ideological grounds for the economic marginalization and exploitation of women.

By the 1980s, female workers made up 43.5 % of the total labor force, and were concentrated in unskilled or semi-skilled, labor-intensive industries, which included manufacturing textiles and clothing, processing tobacco and food, and assembling electronics.[64] These jobs were severely underpaid, and typically had longer working hours, in comparison to jobs dominated by men. In 1985, women earned, on average, only 46.8 % of what their male counterparts earned in manufacturing industries.[65] Furthermore, women's employment was often regarded as temporary until marriage, which further exacerbated the economic opportunities of married, working-class women.

The economic marginality of women bolstered the material conditions for women's economic dependence on men, which, in turn, reasserted the traditional, gendered division of labor between a husband-provider and a dependent housewife. In this way, the family planning policy enforced patriarchal, gender dynamics. Simultaneously, it structured a normative family configuration that hinged upon patriarchal protection and self-reliance as key factors in a family's well-being. In other words, the economic marginalization of women implicit in South Korea's family planning policy shaped and reinforced structural conditions, so that the well-being of children were ultimately subject to the husband's capabilities and willingness to take care of his own family.

Another major implication of the family planning program was that it highlighted the self-reliant family as the normative patriarchal family. In her book *Human Reproduction of Korean Modernity*, Korean feminist scholar Bae Eun Kyung offers poignant observations about the discourse of the normative family, as dictated by the Planned Parenthood Federation of Korea:

> In the discourse of population management or control, planning a child is part of what a family plans for throughout its life. There are no government or state agencies that will take responsibility for excess population. Based on this assumption, married couples are required to plan for the number of children in their family planning. In cases where a large number of children bring poverty or unhappiness to the family, such conditions are ultimately the family's responsibility and should be resolved within the family. This is the policy implication of the population policies.[66]

As Bae argues, the family planning policy functions as an ideological framework within which each individual family is responsible for its family size. Its underlying message is that self-regulating reproduction is a crucial factor for one's own happiness and achievement, and ultimately essential to the nation's well-being. To ensure that each individual family was able to sustain itself, the government employed family planning as a technology that normalized a self-reliant family. Thus, the narrative of how self-reliant families served as a strong rationale for the perpetual lack of an adequate social welfare system for families.

The narrative of family planning not only lays out a discursive framework but also creates a circulatory logic of disciplining and penalizing families that fall outside the stated norm. Given the ideological premise of a self-reliant family as the standard unit of the nation-state, the very fact that a working-class or single-mother family cannot sustain itself becomes confirmation of a failed duty to engage in responsible family planning, affirms their unworthiness, and, thus, disqualifies them from public assistance.[67] In the national family imperative put forth by South Korea's population policy, anybody who falls outside the normative, self-reliant family unit becomes excess population.

Illegitimate Family: Excess Children from Single Mothers—Extra/Legal

The preceding sections discussed how the South Korean government channeled mixed-race children into overseas adoption, and how the government utilized transnational adoption as a mechanism of social control to eliminate what it viewed as an excess population. Who else comprised this excess population? Or, to put it differently, what were the major characteristics of children in transnational adoption during the 1970s and the 1980s? The abandoned include the children of single mothers, poor mothers, and divorcées; the disabled; and, twins.[68] In what ways, and under what circumstances, did these children become viewed as excess?

Between the 1970s and the 1980s, single motherhood grew considerably from 36 % (a total number of 17,627 mothers) to 72 % (47,153 mothers).[69] The single mother was the most identified source of children for transnational adoption, and, thus, became viewed as a social problem. The dominant image of the single mother tends to be of a young, unmarried woman. My analysis of single mothers, however, focuses specifically on two subsets of single mothers who are often overlooked in the population: those involved in extramarital relationships with married men, and widows, both groups which often remain unexamined or unnamed, as single mothers.

While illegitimacy is often thought to denote young, never-married mothers who become pregnant in a relationship with their young, never-married boyfriends, research findings and anecdotes concerning transnational adoption from South Korea present a different narrative. According to Kim Ji Yeol's seminal research on single mothers in Korea, 16 % of single mothers (20 of 122 women, total) who gave up their children for adoption reported that the baby's father was married.[70] A 1984 report by the Korean Women's Development Institute presented similar findings, indicating that 14.4 % of respondents (of 758 respondents, total) were involved with married men.[71] Although this particular kind of single mother is rarely discussed in South Korea, examples of it are common in personal accounts and anecdotes, and documented in literature.

For example, Katy Robinson, a Korean adoptee and an American journalist, wrote in her memoir, *Single Square Picture*, that she explored her past in Korea and identified her married birth father and unmarried birth mother.[72] In 2004, the *Los Angeles Times* featured the story of an adoptee's search for his missing past and his discovery that he was a son of Lee

Won Man, a former chairman of KOLON, a multi-industrial conglomerate (*chaebol*), and put up for adoption in the US without the consent of the baby's mother—his mistress.[73] For a woman to get involved with a married man produces the condition of possibility in which the birth of a child is immediately outside the man's marriage, instantly marking the child as illegitimate. Illegitimacy was a major factor in the decision of many women to give up their child to adoption.

Yang Sook Ja, a 70-year-old birth mother whom I met in August 2005, was one such single mother. She had insisted that we meet outside, rather than in a café, or in any other enclosed place, to ensure the privacy of our conversation, or perhaps, of her life story. We met in front of an arts center in downtown Seoul and spoke for two hours in a stairwell. Born in North Korea, she had fled to the South and begun working as a black-market retailer in US camptowns during the Korean War. Before she got married, she sold US Post Exchange (PX) merchandise, which are goods that have been smuggled out of US military bases. When she was 40, she divorced her husband, due to his serial infidelity, and left behind her three children. Here is her adoption story:

> Let me tell you a shameful story. I became involved with a married man after my divorce. That's the child's father. I wanted to terminate the pregnancy. The baby's father was opposed to abortion, so I wasn't able to. Though I wasn't rich, I didn't have much trouble managing my life, financially. But then, when the baby came along, I couldn't continue to work. There was no economic support from the baby's father, either. One day, I had a big argument with him. I remembered that my sister told me that her friend took her two children to an adoption agency. So I went to seek some help and consult with someone. They gave me baby formula ... What worried me more than my financial situation was the possibility that my child would blame me for causing him to be born to an unwed mother, which would cause him to be subject to much social discrimination. Wouldn't it be better for him to go abroad and live in a country free of such discrimination?[74] (Yang Sook Ja, born in 1935, had a child adopted in 1976)

Along with economic difficulties, Yang Sook Ja's worries about her child's prospects included a consideration of potential, future anger that her son, as an illegitimate child, might direct at her. The lifelong struggles faced by an illegitimate child and the stigma against women involved with married men raises many questions about the consequences of such relationships.

Lee Mi Sun, another birth mother who had a child from a relationship with a married man, provided more context and details. When she was 28, Lee Mi Sun was working at a computer-related company in Busan. It was not her hometown, so she was renting a room. One day, her elderly landlady approached her, and suggested that she go on a date with a man, whom Mi Sun did not find interesting. She refused, but he kept pursuing her. One day, in the pouring rain, he waited outside her building for hours. She felt so sorry for him and finally came outside to urge him to leave. He begged her to sit down for a cup of coffee. She agreed. Then, he begged her to go to an inn, for warmth. She resisted. For 30 minutes, he pleaded with her. Before leaving with him, she warned him that if anything happened, she would jump out of the second-floor room. Despite her threat, he sexually assaulted her. She lamented to me that she could not do what she had threatened. This is how Lee Mi Sun got involved with the father of her adopted child, by rape.[75] Her adoption background, in light of fears about illegitimacy, is elaborated as follows.

> I didn't know he was married until we started living together. Once I learned of his being still married, I wanted to separate from him immediately. He kept saying that he's been separated from his wife for a long time, and would soon file for divorce. Because I was already... with him, I couldn't leave him, so I continued to live there. Then I found myself pregnant. At that time, if a baby was born outside of marriage, then he or she couldn't have a proper family registry, under the father's name. Instead, the baby would be registered in my household as a cohabitant, not as my child. If he was registered with his father and his legal wife, the child would be mistreated by his wife. That was my worry. Both situations were unbearable to me. So I went to Holt in my sixth month of pregnancy. ... He is the child of a mistress. His status of "illegitimacy" would follow him everywhere, from school to the workplace, interfering with any opportunities that might come his way. His illegitimacy would preclude him from working as a public servant or at big corporations ... If I had wanted to be selfish, I would have hidden him and raised him myself. But for his sake, I chose adoption.[76] (Lee Mi Sun, born in 1956, her child was adopted in 1986)

Both Yang Sook Ja and Lee Mi Sun took the initiative to contact the agency and originated the plan for adoption. As they both clearly articulated, the child's illegitimacy, as well as legal misrecognition, were major reasons influencing the decision to relinquish the child. Before 2005, when the *hojuje*, the nation's patrilineal family registration system, was abolished, a woman's parental relationship to her child was legally recognized only via the child's biological father. Having been involved in relationships with married men, Yang Sook Ja and Lee Mi Sun could not register their children under the father's family name. When a father registers his child, due to the prerogatives of patriarchal kinship, a child's registration under the father's *hojuk* (family registry) automatically renders the father's legal wife as the child's mother, as opposed to the child's biological mother, with or without his wife's consent. Under South Korean family law, if these unmarried mothers had wanted to raise their children, the children would legally be designated as illegitimate.[77]

Given the patriarchal prerogatives of South Korean family law, a child's out-of-wedlock status is a failure of paternal recognition, and thus should be read as the father's responsibility, or lack thereof. And yet, as was the case with Yang Sook Ja and Lee Mi Sun, both single birth mothers who were not even legally recognized as mothers of their children, women are exclusively subject to take complete responsibility for their children. There is absolutely no legal framework that enforces married men to legally recognize their child, not to mention, provide child support. Yang Sook Ja and Lee Mi Sun reached their decision to give up their children for adoption, after negotiating between legal persecution (illegitimacy) for their involvement with married men, and their maternal responsibility for their child's grim future prospects. Through these means, Yang Sook Ja and Lee Mi Sun separated from their children and became birth mothers. I argue that the transnational adoption practice from South Korea has removed countless numbers of children born from extramarital affairs with married men. By removing this excess population, the transnational adoption practice reinforces the imaginary of the normative, modern, nuclear family, rooted in sexual fidelity and patriarchal authority, as well as in the patriarchal regulation of women's sexuality and reproduction.

Excess children may not always be illegitimate by birth, but rather, also include "legitimate" children born within a marriage. Widows, like mistresses, are another overlooked group among single mothers. In January 2011, I met with Kim Sun Ae, a widowed birth mother at a weekly English class offered by Global Overseas Adoptees' Link (G.O.A.'L), an adoptee self-advocacy organization founded in 1997. G.O.A.'L's weekly English classes began in 2010 in response to the most frequently noted difficulty stemming from a reunion between an adoptee and a birth family. Kim Sun Ae's weekly English class was comprised of four birth mothers and one birth father, all of whom had reunited with their adopted children. Kim

Sun Ae reunited with her daughter, raised by a French couple, in 2007. Her adoption story goes as follows:

> I met my husband soon after I graduated from high school and followed him to Kwangju. After a year or two, I became pregnant and filed for marriage in order to register my daughter's birth. Soon after, he died of lung disease. Then I went back to Seoul, my hometown, with my newborn daughter. My parents, at the time, would sell vegetables off of a cart in a market. I immediately had to find work, but could not actively look because of my daughter; at the time, she was 5–6 months old. ... There was no one from whom I could receive assistance. ... After returning to Seoul, there was a gathering with my high school classmates, one of whom worked at the Holt agency and affirmed that such children would be better off if they were placed in overseas adoption. She knew my situation was quite difficult and suggested adoption. At that time, I also started seeing a guy [whom she later married] who had never been married. I talked about my daughter, and even brought her along a couple of times to see if he would be willing to raise her. There was no gesture from him that he was willing to take in my daughter as his own. Instead, he seemed a little bit reluctant. He was the eldest son. For his mother, he could hide my previous marriage, if I didn't have a daughter. But ... but with a daughter, he wouldn't be able to ... He seemed to be debating whether he would marry me or not. Then, the adoption agency, which I had once consulted for my daughter's possible adoption, kept contacting me. So I placed her into adoption.[78] (Born in 1954, her daughter was adopted in 1978)

Kim Sun Ae became a widow with a 5-month-old baby at 24. As she expressed, in the absence of any family support, she had to make a choice between raising her child without hope of marriage and the prospect of a new marriage by relinquishing her child. As a young woman, she did not see herself as being able to raise her daughter alone, primarily due to a lack of economic opportunities. She recalled, "Then, there were not many jobs available for women. I had to remarry ... [for survival]."[79] At the time, women's occupations were very limited, ranging from telephone operators to factory workers to domestic workers; and, often such work was viewed as temporary until marriage, even as working-class women typically were never exempt from paid work.

This assumption reflects how traditional gender roles, in which women were expected to be chaste until marriage, and, then, afterward to primarily serve as wives and as mothers, constrained employment opportunities for women, for in order for Kim Sun Ae to even consider remarrying, she had to conceal her previous marriage; and, while her previous marriage could be hidden from her in-laws, her child could not be so easily concealed. At the time, it was quite common for a widow—or even a divorced woman—if she had custody over a child, to leave a child from a previous marriage in the care of her own parents. However, Kim Sun Ae was unable to do so. That is how her daughter, while born to a legitimate family, became an excess child. Without a husband's or a father's protection, Kim Sun Ae and her child became an insufficient, unreliable family unit, and there was little possibility for them to be reinserted into a normal family, while remaining a family unit. To survive, Kim Sun Ae decided to secure the possibility of marriage, and to put her daughter up for adoption.

Excess Children from the Poor

In addition to *kijich'on* mothers and single mothers, the third category of birth mothers comprises women from poor, working-class families. Their adoption background is often described as simply poor, as if poverty, alone, provides the most concrete answer to how and why children from poor families became excess. Yet, the adoption stories of working-class, poor mothers point to the prevalence of domestic violence and spousal neglect as a catalyst, aggravating an often already difficult and stressful situation into an unbearable and often life-threatening one. It is often when a family is in such a crisis that a child is put up for adoption.

In July 2010, I met Park Mi Hee, 58, a soft-spoken birth mother, in a street campaign called "I am looking for my family" that was organized by G.O.A.'L. Park Mi Hee was looking for her daughter from whom she had been separated after her divorce; her daughter was three when she last saw her. She got married in 1973, after having two pregnancies and two abortions from a relationship that had begun with rape; she consented to marry her daughter's father after he threatened to kill her entire family. A relationship that had begun in violence became a marriage that was bruised by violence throughout. She told me that the severity of the abuse made her think, "*Even if I kill him, I am not guilty.*"[80] She recounted her adoption story, as follows:

> Another night of beating. His beating was bad. At night, he would choke me, run around, yelling at me with a knife like a crazy person… At that time, I would rather have died than be beaten. I fell from the second floor, in running away from my ex-husband's bouts of beatings. That incident paralyzed me

from the waist down for the next several months. At that time, he was seeing another woman. One day, he came to the hospital where I was being cared for, and dragged me to his hometown residential office to file for divorce. I was glad, but didn't know that he would take custody of my 3-year-old daughter. Some time passed. He came to my parents' house to take my daughter. I protested. But he took the baby. To stop him, I dragged my limping leg into a wide street busy with traffic. That's the last time I saw my baby.[81] (Park Mee Hee, born in 1953, her daughter was adopted by French parents in 1979)

Park Mi Hee's account reveals the influence of domestic violence on transnational adoption.

Indeed, domestic violence is a prevalent, yet widely underreported, form of violence by husbands against wives, and manifests the vulnerability of women to physical violence in the private domain of the family. According to research conducted in 1983 by the Korea Women's Hotline, 42.2 % of 708 respondents experienced physical abuse in their marriages; 14 % was recorded the previous year.[82] Another study by Lee Soon Hyung reveals that 60 % of respondents experienced domestic violence; of those, 28.5 % suffered regular beatings, causing serious physical and psychological harm.[83] Despite its prevalence and serious physical dangers to women, domestic violence has long been treated as simply a private, spousal dispute that should not be interfered with. This stance toward domestic violence only reifies the husband's patriarchal authority within the family sphere.[84] As a result, in 1984, 90 % of battered women did not report their situations to anyone.[85]

Battered women were not the only ones to take part in the concealment of domestic violence—such concealment was also achieved with the coordinated efforts of neighbors, law enforcement, hospitals, and the law. As recounted by Park Mi Hee, she did not tell anyone about being beaten by her husband, and experienced neighborly indifference. She said, "Then, we were living just next to the landlord. Probably, they must have heard the noise [of being assaulted]."[86] Yet, no one ever checked on her safety, or tried to intervene. Even when domestic violence was reported to the police, the police rarely came. If they did come, the police often spoke only with the perpetrator, aggravating the situation.[87] Furthermore, doctors did not ask about the origins of the injuries when women were brought into the hospital because of domestic violence. All of these institutional and personal responses that condoned domestic violence culminated in the absence of any legal framework to protect victims until 1997.[88]

Without any legal protection, Park Mi Hee fled the marriage, but then suffered the termination of her parental rights through divorce. Until a 1989 revision to *Family Law*, divorced women automatically lost custody of their children, often lacking even visitation rights. Consequently, her husband took full custody of the child and exercised his exclusive parental rights. She was unable to legally or physically resist. Many years after separating from her child, she learned of her daughter's adoption by French parents.

Similarly, Jang Yeon Ja, another birth mother, had not been informed of her child's adoption. Back in 1976, when she found out that she was pregnant after being raped, she went to see the baby's father, who was living with his four siblings and grandmother, in a dilapidated neighborhood in Seoul. So began her brief marriage. Her husband did not seem to have a job, and she did not know what he did with his days. To compensate for his lack of income, she often skipped meals; her child became undernourished. To survive, she took odd jobs, such as peeling dried fish at home, or working in a restaurant kitchen, with her son tied to her back. Her efforts to survive, however, were disrupted by her husband, who seized her wages. Finally, she left the marriage. She explained the circumstances of her departure, as follows:

> He sold everything, including the stereo, his own suits, ... I later found out ...[it was] because of horse gambling. ... One day he asked me to follow him. We were so poor. [Because we were always hungry], I could not properly nourish my child. Finally we arrived at a place where people sold their blood. As soon as a nurse saw him, she said, "I have already told you that you can't sell any more of your blood." The baby's father pointed at me, holding a baby, and told the nurse, "Today, it is not me, but her." I immediately ran away from that place, and went home. That very same night, he asked me to go somewhere and borrow money for him. So, I left home and the baby.[89] (Jang Yeon Ja, born in 1958 (est.), her son was adopted to the US in 1976)

Thus, Jang Yeon Ja fled for her survival, as her husband's gambling started to spin out of control and to pose a threat to her life. She searched for a job, fully intending to take back possession of her child. But not even one month had passed when she learned that her baby was gone. Her husband did not want to be responsible for the child, and had left the baby at her parents' house. However, her parents could not take in their grandson because they were caring for a child with special needs. So, in her absence, the baby was returned to the father. Her brother-in-law, though she used the phrase, "baby's father's brother," and her own aunt, along with her own mother, decided to place the baby into adoption. Her abusive marriage was dissolved, once the baby had been sent away. For the next 30 years, she knew nothing of her child's whereabouts, until he came from the US to look for her in 2005. Jang Yeon Ja's adoption case highlights the lack of supports for working-class families in crisis.

South Korea's lack of social services transferred social welfare functions to the individual family. Yet, in reality, many working-class families share similar economic backgrounds with their close relatives, all of whom manage their households at a subsistence level. Such common conditions leave little room to offer, and/or receive, any financial assistance from their kinship network in a time of crisis. In other words, when the nuclear family fails, there is no support system that enables the family unit to remain intact.

When speaking with Shin Young Eun, introduced at the beginning of the chapter, she lashed out, "Who's helping us? Do I have skills? Do I have in-laws who could help us? Or my brothers? No one was able to help. I wished, I wanted to have someone who could listen to my stories."[90] Consequently, Shin Young Eun gave up her children when they were six and eight. Like so many of her fellow birth mothers, she suffered from economic challenges, and an abusive environment. She detailed the desperate texture of her economic reality, as follows:

> Before I sent my children away, there was nothing I didn't do for a living. There was no rice at home and for two days, I didn't eat ... He still didn't go out and look for work. One day I went out to borrow some rice from a store. While walking, my shoes fell apart. I was in my early 20s. I felt so embarrassed that I stopped walking when pedestrians came into my view. I dragged my feet home when no one was around. ... Another time, the rent was past due. We didn't have money. So we locked the door, and stayed silent inside all day until dark, as if we weren't there, not being able to cook or eat because the landlord would come, asking for the rent.
>
> For me, I could have lived with my sons, if my ex-husband had not come once in a while to steal from us. My husband didn't provide for us and couldn't stay employed. So one day, I took my two boys and found work in the kitchen of a bar. The three of us lived in the basement [of the bar] with no windows.... My then-husband came back and asked me for money. I didn't have any money to give him. He then stole the money that I was supposed to spend on food. I really wanted to separate from him....

> I had been laid off from my job because of my husband. One day I went to a motel with my children because we didn't have a place to go. I wanted to die with my kids there. As I was strangling my boys, I realized that, if I wanted to die, I should do it myself. [For my children], I should give them an opportunity for life, a life different from mine. So I decided on adoption for them. Had I known that I would live this long, I would have never placed them in adoption. But I was going to terminate my life. There was no other choice for me, either we died together or I sent them away.... So I decided... [91] (Shin Young Eun, born in 1960; her two boys were adopted by a French family in 1987)

Although Shin Young Eun had been living with her children apart from her husband, she soon realized that her two children were an excuse for him to return and take advantage of her. His irresponsible behavior, combined with the economic strain of earning a living, precipitated her emotional devastation to the point at which she wanted to kill her children and to give up her life altogether. Park Mi Hee, Jang Yeon Ja, and Shin Young Eun became birth mothers in the process of, or subsequently after their family's disintegration, in part due to the need to run away from their abusive husbands, for their survival. As a result, all three were finally released from abusive, violent, and life-threatening relationships, but faced the loss of their child(ren) in return.

Some birth mothers, however, could not leave behind their destructive and abusive relationships, even after giving up a child for adoption, because they had to take responsibility for the children who remained. Jung Yoon Sook, 58, a gregarious, motivated student in G.O.A.'L's weekly English class, married an ex-military official whom she met on the train at 18, right after graduating from high school. It had not been too long since she had lost her mother, and her father had remarried, immediately after his wife's death. Her husband showed irresponsible behaviors from the beginning of the marriage, yet it lasted for almost 30 years. She delivered a total of nine children from the marriage, and had sent away the youngest three for adoption—two to the US, and the third to domestic adoption.

When I asked why she had so many children, Jung Yoon Sook said, "It is a part of life's irony," adding that she had worked as a local agent who recruited wives for sterilization during the family planning campaign of the 1970s and the 1980s.[92] She said, "I grew up with only one sibling, and always wanted to have a big family."[93] Despite the financial difficulties and marital conflicts, she found her children to be a gift from God and felt proud of her fertility. But the placement of her three children into adoption remained a secret in her family until 2007, when she reunited with her first adopted son, Phil, from the US. After the reunion, she contacted her second, adopted son, who had also been raised in the US, only to learn that he was not interested in searching for his Korean family. She told me the following:

> Look. I have a hairless spot because my ex-husband used to pull my hair during his bouts of beating. He yanked my hair by hand. So, there is no hair. He never worked. Instead, he lied to people to borrow money, which he spent going to bars, basically taking care of himself—his appearance and his spending money. I then had to pay back his debts. So, I worked days and nights, raising six children alone. When my water broke, I was working at a Japanese restaurant where the owner had given up her child for adoption. So she introduced me to an adoption agency run by nuns, where I gave birth to my boy and left him there…because I had to go back and work again.[94] (Jung Yoon Sook, born in 1948, her first child was adopted in 1982; the second, in 1985; and the third, in 1987)

It was 1982 when she placed her seventh child, Chiseng, later renamed Phil, into adoption. She did not elaborate on why she decided on adoption. Perhaps it had been clear to her that she would be unable to raise additional children in her family environment. In addition to being subjected to regular beatings, owing to her husband's deceitful behaviors and financial irresponsibility, she was also burdened by her husband's debts. She did a variety of odd jobs to manage her household, including piecemeal work at home, farm work, restaurant work, milk delivery, and selling children's clothes. In an affront to her efforts to provide for her family, her then-husband went directly to her employers and was given her wages upon asking for them. Despite constantly working, she could not properly feed, not to mention educate, her remaining children.

Furthermore, her husband's destructive behavior negatively influenced her relationship with her extended family. He would lie to relatives, friends, and family members, to borrow money without ever paying back anything, thereby causing tensions between her and her family. As a result, she lived not only in poverty but also in isolation. When she discovered she was pregnant with her seventh child, there was no family or friends from whom she could seek help, and only her restaurant employer knew that she had placed the child into adoption. To Jung Yoon Sook, leaving a baby behind after delivery was a way for her to survive, by allowing her to *go back to work*.

My examination of the adoption accounts of working-class, married birth mothers reveals intercalated layers of violence by which children became excess. The most immediate factors included widespread poverty and domestic violence. Yet, such poverty does not simply refer to a scarcity of resources, but also reflects the absence of a male provider. In the preceding stories, the husband's failure to provide for the family was not just limited to a lack of employment, but, more pointedly, his control over her limited income, and his exploitation of the wife's reproductive and productive labor, thereby further exacerbating the family's economic circumstances.

These factors—unsteady employment, addiction, marital infidelity, indifference to one's family, or any combination of these—often compounded by everyday domestic violence, all transform an already challenging and stressful life into a life-threatening environment. Thus, working-class, poor mothers are forced to bear the impact of such violence, all alone, without virtually any protection. These are often the circumstances under which birth mothers made the decision to separate from their child, whether the decision was to leave behind a child or to place the child up for adoption. These birth mothers' accounts of life circumstances, leading up to the separation from their children, texturize the underlying material conditions of poverty that shape their decisions, and affirm the strong connections between child relinquishment, domestic violence, and patriarchal pressures.[95]

2.4 Transnational Adoption: A Securitizing Mechanism for Nation and Family

So far, this chapter examined the key role and influence that foreign aid organizations have wielded in the development of transnational adoption and of the family planning policy, both of which originated in Cold-War era geopolitics and capitalist imperatives. Framing the origins of transnational adoption as a population removal policy to deal with an excess population of mixed-race children after the war, this chapter critically examined how South Korea has continuously participated in, and even accelerated the engagement of, transnational adoption during the 1970s and 1980s. I argue that the transnational adoption practice has continuously removed excess children from South Korea.

The development of South Korea's transnational adoption practice, interlaced with the family planning policy, reveals the entrenched history of foreign aid's involvement in two major areas of population policy in postwar Korea: child welfare and population control. Foreign aid's involvement in two disparate aspects of population policy appears inconsistent and somewhat contradictory, as reflected in the concern with orphan care on the one hand, and with restriction of women's reproduction, on the other. This inconsistent approach to foreign aid's involvement in population policies, however, was streamlined along and converged with the US's Cold-War era geopolitics and South Korea's economic interests. My close investigation of foreign aid's involvement in both transnational adoption practice and the family planning policy complicates the interpretation of transnational adoption practice as a humanitarian practice of salvation. A close examination of the birth mothers' accounts fleshes out the various contexts and processes by which a child became an excess child during the 1970s and 1980s due to the absence of a legitimate paternal figure for the child. As shown in the birth mothers' accounts, such an absence is not just an effect of a father's natural death, but rather, more often, an active form of refusal, whether shown in the absent GI father of a mixed-race child, or in a married man's failed fulfillment of parental and marital responsibilities. Often this failure of paternal responsibility is accompanied by appalling degrees of violence against women; such violence includes paternal abandonment or neglect; the social stigma against single mothers and their children; and life-threatening domestic violence. While gender-based violence is committed by individuals, it is also reinforced and carried out by institutions, such as the law, government, economy, and the family.

I argue that the transnational adoption practice was a deliberate policy of population management to control an excess population during the 1970s and the 1980s, and that it was orchestrated by South Korea's family planning policy. As the key institution that directly regulated women's reproduction for national security development, the policy operated as an effective mechanism through which to establish a normative patriarchal family and to rationalize the lack of social welfare. Grounded in a self-reliant family as the cornerstone of the nation-state, the family planning policy justified South Korea's absence of a social welfare policy, naturalizing the concept that each individual family must take care of itself.[96] In this way, the family planning policy was a powerful institutional mechanism that rendered mixed-race children, the children of single mothers, and children from working-class, poor families—all of whom lived outside the self-reliant, patriarchal family unit—into an excess population of social pariahs whose continued existence represented a burden on the developmental state. It is in this context that South Korea's transnational adoption practice can be analyzed in terms of family planning. By driving excess children out of South Korea and transferring them into private homes abroad, the transnational adoption practice facilitated South Korea's family planning policy—more accurately, it pursued a population reduction policy which favored a decreased population, so as to deter foreseeable costs in social welfare.

Understanding the transnational adoption practice as a part of South Korea's family planning policy frames the birth mothers' act of surrendering the child as an act carried out to fulfill the imperative of national/family security. From a national security standpoint, birth mothers, through their participation in transnational adoption, joined millions of Korean women who have been mobilized to use contraceptives, so as to prevent the rise of an excess population. By using transnational adoption as an emergency solution to a family crisis, these women regulated their excess reproduction, belatedly. Their belated participation in population control qualifies them to be dutiful mothers. Seungsook Moon argues that these women contributed to the building of the modern nation "by the patriotic control of their fertility."[97] In so doing, they became virtuous maternal subjects who sacrificed their motherhood for the family and the nation. Through the family-planning mechanism of child relinquishment, the birth mothers were able to rectify their nonnormative families and to help secure the normative ideal of the self-reliant, self-sustainable patriarchal family unit. Hence, numerous Korean birth mothers have voluntarily, and involuntarily, helped to secure the idea of a modern national family and thus served South Korea's national security agenda. In turn, they became a virtuous maternal subject, and I argue, a virtual mother.

The next chapter reviews the adoption backgrounds of birth mothers since the post 1980s, and examines exclusively single mothers who are young and have never been married, and their trajectories of becoming birth mothers. By focusing on how the maternity home serves as a unique, social service agency for single mothers, and as a regulatory, discursive, and administrative auxiliary institution, the chapter examines the institutional life cycle via which one becomes a birth mother, thus uncovering the peremptory logic of social governance over single, pregnant women. It argues that the transnational adoption practice has been employed to control and regulate the sexuality and reproduction of single mothers, and that it has continuously and preemptively been functioning as a mechanism of population management for decades.

Notes

1. Her journal entry for October 22 marks the date of her divorce.
2. In 1987, a total of 7947 Korean children were placed in overseas adoption. ("Republic of Korea: Overseas Adoption Statistics (1958 – 2011)", Seoul: Ministry of Health and Welfare in South Korea).
3. Although the 1960s and 1970s are commonly viewed as a distinct era compared to the 1980s, I view the 1970s and 1980s as one continuous period in the context of transnational adoption. This is because the post-1990s marks a sea change in terms of national family planning policy and adoption demographics.
4. Analyzing South Korea's transnational adoption in terms of South Korea's population control policy is not an original approach. See Byung Hoon Chun, "Adoption and Korea," *Child Welfare* 68 (2): 255–260; Tobias Hübinette, "Comforting an Orphaned Nation: Representations of International Adoption and Adopted Koreans in Korean Popular Culture," (PhD diss., Stockholm University, 2005); Eleana Kim, *Adopted Territory: Transnational Korean Adoptees and the Politics of Belonging* (Durham: Duke University Press, 2010); Sarri R.C., Baik, Y. and Bombyk, M. "Goal Displacement and Dependency in South Korean—United States Intercountry Adoption," *Children and Youth Review* 20 (1–2):87–114.
5. For this chapter, I selected 16 birth mothers who had at least one child placed into adoption in the 1970s or the 1980s. The women's ages ranged from 44 to 70 at the time of the interview. Thirteen birth mothers have reunited with their children. Two birth mothers are currently searching for their children, or, more accurately speaking, are waiting for their children to contact them. They have diverse marital, educational, familial, occupational, and socioeconomic backgrounds. At the time of the interview, eight birth mothers were single, half of those by divorce, and three by death; one had never been married. Two birth mothers were still legally married, but remained separated from the birth father. Of the six married birth mothers, two were still married to the father of their adopted children. All but one of these women had other

children, who are either half or full sisters and brothers to the adopted child. Among those, one birth mother adopted a daughter almost two decades after her sons were placed into adoption. At the time of adoption placement, four were unmarried, and the rest were married or widowed. Some birth mothers had been young, just turning 20 at the time of adoption, but the majority had been married and were in their twenties and thirties.

Twelve birth mothers identified financial difficulties as a significant, if not threatening, factor in their lives. Two birth mothers had a middle-class background and were living comfortably. The birth mothers' occupations varied, including a domestic worker, an insurance salesperson, a shaman, a home attendant for the elderly, and several small business owners (of a restaurant, a lingerie store, and an accessories store).

The age of the adopted child at the moment of separation also varied, from soon after birth to a child who was fourteen years old. Eleven birth mothers reported that one, either the first or the last, of her children was placed in transnational adoption. Four birth mothers had sent multiple children into adoption.

6. Although the Korean War is commonly understood as having begun on June 25 in 1950, there has been much analysis that locates the origins of the Korean War in the division and military occupation of Korea in 1945, when the US and USSR installed its occupation governments in the South and North of the country, respectively. See Grace M. Cho, *Haunting the Korean Disapora* (Minneapolis: University of Minnesota Press, 2008), Bruce Cummings, *The Korean War*, (NY: Random House, 2011); Dong-choon Kim, *Chônchaengkwa sahŭi* [Korean war and society], (Seoul, Korea: Dolbaegae), 72;
7. Charles Armstrong. "Introduction," *Journal of Korean Studies 18*, no. 2 (2013): 180.
8. Giorgio Agamben, *State of Exception* (Chicago: University of Chicago Press, 2005).
9. Ibid., 2.
10. Dong-choon Kim, *Chônchaengkwa sahŭi* [Korean war and society], 72.
11. Jae-Jung Suh, "Truth and Reconciliation in South Korea: Confronting War, Colonialism, and Intervention in Asia Pacific." *Critical Asian Studies 42*, no. 4 (2010): 512.

12. Won Kyu Choe, "*Oeguk min'gan wŏnjo tanch'e hwaltonggwa han'guk sahoe saŏp palch'ŏne mich'in yŏnghyang*", [Activities of Foreign Voluntary Agencies and Their Influences upon Social Work Development in Korea]", (Ph.D. dissertation, Seoul National University, 1997), 74; Arissa Oh, *To Save the Children of Korea: The Cold War Origins of International Adoption* (Stanford: Stanford University Press, 2015); Soojin Pate, *From Orphan to Adoptee: U.S. Empire and Genealogies of Korean Adoption* (Minneapolis: University of Minnesota Press, 2014).
13. Consequently, the Korea Association of Voluntary Agencies (KAVA), the association of these foreign aid organizations in Korea, was often referred to as South Korea's second Ministry of Public Health and Welfare.
14. Choe, "Activities of Foreign Voluntary Agencies," 74.
15. At the time, 40 % of the population suffered from hunger and malnourishment. In the face of postwar poverty, many working-class families utilized these orphanages as a temporary childcare system where their children could receive subsistence and medical attention. Because of this phenomenon, many children living at these orphanages were not orphans in the strict sense.
16. In *From Orphan to Adoptee*, Pate identified this dramatic increase as being due in part to US soldiers working closely with aid organizations. This participation was part of a US military project to rehabilitate their image in South Korea, since it had been damaged during the war.
17. Choe, "Activities of Foreign Voluntary Agencies," 138.
18. Ibid., 143-147.
19. Arissa Oh, "War Waif to Ideal Immigrant: The Cold War Transformation of the Korean Orphans," *Journal of American Ethnic History* 31, no. 4 (2012): 35.
20. Choe, "Activities of Foreign Voluntary Agencies," 154.
21. Hyun Sook Han, *Many Lives Intertwined* (St. Paul: Yeong & Yeong Book Company, 2004), 97.
22. Choe, "Activities of Foreign Voluntary Agencies," 174.
23. Until the late-1960s, the Seventh Day Adventist Church, the Catholic Relief Service, Holt Adoption Program, the Pearl Buck's Welcome House, Unitarian Service Committee of Canada, and

Christian Reform Korean Mission continued to recruit children for adoption. See Hübinette, "Comforting an Orphaned Nation."
24. Doyoung Kim, 1972-2002 *tongbang sahoe pokchihoe 30 nyŏnsa* [30-Year History of Eastern Social Welfare Society], (Seoul: Eastern Social Welfare Society, 2002), 8.
25. From the mid-1970s onward, the proportion that foreign aid organizations contributed to South Korea's national welfare budget fell drastically to 14 % in 1980 and reached 2 % in 1992.
26. Pate, *From Orphans to Adoptees*, 36.
27. Klein, *Cold War Orientalism*, 152.
28. Ibid., 154.
29. Hosu Kim and Grace M. Cho, "The Kinship of Violence," *Journal of Korean Adoption Studies* 1, no 3 (2012): 7–25.
30. Hübinette, "Comforting an Orphaned Nation," 60.
31. Bum-Ju Whang. *50 year History of Holt Children's Services, Inc.* (Seoul: Holt Children's Service, 2005), 158.
32. Ibid, 150.
33. Kyung Tae Park, *Sosuja wa Hankuk Sahoe* [Minority Groups in Korean Society], (Seoul: Humanitas, 2006), 206.
34. Kim and Cho, "Kinship," 10.
35. Ji-Yeon Yuh, *Beyond the Shadow of Camptown: Korean Military Brides in America*, (New York: New York University Press, 2002), 26.
36. Cho, *Haunting the Korean Diaspora*; Katharine Moon, *Sex Among Allies* (New York: Columbia University Press, 1997); Yuh, *Beyond the Shadow of Camptown*.
37. Moon, *Sex Among Allies*.
38. For example, mixed-race men are not eligible to serve in South Korea's military, which is otherwise mandatory for all South Korean men.
39. Eun Hye Shin and Hyun Hee Kim, "Report on Former Kijichon Sex Workers in Gyeonggi Do." Conference Proceedings. (Seoul: *Haessal Sahoebokjihoe*, 2008), 61.
40. The Ministry of Health and Welfare's statistics on mixed race children were officially recorded only up to 1973. "Republic of Korea: Overseas Adoption Statistics (1958 – 2011)", Seoul: Ministry of Health and Welfare in South Korea.
41. Grandmother Kang, in an interview with the author, January 10 2012.

42. Ibid.
43. Im Soon Ja, in an interview with the author, January 3, 2012.
44. A contract marriage is a living arrangement in which a serviceman provides a sex worker with living expenses in return for a monogamous relationship.
45. Margo Okazawa-Rey, "Amerasian Children of GI Town: A Legacy of U.S. Militarism in South Korea," *Asia Journal of Women's Studies* 3, no.1 (2003): 89.
46. At the time, Im Soon Ja owned two houses and was able to live off of the rent she collected.
47. Han, *Many Lives Intertwined*, 98.
48. Han learned later that her appearance brought panic to local mothers who yelled, "Quick! Hide your children! Mrs. Shim is coming!" (Ibid., 99).
49. Kim, *Adopted Territory.* 48
50. Kim and Cho, "Kinship," 10.
51. Put forth in the language of economic growth, the family planning policy was essentially a population control program to preserve resources and promote economic growth.
52. Eun Kyung Bae, *Hyŏntae hankukui inkan chaesangsan* [Human Reproduction in the Korean Modernity: Women, Motherhood, and Population Control Policy] (Seoul: *Sikanyŏhaeng*, 2012), 89.
53. Ibid., 90
54. Ibid., 93.
55. The International Planned Parenthood Federation, the UN Family Planning Agency, the Population Council, the US Agency for International Development, and the Swedish International Development Agency provided financial and technical assistance to the development and implementation of South Korea's family planning policy.
56. Bae, *Human Reproduction*; Leslie Bier, "The Family is a Factory: Gender, Citizenship, and the Regulation of Reproduction in Postwar Egypt," *Feminist Studies* 36, no. 2 (2008): 404–32; Leslie Dwyer, "Spectacular Sexuality: Nationalism, Development and the Politics of Family Planning in Indonesia" in *Gender Ironies of Nationalism: Sexing the Nation*, (New York: Routledge, 2000), 25-62 ; Seungsook Moon, *Militarized Modernity and Gendered Citizenship in South Korea* (Durham: Duke University Press, 2005).

57. Address by President John F. Kennedy to the UN General Assembly, September 25, 1961, US Department of State (accessed on January 15, 2015). [www.state.gov/p/io/potusunga/207241.htm].
58. Rhew Dahl Yeong, quoted in Bae, 92.
59. Bae, *Human Reproduction*, 93.
60. Bae, *Human Reproduction*, 94.
61. Moon, *Militarized Modernity*, 83.
62. Ibid.
63. Ibid., 76.
64. Ibid., 70.
65. Ibid., 77.
66. Bae, *Human Reproduction*, 187.
67. The modern nation-building project posits all citizens as being equipped with an ethos of self-sufficiency, self-reliance, and a dedication to work. As a consequence, those who have not achieved self-sufficiency and self-reliance are considered to be economically and morally incapable. The very need for public assistance undermines a person's worth as a citizen, inscribing that person as a failed national subject that is undeserving of public assistance.
68. Twins and children with special needs constitute a disproportionate number of the children adopted overseas. In South Korea, there are many superstitions about twins. For example, fraternal male and female twins often were seen as a bad omen for the family. There were fears that they could be harbingers of incest, or that the twin daughter would steal the "luck" of the twin son. In a similar vein, children with special needs long have been considered as shameful to the family and as a burden to family funds.
69. Kim, *Adopted Territory*, 25.
70. Kim Ji Yeol, "*Mihonmoe kwan han Kijojŏk Yŏngu*" [An Analytic Study of the Unmarried Mother in Korea]", (Masters' thesis, Ewha Women's University, 1974).
71. Korean Women's Development Institute. *Mihonmo silt'aee kwanhan yŏnku* [Study on the Unwed Mother with Special Reference to the Analysis of Factors relating her Occurrence and Welfare Measure]. (Seoul: KWDI, 1984).
72. Katy Robinson, *A Single Square Picture: A Korean Adoptee's Search for Her Roots* (New York: Berkley Books), 16.
73. Nora Zamichow, "Searching for Missing Pieces of a Painful Past," *Los Angeles Times*, November 28, 2004.

74. Yang Sook Ja, in an interview with the author, August 12, 2005.
75. Of the 16 birth mothers mentioned in this chapter, four reported that their relationship with the baby's father started with being raped. Dorow (1999) indicates that about 10 % of adoptions in South Korea in the 1990s were from pregnancies caused by rape. The experiences with sexual violence among the birth mothers mirrors a widespread, yet under-reported phenomenon of sexual violence in South Korea, which has the world's third highest report of rapes nationally. Despite its alarming rate, discourse around rape is focused on a woman's lost chastity, rather than on its violent, criminal nature. Korean Women's Hotline, the first women's organization with the aim to eradicate gendered violence, which was established in 1983, critically observed in a newsletter, "Unless a women takes her life over her lost chastity, rape victims take blame in our society where chastity is considered an utmost value in women" (1986. 2. 28, p. 4). This widespread traditional ideology of a woman's sexuality, along with the misogynistic interpretation of rape, served to foster cultural tolerance, if not acceptance, of sexual violence against women and persisted in the absence of a legal framework. It was not until the 1980s that a perpetrator could be indicted on criminal charges. Against this cultural, legal, and social background, none of the birth mothers above either reported their rapes or sought help, and instead were compelled to marry the men who raped them. Although the common thread of sexual violence may not directly explain why children were placed into adoption, these accounts suggest a glaring power asymmetry and double standards in gender roles governing family life.
76. Lee Mi Sun, in an interview with the author, August 8, 2010.
77. According to Lee Mi Sun's account, the methods by which she could turn her illegitimate child into a respectable and recognizable member of society with legitimate parentage included two options: (1) to make his existence known to the father's legal wife, so the child could be registered under his family registry; or, (2) to ask either her male siblings or her father to register the child in their household, turning her relationship to her child to that of an aunt or a sibling, in the eyes of the law. In either case, she was not legally eligible to be the mother of her child.
78. Kim Sun Ae, in an interview with the author, January 17, 2011.

79. Ibid.
80. Park Mi Hee, in an interview with the author, June 30, 2010.
81. Ibid.
82. Korea Women's Hot Line, *Hankuk yosŏng inkwŏn untongsa* [History of korean women's rights movements], ed. Korea Women's Hot Line (Seoul: Hanul Aacademy, 1999), 112.
83. Lee Soon Hyung, "*pubugan kut'ahaengdonggwa kwallyŏnbyŏnsu*, [Spousal Abuse and its determinant variables]" [*Duk Seong Yeo Ja Dae Hak Non Mun Jip*] 17, 143–158.
84. Domestic violence in South Korea is now recognized as a crime and can be addressed through the justice system. The Ministry of Gender Equality and Family launched a national comprehensive investigation of domestic violence that occurs every three years. As of 2008, there are over 300 family counseling programs and 70 shelters. Despite this, the overall domestic violence rate has not shown any solid sign of decline. The 2010 report indicates that 15.3 % of women respondents (from a total of 1194) experienced physical violence from their husbands within the past year. The majority of those women (62.7 %) did not seek help. Women who did seek help reached out to family, relatives, friends, and neighbors first. Only 8.3 % called the police. Over the past 30 years, public recognition of domestic violence has increased to the point of establishing a state agency to address the issue. While this has led to greater public awareness of domestic violence as a crime, such awareness has not translated into any meaningful change in the occurrence of domestic violence.
85. Myung Hee Kwon, *1984 nyŏn sang panki salye yŏnku* [The First Year Report of the Korea Women's Hotline, A Case Study of the First half of 1984]; Eunhye Shin, *1983 nyŏn habangi saryeyŏngu, Hankuk Yŏsong ŭi chunhwa, Kaewon 1 Chunyŏn Kinyŏm Pogosŏ* [The First Year Report on the Korea Women's Hotline, A Case Study of the Latter Half of 1983], (Seoul: Korea Women's Hotline, 1984).
86. Park Mi Hee, in an interview with the author, June 30, 2010.
87. Kim Soon Hyung's investigation found that 57.89 % of police officers told the couple to resolve the conflict within the family. Often, police only listened to the husband's account and ignored the wife (295, 2000).
88. South Korea's first domestic violence law, *The Prevention of Domestic Violence Law*, was implemented in 1997.

89. Jang Yeon Ja, in an interview with the author, August 10, 2005.
90. Shin Young Eun, in an interview with the author, January 18, 2011.
91. Ibid.
92. Jung Yoon Sook, in an interview with the author, January 19, 2011.
93. Ibid.
94. Ibid.
95. Brian, *Reframing Transnational Adoption*, x.
96. Only one of the birth mothers I interviewed expressed any sense of disappointment in the government or attributed their adoption decision to an inadequate welfare policy. For birth mothers growing up in postwar, poverty-stricken South Korea, the policy of "First Development, Later Distribution" was seen as necessary for economic development and for the nation's well-being.
97. Moon, *Militarized Modernity*, 89.

CHAPTER 3

Maternity Homes, the Birthplace of the Virtual Mother

The previous chapter examined the historical, military, geopolitical, and economic links between the development of transnational adoption and South Korea's national family planning policy, and established the platform for a critical analysis of transnational adoption as a technology of population control. By examining the structural determinants under which numerous working-class women became birth mothers during the 1970s and the 1980s, Chapter 2 argues that birth mothers participated in transnational adoption as part of a national, population control measure, thereby serving national and family security under the developmental state. In this chapter, I focus on single mothers, the largest and fastest growing population of birth mothers from the 1980s to the mid 2000s, and discuss the elaborate system of social governance through which the transnational adoption practice has been deployed as a biopolitical, preemptive measure against single mothers and their "illegitimate" children.

Single mothers constitute the great majority of all birth mothers involved in transnational adoption from South Korea. More than 120,000 children, or two out of three adoptees, were, or are, children of single mothers. Single mothers are referred to as *mihonmo*,[1] which literally means "not-yet-married mothers." Due to the high rate at which children of *mihonmo* are sent away for adoption, the term has become synonymous with *birth mother*. The conflation of these two categories in common parlance, however, misrepresents the population of South Korean birth mothers as comprised entirely of single mothers.[2] But more

© The Editor(s) (if applicable) and The Author(s) 2016   79
H. Kim, *Birth Mothers and Transnational Adoption Practice in South Korea*, DOI 10.1057/978-1-137-53852-9_3

importantly, it introduces the expectation that a single mother should relinquish her baby to adoption.

To examine how single mothers are rendered into birth mothers, I analyze a critical historical juncture during which single motherhood increasingly accounted for the children placed into transnational adoption. This period occurred between the 1980s and the mid-2000s, when children born of single mothers accounted for 80 to 90 % of all transnationally adopted children.[3] This rising trend persisted until 2007, when a series of significant changes took place; these included an increase in domestic adoption and a parallel decline in transnational adoption; the abolishment of *hojuje* (patrilineal family law); a shift in government policy from population control to pronatalism; and, a revision of adoption law. A critical examination of this historical period sheds light on how social governance has used adoption to regulate single mothers.

According to recent adoption scholarship, South Korea's practice of transnational adoption has long functioned as a biopolitical technology—that is, a technology of regulating and managing various perceived population crises.[4] Drawing upon Michel Foucault's notion of biopolitics, Tobias Hübinette[5] and Eleana Kim[6] identify state racism as a key organizing principle of the practice, in that transnational adoption is intended to drive out 'impure' and 'disposable' children (e.g., mixed-race, disabled, or illegitimate children) from South Korea.

Regulating the population of excess children via transnational adoption involves the state's regulation of a woman's reproduction. Barbara Yngvesson describes it thus: "Transnational adoption is likewise a dimension of biopolitics, in which ... certain adults are entitled to become parents and raise children *while others are discouraged or prohibited from doing so*."[7] Yngvesson's keen insight into the inequality that underlies transnational adoption sets the stage for a critical inquiry into the structural factors that play a role in the unwed mother's overwhelming 'choice' to relinquish her baby to adoption.

Among the various institutions that facilitate single mothers to choose adoption, I privilege maternity homes as a principal site of population management.[8] Since the 1980s, the maternity home has developed into a key social welfare institution that provides various practical and emotional supports and services for single mothers. Like orphanages and adoption agencies in Korea, maternity homes are a social service agency that originated in foreign aid organizations established by Christian missionaries. Despite, or perhaps because of, the supports supplied by maternity homes, a great majority of the residents give up their child for adoption. This high relinquishment rate begs a critical analysis of the regulatory functions that maternity homes have undertaken over the past 30 years. Therefore, this chapter examines the maternity home as a hub where various techniques of social governance have merged to curb single motherhood by regulating the population of single mothers and their excess babies via transnational adoption.

This chapter draws primarily upon in-depth interviews with three birth mothers, a single mother, and three maternity home directors; the interviews were gathered during three site visits that took place over ten years. In addition, I employ archival research; a secondary analysis of existing Korean literature, including government reports on birth mothers; a content analysis of maternity home websites; and, a discourse analysis of collections of letters written by birth mothers. Through multiple modalities of exploration, this chapter examines how the maternity home developed from a disciplinary institution wherein unwed mothers felt pressured to "choose" adoption into an administrative and discursive technology that initiates, mediates, and secures the unwed mother's decision to select adoption for her baby.

This chapter explores the ways in which maternity homes function as conduits for, and corollaries of, a systematic regulation of the population, by asking the following two questions: (1) In what ways has the maternity home operated in tandem with various social institutions to constitute a biopolitical security apparatus to control the population of single mothers and their children through the process of transnational adoption? (2) Through what processes has the maternity home produced both the figure of the single mother, a subject who is depicted as unworthy of motherhood, and the figure of the birth mother, a subject who self-regulates and self-controls her 'illegitimate' reproduction via the 'rational' decision to give up her child for adoption?

By addressing these two questions, I hope to illuminate the various constitutive forces of this welfare agency in its regulatory role of containment, classification, and circulation of populations. Alongside this regulatory role, maternity homes articulate a subjectification of the birth mother in the form of pre-natal alienation before the baby's birth, leading to her virtual existence afterward. This chapter, therefore, offers a nuanced and complex analysis of the processes involved in transnational adoption, which, as Hübinette astutely observes, has been "one of the most successful *self-regulating and self-disciplining* biopolitical technologies of social control" over the population of single mothers and their children in South Korea.[9]

3.1 South Korea's Adoption History and Maternity Homes (1980s to mid-2000s)

The 1980s marked a peak-time in South Korea's transnational adoption history and its increasing association with single motherhood, as the majority of adoptees were born to single mothers, in contrast to previous decades when birth mothers had been largely poor, working-class, married women and widows. Global adoption statistics reveal that the number of Korean-born children exceeded 20 to 30 % of all children adopted transnationally during the 1980s.[10] Despite this stunning figure, South Korea's activity in transnational adoption garnered little attention for 30 years, either from its own citizens or from the international community.

The practice first came under wide scrutiny in 1988, as South Korea was preparing to host the 1988 Summer Olympics. In the lead up to the international sporting event, Western media outlets criticized South Korea's practice of transnational adoption, characterizing it as a baby export business.[11] In the face of such criticism, the Korean government intervened and sought to reduce the number of children being sent overseas.[12] Since then, transnational adoption has remained a controversial social issue in which single mothers are blamed for failing to meet standards of sexual propriety. The population of *mihonmo* has been identified as culpable for this "national shame."

Over the next two decades, the South Korean government continued to engage in various programs aimed at decreasing the number of children available for transnational adoption. Its major efforts were concentrated on increasing domestic adoption, as it continued to avoid implementing a broader social policy to support single mothers and their children. The government introduced a quota system that prioritized domestic adoption; it also launched a campaign to promote domestic adoption, by offering incentives, such as tax benefits, healthcare benefits, and government subsidies to its participants. In turn, the number of children placed in transnational adoption continued to fall—this number reached over 2000 in 2005 and was finally outnumbered by the number of domestic adoptions in 2008. Meanwhile, the proportion of single mothers involved in transnational adoption grew from 72 % in the 1980s to 92 % in the 1990s to 98 % in 2005.

The high proportion of *mihonmo* in South Korea's annual adoption statistics should not be mistaken as a reflection of their demographic prevalence or as simply a general trend. South Korea's nonmarital birthrate has remained constant, hovering at less than 10,000 per year, one of the lowest among countries of comparable economic standing; babies born to single mothers comprise 0.6–1.6 % of all live births in South Korea. The comparatively low proportion of single mothers may be a manifestation of the hostile cultural, legal, and economic environment against 'illegitimacy,' but can also be explained by the high rate of abortions in South Korea. Abortion in South Korea, according to Eunshil Kim, has long and widely been used for population control.[13] Although South Korea has had anti-abortion laws, the government did not enforce them, and thus facilitated abortion as a self-regulating mechanism against a population of single mothers.[14] According to a 2009 report, over 95 % of the 150,467 "out-of-wedlock" pregnancies in 2005 were terminated.[15]

Given these factors, what systematic forces lead the majority of single mothers—a small fraction of the population—to give up their babies for adoption? Despite changing social attitudes toward premarital sex, there remains a robust, normative family ideology rooted in the traditional patriarchal family, which upholds a double standard over, and cultivates social stigma against, single mothers. In addition, the South Korean government has continued to operate an inadequate social welfare policy in favor of developing national economic security. Even in the late 1990s, when the South Korean government slowly expanded its social welfare programs, the welfare budget for women remained a negligible 3 to 4 % of its annual social spending, well below the average of countries with comparable economic standing.[16]

Facing social stigma and a lack of social supports, single mothers are most likely to choose abortion or to abandon their child. In response to this problem, the maternity home has emerged as a unique social service for single mothers in South Korea. The first maternity home, originally named *Kusekun Yŏchakwan* (Salvation Army's Women's Center), later renamed *Duri Home* in 2009, was established by the Salvation Army in 1926 during the Japanese occupation. *Duri Home* initially offered shelter to homeless women and prostitutes, and expanded their services to include single, pregnant women in 1966. The second maternity home, *Ae Ran Won* (House of Grace), established by an American Presbyterian missionary, Eleanor Creswell Van Lierop, was built in 1960. At its beginning, *Ae Ran Won*, provided a shelter for camptown sex workers and run-away girls. In 1973, *Ae Ran Won* began offering services for single, pregnant women. The third maternity home, *Maliaŭi Chip* (The House of Mary) was founded by the *Sisters of the Good Shepherd*, a Catholic organization, in

1979. It is noteworthy that all these maternity homes, as with numerous orphanages in postwar South Korea, were first established and funded by foreign Christian organizations; later, they fell under Korean management, but were still affiliated with the same religious organizations. During the 1980s to the mid-2000s, the number of maternity homes grew from three to 18 facilities. This rapid growth can be directly attributed to the establishment of maternity homes by adoption agencies.[17] As of the mid-2000s, ten, or more than half of all maternity homes, were run by only three adoption agencies, Holt International Children's Service (HICS), Social Welfare Society (SWS), and Eastern Children's Welfare Society (ECWS), all of which were founded by devout Christians who regarded adoption as an "act of God's love" and a Christian's duty for salvation. As examined in Chapter 2, almost all adoption agencies and numerous orphanages were established upon the initiative of a foreign aid organization; almost all maternity homes shared their roots in a foreign Christian organization, and followed a Christian mission and ethic.

Corresponding to the rapid growth in such institutions, the number of residents served annually rose from several hundred in the 1980s to more than 2500 by the mid-2000s.[18] The maternity home residents constituted 31 to 43 % of all births outside marriage, and a great majority of these single mothers, as many as 70 to 95 %, chose to give up their newborns for adoption.[19,20] A crude estimate of the proportion of children relinquished at, and transferred from, maternity homes into adoption placement indicate that such children constituted up to 40 % of all adopted children in 2005.[21]

Maternity homes, whether established as a charitable organization or as part of an adoption agency, have long maintained proximate working relations with adoption agencies. For instance, in 1982, the *Daily Economics* reported that *Ae Ran Won* provided services to single, pregnant women who agreed in advance to give up their unborn children to an adoption agency.[22] In return, *Ae Ran Won* and other maternity homes regularly received donations from adoption agencies.[23] Additionally, maternity homes and adoption agencies often share employees; it is not uncommon for an adoption agency worker to work at a maternity home, or vice versa.

While maternity homes and adoption agencies are highly interdependent, it is especially the case for maternity homes that were established by adoption agencies; here, the two organizations are close to the point where the boundaries between the two have become blurred. Quite often, one finds maternity homes located in the same building as the founding adoption agency, or within walking distance of it.[24] In 2004, when I visited *Hye Rim Won*, an SWS-affiliated maternity home in Daegu, its main office shared space with the local adoption center. This historical, physical, administrative, and geographical proximity should not be interpreted as simply a natural consequence of organizational development, for a 1975 revision to adoption laws mandated adoption agencies to take financial responsibility for orphanages and other welfare institutions, in order to continue the practice of overseas adoption. This partial-to-full dependence on adoption agencies to manage orphanages placed the maternity homes in the precarious condition of promoting "adoption facilitation rather than family preservation."[25] In this light, adoptive parents overseas can be viewed as subsidizing South Korean welfare institutions, including maternity homes.[26]

3.2 Homes for "Unwed Mothers": A Biopolitical Welfare Institution

In order to understand the phenomenon of how single mothers became overwhelmingly associated with adoption, I begin with Michel Foucault's concept of biopolitics.[27] Foucault argues that biopolitics is a technology of power over life that renders certain populations into a political problem. In the field of biopolitics, any event that "sapped the population's strength, ... wasted energy, and cost money because ... treating them was too expensive," is subject to regulation and intervention.[28] Drawing upon Foucault's idea of biopolitics, I examine the phenomenon of single mothers and their "out-of-wedlock births" as a perceived social illness, risk, or liability for the population.

Foucault describes sexuality as "a field of vital strategic importance" in biopolitics. He writes, "Sexuality exists at the point where body and population meet. And so it is a matter for discipline, but also a matter for regularization."[29] By highlighting the procreative effects of sexuality, Foucault focuses on the domain of sexuality as a crucial site for security where disciplinary power over individuals intersects with, and is articulated into, a regulatory power over the population. What permeates the membranes of these two techniques of power is the idea of norms, which takes effect in its optimization of all elements of life at the level of population. Norms are not a fixed constant; rather, they function as a modality of optimizing life, which entails a complex interplay of power to maximize the level of security for the population.

Then, what procedures does the regulation of the population entail, and what kinds of subjectivity does it produce? Jesook Song, in her analysis of South Korea's neoliberal society, emphasizes the role of civil society, especially NGOs and their partnership with governmental organizations.[30] This partnership illuminates two features of governance in relation to population management. First, the regulatory mechanism of population management is not a direct intervention of the state, but rather involves a multiplicity of social institutions and actors. Second, various social institutions and actors employ certain techniques and efforts to produce self-governable and self-responsible subjects, who make the most "rational" choice for themselves, thereby serving as a normative force for the population. In other words, coordinated efforts from social institutions and actors, as well as the subjectification of a normative individual, operate as mechanisms of population management.

Understanding these two dimensions as a biopolitical security apparatus for population management, I frame the maternity home as a key departure point—one of the earliest and the most comprehensive—from which to understand the regulatory mechanism that governs the single-mother population. Rooted in the Christian ethic of the sanctity of life and its mission of salvation,[31] maternity homes operate in tandem with other social institutions, such as the church, family, the law, social welfare agencies, adoption agencies, and actors, such as family members, social workers, medical doctors, and adoption professionals. The maternity home stands in defense of life, that is, the baby's life. Yet, the life-saving mission does not just refer to protecting the baby from a potential abortion or from a hostile environment; it also involves providing guidance to the baby's mother. Central to its guidance is the production of a virtuous birth mother who chooses adoption for her baby, thereby functioning as a self-governable and self-responsible subject who upholds the national/family security apparatus.

Rendering the maternity home as a dynamic, constitutive political field that enacts a disciplinary and regulatory power on a population, I draw upon Foucault's notion of site and biopolitics. "[This] problem of the human site," Foucault writes "[is] that of knowing what relations of propinquity, what type of storage, circulation, marking and classification of human elements should be adopted in a given situation in order to achieve a given end."[32] To scrutinize the maternity homes' long association with adoption, I examine three functions of the maternity home: (1) the *containment* of women's deviant sexuality and reproduction; (2) the *classification* of single, pregnant women's bodies into unfit mothers; and, of their babies' prospective life in Korea, as grim; and, consequently (3) the *circulation* of babies and their birth mothers via adoption. By analyzing how adoption serves as a regulatory mechanism over the population of single mothers, I discuss the paradoxes of motherhood at play in the maternity home, whereby single, pregnant women attain the subjectivity of motherhood by renouncing their motherhood. Thus, I argue that transnational adoption has been deployed to regulate the population of single mothers via the maternity home, thus giving rise to the virtual existence of birth mothers.

3.3   Two Mothers: 1983 and 2005

It was 1983. I was only 18 years old, working at a factory, handling fur. I found myself pregnant while dating the baby's father, whom I knew from my hometown. Initially, I thought about having an abortion. But I didn't have enough money. So, for the next four months, I saved up money for medical expenses and went to a hospital. There, I was told to wait until a later stage of pregnancy because a termination might jeopardize my health, suggesting that I would still be able to induce the baby still-born at the eighth month. Finally, when I went to a hospital to terminate the pregnancy at the eighth month, another doctor, now, I suspect, a good Christian, criticized me for trying to murder the baby and refused to provide any medical services. My boyfriend and I didn't have a place to go with the growing belly ... So he took me to his older brother's house where I stayed for another month. One day, his brother's wife took me to a midwife facility[33] where I then was taken in a van, without my own or my boyfriend's consent, to a home for unwed mothers run by a Christian organization. I didn't know where I was until I saw numerous pregnant women. No one told me. ... The baby arrived a month after the expected due date. ... Some time, a day or two, passed. An adoption agency worker came by and took the baby. Though I didn't think consciously about adoption for my baby's future, what seemed certain to me was that raising a child as an unwed mother was unimaginable. There, they all sent their babies away. There was a tacit agreement that the baby would be given up for adoption upon my entry. No consulting! We made some paper flowers, sewed, and a few went into training to become hair stylists. I was there for about three months, during which time my boyfriend thought I was missing. No one knew where I was. I was not allowed to go outside. The only place that I was allowed to go to was a church affiliated with the facility. That's where I gave birth and "decided" on adoption. I was unmarried.[34] (Lee Soon Young, her son was adopted to France in 1983)

In 2005, I found myself pregnant a month after I broke up with my boyfriend. Considering abortion as an option, I went to see a doctor who, unlike many others, didn't ask about my marital status. Instead he just performed an ultrasound exam. I was in my mid-30s. [After the exam,] I wanted to keep my baby, but didn't want to disappoint my family. Marriage to my ex was out of the question. Days passed and months went by while I tried to reach a decision. My friends or colleagues who knew of the pregnancy persuaded, begged, coaxed me to terminate the pregnancy. By the sixth month, I fled the pressure and disdain of my friends and went to a home for unwed mothers. When I asked if services were available, I was asked whether I wanted to keep or give up my baby. "There is no availability, if you want to keep your baby after delivery in our facility" was the answer. I said, "I haven't decided yet." They told me, "Then, one spot is available for you." Every month, adoption agency staff members visited the home and offered monthly adoption workshops in which the advantages and disadvantages of domestic and foreign adoption were explained, and followed by a Q & A. After a long period of hesitation, when my mind was moving more towards adoption, I set up an appointment with staff members from all three adoption agencies. On the first day of meeting for one-on-one conversations, each adoption agency case worker showed up with adoption paperwork when visiting me at the unwed mothers' facility. Since it was before the baby's birth and I had not finalized my decision, I refused to sign the paperwork. Finally I decided on one adoption agency that promised open adoption, which is foreign adoption. The delivery date came earlier than expected. My baby was born a few hours past midnight. The very next morning, an adoption agency worker came by and asked for my signature on two items of paperwork, one being the adoption authorization, and, the other, relinquishing my custody. In the hallway, I signed both documents, and was instructed to write, "I, Choi Hee Sun, will take sole legal responsibility for this adoption made without the baby's father's consent."[35]

I met these two women, Lee Soon Young and Choi Hee Sun, in 2011, while collecting the oral history of Korean birth mothers. Lee Soon Young, 46, is now a mother of two and married to the father of her first child. She reunited with her first son, who now lives in France, in 2005, 22 years after she gave him up for adoption.[36] Choi Hee Sun, 40, is a single mother raising her six-year-old son, and has been actively involved in the Single Mothers' Movement since 2007. Her advocacy work includes providing public education to fight the social stigma of single motherhood, urging lawmakers to increase social welfare for single parents, and organizing birth mothers.[37] Soon after I met her, Choi Hee Sun confessed that she initially gave up her baby for adoption in 2005, and then reclaimed him one week later, with support from a maternity home staff member. Reclaiming one's child was a very uncommon practice at that time.

While the two women's final decisions were quite different, both of their accounts, occurring over 20 years apart, illustrate the systematic mechanisms at work in maternity homes that lead to a great majority of single mothers relinquishing their child to adoption. A close examination of their experiences illuminates the institutional development of a disciplinary and authoritative operation into a self-regulating and self-controlling one. Their accounts resonate, to a great extent, with many other birth mothers who chose adoption primarily because they were not married. Of the eight single birth mothers I met, whose ages ranged from their early 20s to the 70s, four birth mothers stayed at a maternity home; the other four did not stay at a maternity home, nor did they make the decision to place their child into adoption from within a maternity home. Yet, the birth mothers' stories of adoption include any combination of major social institutions—the church, the law, medical facilities, and adoption agencies—that influenced their adoption decision. In other words, a careful analysis of their experiences demonstrates not only the conditions and limitations of maternity homes, but also the panoply of social governance that leads birth mothers to view adoption as the inevitable, logical solution for a baby born out of wedlock.[38]

Containment: Exclusion by Inclusion

Both Lee Soon Young's and Choi Hee Sun's sexual transgressions, and their subsequent failures to abort the pregnancy,[39] resulted in rejection and hostility from their own communities (i.e., their family, friends, neighbors, the workplace, and school).[40] Lee Soon Young had to quit her job and leave her work-based dormitory, while Choi Hee Sun suffered constant pressure to terminate her pregnancy, from both work associates and friends. Additionally, neither woman could seek financial aid from their families, not just because of their working-class backgrounds but also out of fear of shaming them. Without a job or support from family, supports which are indispensable in the structural absence of public provisions, unwed mothers, such as Lee Soon Young and Choi Hee Sun, find themselves hopelessly excluded and ostracized from society.

In a strict sense, the two women did not actually *choose* to enter a home for unwed mothers. Both of their entries, in fact, were mediated and facilitated by a combination of family members and medical institutions. Lee Soon Young's entry was required by law, since under the *Law Against Morally Depraved Behaviors* (*Yullakhaengwi Pangjibŏp*), one is supposed to report sex workers and poor and working-class women who are *likely to engage in sex work* to a municipal authority, so that these women can undergo rehabilitation. The very same law provided the legal foundation for maternity homes from 1961 to 1989. Under this law, she was identified as a potential sex worker because of her out-of-wedlock pregnancy and poor economic status, and thus was handed over to a maternity home. Her entry was not an extra-legal act committed by family, medical personnel, or maternity home employees; rather, it was the result of lawful procedures, orchestrated by dutiful citizens and medical professionals under the mandate of the *Law Against Morally Depraved Behaviors.*

A temporary, full-time residency is mandatory to receive any support from a maternity home. Upon their entry, both women fully submitted themselves to the control of the institution, for which they received support for their pregnancy and the baby's delivery; Lee Soon Young recounted that she had to submit all her belongings, including her clothes, to the office upon admission. This residential requirement allows maternity homes to exert maximum control over single, pregnant women and, thus, to subject them to its institutional premises, procedures, daily regimens, regulations, and supervision. Maternity homes, thereby, contain single mothers and their pregnancies.

Under the *Law Against Morally Depraved Behaviors*, maternity homes were prescribed primarily as a job training facility for vulnerable women, in order to prevent them from succumbing to prostitution. According to the law, residents must be provided with job training, and given round-the-clock supervision. Lee Soon Young, who had previously worked at a fur factory, continued to engage in such light manufacturing work, practicing the skill of sewing, cross-stitching, and making paper flowers. Even after 1989, when the *Law Against Morally Depraved Behaviors* was no longer in effect, job training continued to be an integral part of the daily regimen at maternity homes. While presented as practical measures to prepare for the future, these training sessions can still be construed as disciplinary measures aimed at containing single, pregnant women's bodies.

The maternity homes are temporally enclosed, finite environments in which single, pregnant women are cared for until their 'illegitimate' babies are born.[41] A majority of maternity homes, particularly those affiliated with adoption agencies, were not equipped with childcare units until 2007, when the South Korean government mandated that maternity homes provide childcare facilities. Prior to this law, even those maternity homes that were equipped with childcare facilities were limited in number, and often unavailable.

Choi Hee Sun entered the maternity home in 2005. Upon her contacting the home, the facility immediately attempted to ascertain her plans for the infant to determine whether or not to provide institutional support. In other words, a single pregnant woman's access to institutional aid was dependent on her willingness, or, at least, openness, to putting her unborn child up for adoption. The conditional acceptance of the agency's terms was a commonplace practice in maternity homes. This trend could simply reflect the structural conditions of maternity homes, which lack services for women who want to raise their children. Yet, it is hard to deny that a lack of childcare at maternity homes has worked to contain, if not predetermine, the choice of adoption for single mothers.

One can stay at a maternity home for up to six months; if desired, the stay can be extended for an additional six months. A great majority of expectant mothers, such as Choi Hee Sun, seek entry during their last trimester and stay for an average of one to three months.[42] During their brief stay, these young, single women, usually first-time mothers, must make life-altering decisions about their pregnancies. Since maternity homes do not allow children, residents are unable to take their babies back to the maternity home after giving birth at a hospital. If a resident cannot decide what to do with the baby by the end of her pregnancy, she is usually deemed unfit to parent due to this ambivalence.[43] A birth mother, Seo Chae Rim, 21, described her adoption circumstances:

> Immediately after my delivery, a staff at the maternity home told me that I should call the adoption agency. I had been unsure of what to do, up to the point of my delivery, which came unexpectedly. I was getting a regular checkup, and the doctor told me that my uterus was opening, so I was then admitted to a hospital to give birth. I didn't have anything on me for the baby. Had I brought something that I could wrap around the baby, I might have considered [keeping him] ... But I had nothing. I couldn't take my baby back to the facility. So I called the adoption agency.[44] (Seo Chae Rim, her son adopted to the US, 2005).

While the *Law Against Morally Depraved Behaviors* and the lack of childcare facilities at the maternity homes regulate the physical dimension of containment, Christianity regulates the residents' spiritual dimension. Maternity homes incorporate Christian ethics and practices into their daily programs. Residents are asked, and encouraged, to pray before each meal, and to participate in a weekly, Bible studies' class and a Sunday service. The church delivers anti-abortion sermons, and organizes a "pledge of purity" ceremony, and baptism for newly proselytized residents.[45] During the pledge, residents swear in God's name that they will not engage in premarital sex, and, at the end, are given a ring to wear as proof of their pledge.

At the heart of all these technologies of containment lies the regularization of single mothers' sexuality and their reproduction. Lee Soon Young described her decision to follow the adoption pathway as a tacit agreement upon her entry into the maternity home. The spatial politics of exclusion by inclusion disbarred her potential to be a mother before she could even become one. Meanwhile, Choi Hee Sun's account suggests that the temporal structure of these facilities logistically pressures single, pregnant women to choose what is most readily available, that is, adoption placement. Within the group home, the spatial and temporal logic of inclusion excludes single mothers from the possibility of motherhood. Then, the next question is through what particular ways does the logic of containment render adoption as the only honorable and rational choice?

Classification of Single Mothers: From Unfit to Sacrificing Mothers

Upon their entry, "unwed mothers" must fill out an application and provide comprehensive background information. New residents must detail their work history, educational background, religious practices, socioeconomic status, medical history, abortion history, previous pregnancies, and any past substance use. The application also inquires into their relationship with their family and the baby's father, as well as their general understanding of pregnancy and childbirth. Finally, the application inquires into plans for the baby's future. There are three options: relinquishment, full parental rights, and undecided—listed in that order. During their stay, residents undergo psychological and personality testing, IQ testing, and several other forms of emotional and intellectual assessment. These records are kept in a permanent file for each individual resident. These files, accumulated over the last 30 years, constitute the primary body of knowledge about the *mihonmo* population, and further, underlie the very production of the category, serving as the basis for the ongoing management and regulation of women who become *mihonmo*.

Not only do maternity homes directly extract information from the body of unwed mothers, they indirectly facilitate the development of *mihonmo* discourse. As a social welfare site that exclusively serves single, pregnant women, maternity homes have been a rich field for researchers gathering empirical data on unwed mothers. As a result, residents of these homes have been oversampled, and their profiles have determined the characteristics of Korean single mothers in academic literature, cultural productions, and public policy research.[46] By rendering residents as readily available research subjects, these social welfare facilities have served as social laboratories for the *mihonmo* population.

The figure of the unwed mother is consistently presented as an unfit mother.[47] From the emergence of the single mother as the representative birth mother, she is depicted as inadequate for the task of motherhood because of her low socioeconomic status, her unmarried status, her immaturity, and her unstable, familial background. The greatest indication of her inability to mother is her deviation from prescribed sexual norms.

Mihonmo discourse has not been limited to mothers, but extended to their children. In 1984, the Korean Women's Development Institute stated, in its first comprehensive research report,[48] that the children of unwed mothers were more prone to premature or underweight births, and were highly vulnerable to mental and physical disabilities.[49] A wealth of literature from various disciplines (e.g., medical research, psychology, criminology, and public policy) also identifies children from single-mother households as more likely to develop into juvenile delinquents, due to social ostracism and discrimination.[50] Accepting inadequate social welfare supports and the social stigma against single mothers in Korea as part of an unchangeable status quo, the discourse of *mihonmo* claims that 'illegitimate children' have no viable future in Korea. Echoing the rationale for the first cohort of adoptees (i.e., mixed-race children), the discourse of "no future in Korea" penalizes a single, pregnant woman for her sexual transgressions, and affirms the unwed mother's negative influence on her child, underscoring her unworthiness as a mother.

Even today, scholars, policy makers, and adoption professionals have continued to rationalize, unequivocally, that adoption is the best available choice. Aligned with this adoption-is-best narrative, maternity homes impart adoption knowledge to their residents in two ways: (1) a regular, monthly adoption workshop and (2) a meeting with a Korean adoptee during his or her motherland visit. Maternity homes, in collaboration with adoption agencies, offer a series of monthly workshops, promoting adoption as the best choice for their children's future, as noted in Choi Hee Sun's accounts. In the workshop, single pregnant women learn about the average adoptive parents' profile of being a well-educated, professional, middle-class, European-American, heterosexual couple, and also about two kinds of adoption—transnational and domestic placement. As indicated in Choi Hee Sun's accounts, transnational adoption is presented as "open," which allows for the possibility of an ongoing exchange of photos and letters with the child, as well as a potential reunion in the future; in contrast, domestic adoption in South Korea is closed, which forecloses any of those possibilities.

The information about adoption that is disseminated through these monthly workshops becomes a valid and legitimate truth that is then corroborated by meeting with Korean adoptees who are on "motherland tours."[51] During adoptee visits to maternity homes, birth mothers share the circumstances and dilemmas surrounding their pregnancy, and explain the decision to give up their child to adoption, thereby providing a plausible past that many adoptee participants may have experienced, but have no memory of. Adoptees then share what expectant mothers are most curious about—their lives as adoptees. Via this meeting, expectant mothers come to relate the adoptees they meet with their babies-to-be. By and large, the adoptees' lives are presented as successful and happy, thus turning abstract ideas of adoption, particularly of transnational adoption, into embodied, rewarding lives. Such meetings work to convince single, pregnant women that adoption will afford their child better life opportunities.

The maternity home's efforts to produce a specific kind of understanding about adoption often culminates in a confession by birth mothers that actively claims that adoption is their expression of motherly love. Since 1999, maternity homes have published four edited volumes of autobiographical essays and/or letters, written by residents.[52] Rupa Bagga-Raoulx indicates that these writings have been used therapeutically as part of maternity home regimens to help birth mothers express their feelings and hopes and fears for the child's future; often, the residents are encouraged to keep journals.[53] These writings are submitted to staff members and counselors, but also, at times, shared with other residents, and placed into the resident's personal file. The residents' writing collections are, therefore, an invaluable source for understanding what is most commonly or normatively believed within maternity homes.

A majority of these writings are delivered in the form of letters, which are addressed to children who are either intended for, or already relinquished to, adoption. The narratives, telling of the adoption backstory and the birth mother's decision-making processes, resound with the single mothers' pain, shame, and guilt.[54] They also express their love toward their baby, and their desire to reunite with the child in the future. This desire is often expressed in religious terms.[55]

One of the most prevalent themes in the letters is the most powerful rationale for adoption: the possibility of a better life. The book *I Wish You a Beautiful Life*, an edited volume of letters from residents of *Ae Ran Won*, originally published in English, is the most well-received collection. In it, one letter reads:

> As your mother I was always concerned about you. There was no way for us to live together. I gave birth to you, so I had the responsibility to provide a wonderful environment for you. I preferred to say good-bye to you, rather than to live with you, if that decision could bring you better opportunities. … Therefore, adoption was my gift to you.[56]

In this passage, the mother's decision to relinquish her baby is rationalized through the profound belief that adoption will provide "better opportunities" and this expectation is expressed, using the language of gift-giving. Here, relinquishment is depicted not as abandonment, nor as a denunciation of the unwed mothers' motherhood; rather, it is presented as the supreme affirmation of a mother's love and sacrifice. Throughout these confessional letters, unwed mothers perform as repentant birth mothers who confess their mistakes, and eventually display their love toward their baby, by making the greatest maternal sacrifice.

While the birth mothers' letters suggest a firm belief in a better life associated with the child's adoption, I argue that there is a noticeable gap in the substance of what constitutes a "better life." The discourse of a better life through adoption automatically registers a devaluation of the birth mother's life and her own future, in comparison to the life worth and future of unknown adoptive parents in the US, or other western countries. Likewise, the better-life-through-adoption promise revalorizes the child's worthless life *before* adoption to a worthwhile life *after* adoption; thereby, it suggests that the value of the child's life is commensurate with the parents' capacity to invest in financial, moral, and educational resources for that child's future. Such betterment of the child's life is expected to be measured by positive educational and financial outcomes that serve as clear indicators of a "good life." The profound belief in a better life depends on absolute trust that the middle-class, normative, European-American family life is the best environment for the development of these excess children.

Over the course of their development, maternity homes have participated in and facilitated the knowledge production of *mihonmo*, as well as of adoption. Such knowledge production has produced a discourse wherein single mothers are portrayed as unfit and incapable parents, and wherein the lives of children raised by single mothers in Korea are presented as worthless. This discourse serves as a rationale for presenting adoption as the best alternative for single mothers. Furthermore, maternity homes have radically recast the figure of the single mother who chooses to give up her child for adoption as a virtuous, self-sacrificing birth mother. Through this system of reclassification emerge two figures representing the single-mother population: (1) an incapable, sexually delinquent, unfit mother; and (2) a self-sacrificing birth mother who makes the best possible choice in a challenging situation.

The Circulation of Bodies

Before the introduction of the *Adoption Special Law* (*ipyang t'ŭklyepŏp*) in 2011, the *Special Law on Adoption Promotion and Procedure* (*ipyang chokchin mich' chŏlch'ae kwanhan tŭklyepŏp*)[57] remained the legal framework for adoption. As encapsulated in its title, the law's aim was to expedite and promote adoption. For a child to be eligible for adoption, the law required the child to be an orphan; an orphan was defined as a child whose two parents are dead, incapable, or unwilling to raise the child. In other words, an orphan, in the legal sense, was not necessarily a parentless child; in fact, a considerable number of children available for adoption have at least one living parent. In such cases, the adoption procedure begins by rendering the child into an "eligible orphan." This process requires the complete severance of a child from his or her natal parents, and the subsequent legal transfer of custody from a parent to the adoption agency.[58] This recategorization is a precondition for a child to be eligible for adoption, and provides the background for Lee Soon Young's and Choi Hee Sun's adoption consultation, which took place and was facilitated from within the maternity home.

As indicated by Choi Hee Sun's experience, once she showed interest in adoption, adoption agency workers immediately took the necessary steps for orphan production. Adoption agency workers visited her in the maternity home, offering individual consultations. At the initial intake meeting, representatives from all three adoption agencies presented the mother with adoption paperwork, including forms for the termination of parental rights and the relinquishment of the child. In this way, maternity home residents terminate their parental rights even before the infant is born.

By signing the adoption papers at the facility, a single, pregnant woman agrees to give up all *potential* parental rights and to transfer her *would-be* custody of the baby to the adoption agency; in turn, she becomes a birth mother who is legally dead before giving birth. Thus, the baby is born a legal orphan. Since the maternity home residents are under heavy visitor restrictions and constant monitoring, it is only with the maternity home's permission that an adoption agency worker can meet with an expectant mother and try to sever the unborn baby from her. And, by permitting the preemptive completion of the adoption paperwork at the facility, maternity homes take part in initiating orphan production at the earliest possible moment.

The preemptive completion of the adoption paperwork relinquishing the child's custody is essential to the next step of acquiring possession of the baby. The medical facility's role and its cooperation with the adoption agency are vital to secure a safe physical and emotional separation of the child from the single, pregnant woman. As maternity home residents approach delivery time, they are sent to the hospital to give birth and placed under the care of an ob-gyn. Often, the medical hospital is where they have been receiving their prenatal checkups and treatments. Once the baby is born, medical professionals supervising the baby's delivery do not leave the baby with the mother. Instead, the child is taken away from the site of birth and sent to a separate room under the direct supervision of nurses; meanwhile, the mother can see the child during designated hours, only if she wants. Furthermore, mothers are not allowed to nurse the child after the delivery. In this way, hospitals prevent a mother from further developing any physical or emotional attachment to the baby, and also promote the protocol of completely separating the child from the mother upon delivery.

After the birth of the child, the hospital notifies the maternity home, which then relays the message to the adoption agency, or else, the hospital directly contacts the adoption agency. The streamlined efforts to expedite the child's adoption allow almost no chance for birth mothers to reconsider their premeditated adoption decision. Upon the news of the child's birth, the adoption agency, having full control over the child through pre-adoption paperwork, dictates the amount of time that the birth mother can spend with the baby, as well as when the infant will be separated from her, typically, a range of several hours to two days. An adoption agency caseworker arrives to take the newborn, who has preemptively been processed for adoption.

No birth registration needs to be issued for the newborn,[59] and he or she is taken in as an abandoned baby, legally an orphan from birth. After the baby is taken by the agency, the birth mother returns to the maternity home. Meanwhile, the child remains in foster care until his or her placement in an adoptive family.

A close examination of the delivery of the child, from the single mother to the adoption agency, reveals that an adoption apparatus for excess children is fully in place in South Korea. Since the 1980s, the vast majority of births have taken place in hospitals, accounting for 82.4 % of all births in 1985, and 98.8 % in 1994.[60] The normalizing practice of giving birth in a hospital renders midwife facilities and medical centers, as echoed in Lee Soon Young's and Choi Hee Sun's experiences, as key institutions that detect the population of single mothers and steer them into adoption agencies, with, or without, the help of maternity homes. Once hospitals identify a pregnant woman to be a single mother, it is common for them to immediately ask whether she plans to raise the child, and to introduce her to either an adoption agency or an adoption agency–affiliated maternity home. For example, in 2008, soon after Jun Hae Rin, then 18, confirmed her pregnancy at a hospital in her hometown, a nurse told her of an agency-affiliated maternity home in Kwang Ju, a city an hour and a half away from her hometown; once there, she "decided" on adoption.

After the child's custody is taken by the adoption agency, the maternity home helps to prepare single mothers to return to society without traces of having given birth. Lee Kyung Ae, who worked at a maternity home for 17 years, told me that residents are given a special serial number to access government-subsidized, health benefits. With this temporary serial number, the birth mother receives public relief, and any medical records of pregnancy and delivery are concealed in her official health insurance file. This government-sanctioned omission in the birth mother's health insurance file, combined with the lack of birth registration, means that she does not have any legal or medical record attesting that she gave birth to a child.

The maternity home also conducts a sex education workshop that aims to help residents develop healthy relationships and to engage in 'appropriate' sexual conduct, as well as to impart accurate information about sex and contraceptives, so as to prevent any subsequent pregnancies.[61] To this end, medical doctors affiliated with maternity homes sometimes administer more direct measures of birth control before residents leave the maternity home. For example, Soe Chae Rim, a 21-year-old single mother when I met her in 2012, gave up her first child for adoption at 16. Before she left the maternity home, she was sent to a gynecologist to follow up on her postdelivery recovery. After pressing her on whether she intended to have sex again, the gynecologist advised her to get an intrauterine device (IUD) for birth control, and she acquiesced.[62]

Considering Lee Soon Young's and Choi Hee Sun's experiences, with a focus on how maternity homes circulate babies from unwed mothers to adoption agencies, illuminates core features of the institutional mission of maternity homes.[63] For example, *Esther's Home* describes itself as "a place of consolation for unwed mothers and consultation for the babies' future."[64] Another maternity home, *In Ae Welfare Center* in Kwangju, aims "to help single, pregnant women with their crisis and help them to find their way back to being dutiful citizens."[65] Both statements acknowledge the sexuality of single, pregnant women as deviant, and thus articulate an institutional commitment to rehabilitate these women. Central to the rehabilitation process is a "consultation for the babies' future," suggesting that salvaging the future of the unborn child is the route by which an unwed mother's sexual transgression can be redeemed, thus allowing the mother to "find her way back" to healthy citizenry. By facilitating the circulation of babies from the unwed mothers to adoption agencies, the maternity home rehabilitates the birth-mother population into healthy, dutiful, and potential mothers-to-be.

3.4 Life and Death at the Home for Unwed Mothers: The Birth of Virtual Mothers

So far, we have examined the social governance underlying the maternity home in three following aspects: containment, classification, and circulation. As a unique social welfare agency for single, pregnant women, maternity homes stand at the nexus of a regulatory mechanism that contains the sexuality of single, pregnant women and their unborn children. The practice of containment facilitates the development of a classification system in which the possibility of motherhood and a life with her child is foreclosed to the *mihonmo*. Life for a *minhonmo* and her child is preordained as worthless and devalued, thereby rationalizing the circulation of babies via adoption placement as yielding better life opportunities. By ensuring the circulation of babies and *mihonmo* through adoption, the maternity home has completed a regulatory cycle of securitizing the population against an excess population of single mothers and their children.

The maternity home, as a key social institution in the regulation of single motherhood via adoption, offers a safe and supportive environment for single women who are pregnant; thereby, it acknowledges and endorses single motherhood. However, the underlying tenet of the maternity home and its operation, as illustrated above, continues to be transfer the baby from a single mother to an adoption facility, rather than to advocate for, or even consider, a single mother's right to raise her own child. To put it differently, as a site of crisis management, maternity homes offer comfort and support to the vulnerable population of single mothers, shielding them from the hostile environment against unwed mothers; yet by enclosing them from a regular, normal site for their "other" mothering, maternity homes serve to secure the patriarchal familial order.

To analyze the regulatory mechanism of maternity homes and its effects on pregnant, unwed mothers, I apply Jodi Kim's use of "social death,"[66] a concept Orlando Patterson developed to describe the abject state in which slaves live, without rights and in nonliving conditions.[67] While she clearly acknowledges the differences between working-class, unwed birth mothers worldwide, and slave women, Kim strategically juxtaposes the "natal alienation" experienced by slaves to the adoption circumstances faced by birth mothers, both groups which are often characterized by unassailable structural forces and a system of inequality. She articulates the birth mothers' quality of life as being mired in "profound natal alienation, or the capacity to give life but the severing of rights to claim to parent that life…"[68] Via her observations and analysis of structural conditioning, I understand the life conditions of a single, pregnant woman to be inseparable from her social death, even during her stay at the maternity home, and argue that she is subject to *prenatal alienation*.

Prenatal alienation not only identifies the conditions surrounding adoption, but it also reveals the preemptive nature of social regulation against single motherhood. The temporal logic of prenatal alienation in maternity homes, as shown throughout this chapter, functions as a core principle of population management, as opposed to the earlier deployment of transnational adoption as a post-reproduction measure during the 1970s and 1980s. Single, pregnant women are immediately registered as, and transacted into, birth mothers in their interactions with social institutions, such as the family, maternity homes, medical doctors, and other welfare facilities. Through the logic of this regulatory mechanism, a self-regulating and a self-responsible birth mother subjectivity is produced at the earliest possible moment. The birth mother, therefore, emerges at the death of the potential, single mother, but only in virtual form.

The maternity home alters the conventions of mothering and creates virtual mothering. Virtual mothering is the byproduct of the preemptory, constrictive rubric of social governance by which single, pregnant women relinquish their babies and become birth mothers. Yet, the subjectivity of a birth mother always emerges in a paradoxical form of mothering. Thus, by sacrificing mothering, she becomes a mother. And, by being excluded from mothering via adoption, a birth mother offers her mothering, by wishing her child a better life in adoption. In a sense, she experiences her own mothering virtually—as neither living nor dead— as she waits both for her baby and for his or her adoption. Yet, her virtual status as a mother does not end with the baby's adoption placement. After surrendering the child to the maternity home, hospital, or adoption agency, she is then to return her normal life— her home, work, and school, spaces in which her experiences of pregnancy, birth, delivery, and adoption, are deemed unspeakable. And thus, she remains a virtual mother.

In *Part I, Unbecoming Mothers: A History of Gendered Violence*, I have examined the historical, geopolitical, socioeconomic, and cultural contexts by which working-class women and poor mothers in South Korea, including *kijich'on* mothers, divorcées, widows, and single, young women, became birth mothers. In these two chapters, I have demonstrated how South Korea's unending geopolitical crisis justified, and continues to justify, a perpetual lack of a national social welfare policy, creating a permanent condition for transnational adoption; thus, what began as an emergency relief effort well over 60 years ago has evolved into a surrogate welfare institution for children and mothers existing outside of the normative patriarchal family. Foreign Christian philanthropic endeavors have been vital to the invention and maintenance of such practice, as the initial development of orphanage-based child welfare in the postwar recovery period continued to engage other areas of welfare, such as the development of maternity homes for single, pregnant women, thus shaping key institutional frameworks and creating a pipeline through which to place excess children into adoption placement. These developments were instituted to facilitate the social governance of excess children in South Korea. My critical analysis reveals how the institutional frameworks, national discourse, and, security state practices intersected with personal circumstances, leading *kijich'on* mothers, poor, working-class mothers, and single mothers to become birth mothers. I argue that it is difficult to deny that these birth mothers have served South Korea's national security agenda through the coerced separation from both the child and their own mothering, no matter how willingly or unwillingly.

Notes

1. Throughout this chapter, I use the terms, *unwed mothers*, *single pregnant women*, and *mihonmo* interchangeably in order to provide more nuanced understandings of the population. When using the term *unwed mothers*, I intend to convey the sense of a deeply rooted social stigma. *Single, pregnant women* is a more neutral phrase.
2. Single motherhood is not always considered illegitimate. There are two categories of single-mother households: *pyunmo* refers to a mother whose husband passed away prematurely; and a newly developed category, *pihonmo*, refers to a self-sufficient, unmarried woman who chooses to have a child of her own volition. *Pihonmo* typically have class privilege and are granted sexual freedom.
3. Reflecting growing concern over the low birthrate that began in 2000, the South Korean government began to implement more active supervision and regulation over maternity homes from the mid-2000s onward. Furthermore, from the mid-2000s, a growing awareness about women's equality, as well as adoptee activism for single motherhood, has slowly garnered public concern over depopulation, and increased the support for single motherhood. The patriarchal family registration system which did not recognize a single mother's relation to her child was abolished in 2008. That same year, the government began to subsidize $50 monthly payments to single-mother households. In 2007, under this changed climate, maternity homes were mandated by the government to

provide appropriate accommodations for newborn babies. Consequently, the family preservation rate from maternity homes has been on the rise. Currently, the relinquishment rate from maternity homes has been reduced to 50–60 %.
4. See Natalie Cherot, "Transnational Adoptees: Global Biopolitical Orphans or an Activist Community?" in *Culture Machine* 8 (2008), Tobias Hübinette, "Comforting an Orphaned Nation" (Ph.D. diss., Stockholm University, 2005), Eleana Kim, *Adopted Territory: Transnational Korean Adoptees and the Politics of Belonging* (Durham: Duke University Press, 2010), Jodi Kim, "An 'Orphan' with Two Mothers: Transnational and Transracial Adoption, the Cold War, and Contemporary Asian American Cultural Politics," *American Quarterly* 61, no. 4 (2009): 855–880, Hosu Kim and Grace M. Cho, "The Kinship of Violence," *Journal of Korean Adoption Studies* 1, no. 3 (2012): 7–25, and Barbara Yngvesson, *Belonging in an Adopted World* (Chicago: University of Chicago Press, 2010).
5. Hübinette, "Comforting an Orphaned Nation".
6. E. Kim, *Adopted Territory*.
7. Yngvesson, *Belonging in an Adopted World*, 196 (emphasis added).
8. In South Korea, *mihonmo ui jip*, which means 'home for unwed mothers,' refers to maternity homes. In the chapter, I interchangeably use the terms, 'home for unwed mothers' and maternity homes.
9. Hübinette, "Comforting an Orphaned Nation", 64 (emphasis added).
10. Rosemary C. Sarri, Yeon-Ok Baik, and Marti Bombyk, "Goal Displacement and Dependency in South Korea–United States Intercountry Adoption," *Children and Youth Review* 20, no. 1–2 (1998): 87–114.
11. See Susan Chira, "Seoul Journal – Babies for Export: and Now the Painful Question," *New York Times* (New York, NY), April. 21, 1988, Peter Maass, "Adoptions: Korea's Disquieting Problem; National Embarrassment over Letting Foreigners Take Children," *Washington Post* (Washington, D.C.), Dec. 14, 1988, and Matthew Rothschild, "Babies for Sale: South Koreans Make Them, Americans Buy Them," *Progressive* 52, no. 1 (1998): 18–23.

12. In Korea's adoption history, there have been numerous attempts by the government to slow down and, ultimately, terminate transnational adoption through the promotion of domestic adoption. However, without systematic enforcement, these attempts were unsuccessful.
13. Eunshil Kim, "nakt'ae kwanhan sahoechŏk nonŭiwa yŏsongŭi salm" (Abortion Discourses and Women's Lives in Korea), *hyŏngsajŏngchaek yŏnku* 2(1991), 383 – 404.
14. In 2009, in response to the national population crisis stemming from the low fertility rate, the South Korean government strengthened the legal guidelines for abortion, invoking a heavy fine against, and revoking the medical license of, surgeons who performed the practice.
15. Mijeong Lee, *sahoechŏk p'yŏnkyŏnkwa mihonmo kwanŏlyn t'ongkye* "Social Prejudice against Unwed Mothers and Related Statistics", in *minhonmoŭi hyŏnsilkwa chalip chiwŏn pangan*, (Reality of Unwed Mothers and Support for Self-Reliance), (Seoul: Korean Women's Development Institute, 2010), 12.
16. Joosun Kim, *hankuk mihonmo pokchi sŏpisŭe kaesŏn pangane kwanhan yŏnku* (Study on the Social Welfare Program for Korean Unwed Mothers and Policy Implications), (Master's thesis, Inha University, 2004), 30.
17. Tobias Hübinette astutely observes that the agency's expansion of social services to single, pregnant women was largely tied to the adoption agencies' need to "secure a continuous supply of newborn and healthy babies" against market fluctuation. See Hübinette, "Comforting an Orphaned Nation", 72.
18. Mijeong Lee, "Social Prejudice against Unwed Mothers and Related Statistics", 17.
19. Ibid.,18.
20. The high relinquishment rate of out-of-wedlock births in South Korean maternity homes echoes findings in a study of US maternity homes by Christine E. Edwards and Christine L. Williams (2000). Utilizing field research and interviews with residents in the late 1990s, Edwards and Williams identified two primary functions of maternity homes: (1) to provide support for single, pregnant women; and, (2) to facilitate the adoption of babies after delivery. Noting the high correlation between a single mother and adoption

placement, Edwards and Williams raised critical concerns about the influence of these facilities in their clients' decision-making processes. See Christine E. Edwards and Christine L. Williams (2000), "Birth Mothers in Maternity Homes Today," *Gender and Society* 14, no 1: 160–183.
21. Lee, *Social Prejudice against Unwed Mothers and Related Statistics*, 18.
22. Seung, "Ae Ran Welfare Center", *Daily Economics,* Section 9, March 18, 1982.
23. "Adoption agencies withheld donations to maternity homes when the maternity home starts to promote family preservation". [Yeo Woon Ja, interview with the author, January 3, 2012].
24. In 1986, the Eastern Social Welfare Society, the second largest adoption agency, built its first group home for unwed mothers in its welfare institution complex, just steps away from its own child recruitment center.
25. E. Kim, *Adopted Territory*, 75.
26. Ibid.
27. Michel Foucault, *Society Must Be Defended: Lectures at the Collège de France 1975–1976*, trans. David Macey (New York: Picador, 2003).
28. Ibid., 244.
29. Ibid., 251–252.
30. Jesook Song, *South Koreans in the Debt Crisis: The Creation of a Neoliberal Welfare Society* (Durham: Duke University Press, 2009).
31. Han Sang Soon, Director of *Ae Ran Won* , on its 50-year anniversary said, "From the beginning, guided by Christian ethics, which teaches utmost the value of life, we have devoted ourselves to single mothers who secure babies' life against abortions." See *Ae Ran Won 50 nyŏnsa* [Seoul: The 50-year-history of Ae Ran Won, 2010). 54.
32. Foucault, *Society Must Be Defended*, 23.
33. Midwife facilities are known as *choshanso* (literally, birthing assistance center). Before childbirth became monopolized by hospitals, *choshanso* used to be a popular option, especially for working-class women.
34. Lee Soon Young (birth mother) in an interview with the author, January 14, 2011.

35. Choi Hee Sun (single mother) in a phone interview with the author, March 5, 2011.
36. She admitted, retrospectively: "I don't remember exactly how I felt. But I assume, I must have felt probably somewhat relieved [right after the adoption]."
37. She has been featured in Korean newspaper outlets, and the *New York Times*. For example, see Choe, Sang Hun, "Group Resists Korean Stigma for Unwed Mothers," *New York Times*, October 7, 2009.
38. My analysis of how maternity homes are aligned with the social governance of single motherhood via adoption does not refute the agency of single mothers or mean that all maternity homes and their staff members oppose single motherhood. Despite its long history of promoting adoption for single mothers, a few maternity homes began to advocate for single motherhood. The non–adoption-affiliated maternity home, *Ae Ran Won*, is a great example. Choi Hee Sun's reversal of her adoption decision, as she recalled, was only possible with the assistance of the maternity-home staff, who helped her to contact the adoption agency and to get back her child a week later. Furthermore, Han Sang Soon, the director of *Ae Ran Won*, has advocated for single motherhood and demanded that the government support maternity homes to develop childcare for single mothers who want to raise their children. *Ae Ran Won* opened a group home for residents who decided to raise their own children in 2000, many years before the government began to fund such facilities in 2007.
39. A significant number of residents reported they had either initially considered abortion or missed the opportunity to do so, as did Lee Soon Young and Choi Hee Sun. In 2000, Jamowon's statistics showed that 36 out of the total 112 residents came to the facility because they missed the window for an abortion. The belated acknowledgment of pregnancy, financial reasons, a prospective marriage with the baby's father, anxiety or fear of the surgery, and religious reasons are identified as reasons for delaying the abortion decision. Kim, Joosun. "*Hanguk mihonmo pokchi sŏ bisŭ ŭ i kaesŏ nbangan e kwanhan yŏngu*" [A study on the social welfare program for Korean unwed mothers and policy implications]. Master's thesis, (Incheon: Inha University, 2004), 10.

40. It is customary to expel high school students once their pregnancy is disclosed due to the fear that they will exert a bad influence on other students.
41. There were a few facilities that provided residential and other kinds of supports for single mothers and their newborn babies, prior to the South Korean government's policy shift in 2007. However, the funding for those supports were not provided by the government, and instead these organizations relied on donations from other sources.
42. Young Mi Bae, "*Ch'ŏngsonyŏn mihonmo palsaeng yoine kwanhŏannkuy* [A study on the determinants of unmarried adolescent mothers]," *Proceedings of the International Women's Research Symposium* 10 (2001): 51–80.
43. Namsoon Huh, "Services for Out-of-wedlock Children in Korea," *Early Child Development and Care* 85 (1993): 35–46.
44. Seo Chae Rim (birth mother) in an interview with the author, January 2, 2012.
45. Jin-A Noh, *Mihonmo ŭi chip* –Ae Ran Won, *Church Education*, December 1996.
46. See HyeJung Cheon et al., "Minhonmo poho sisŏle kŏchuhanŭn 10tae minhonmo ŭi kyŏnghome taehan yŏnku" [A study on the experiences of institutionalized unmarried teenage mothers: Pregnancy and sexual behaviors], *Journal of the Korean Home Management Association* 20, no 4 (2002): 1–12; Byung Hoon Chun, "Adoption and Korea," *Child Welfare* 68, no. 2 (1989): 255–260; Ok Ja Hwang and Mi Hyun Yoon, "Mihonmo tŭksŏnh pyŭnhwae kwanhan yŏnku" (The study of the development of the characteristics of unwed mothers in Korea), *Dongguk Journal: Humanities & Social Sciences* 35 (1996): 219–247; Ji Yeol Kim, "Mihonmo e kwanhan kichŏ chŏk yŏngu" [An analytic study of the unmarried mother in Korea] Master's Thesis, (Seoul: Ewha Women's University, 1974); Joo Sun Kim, "*Hanguk mihonmo pok-chi sŏ bisŭ ŭ i kaesŏ nbangan e kwanhan yŏngu*" [A Study on the Social Welfare Program for Korean Unwed Mothers and Policy Implications], master's thesis (Inchoen: Inha University, 2004), Korean Women's Development Institute, "*Mihonmo silt'aee kwanhan yŏnku*" [Study on the unwed mother with special reference to the analysis of factors relating her occurrence and

welfare measures] (Seoul: KWDI, 1984); Young-Mi Lee and Seung-Hee Choi, "The Development and Effectiveness of Group Program to Promote Self-Determination for Teen Parents." *Korean Journal of Family Welfare* 16 (2005): 103–126; Choon Rae Noh and Won Hee Kim, "*Sisŏlkŏchu mihonmo ŭi ipyang kyŏlchŏngyoin e kwanhan yŏngu*" [Predictive factors of baby release for adoption among unmarried mothers]," *Journal of Korean Child Welfare* 17 (2004): 49–79; Kyung Ae Park, et al., "Teenage Childbirth," *Korean Journal of Obstetrics and Gynecology* 18, no. 11 (1975): 923–928; and Mi Hyun Yoon & Jae Yeon Lee, "*Hanguk 10 tae mihonmo ŭi t'ŭkdŏng e kwanhan yŏnku*" [Characteristics of teenaged unwed mothers in Korea], *Journal of Korean Child Welfare* 23, no. 3 (2002): 149–169.

47. Before the 1990s, the unwed mother was a young, uneducated, factory worker from a rural area who, without proper parental supervision, engaged in inappropriate sexual behavior. After the 1990s, the figure of the high school dropout or the runaway came to embody the figure of the single mother.

48. Korean Women's Development Institute (KWDI), *Mihonmo silt'aee kwan-han yŏngu* [Study on the unwed mother with special reference to the analysis of factors relating her occurrence and welfare measures]. (Seoul: KWDI, 1984).

49. In particular, numerous studies after the 1990s reported an increase in the proportion of teenage, single mothers. These studies reported a prevalence of birth defects, premature births, and low birth weights among infants born to unwed mothers, and thus argued that the pregnancy of an unwed mother was more likely to result in a child with a disability.

50. See Young Mi Bae, "*Ch'ŏngsonyŏn mihonmo palsaeng yoine kwanhan yŏngu*" [A study on the determinants of unmarried adolescent mothers], International Women's Research Symposium 10 (2001); Hyejung Cheon et al., "*Mihonmo pohosisŏle kŏchuhanŭn 10 tae mihonmo ŭi kyŏnghŏm e taehan yŏngu,*" [A study on the experiences of institutionalized unmarried teenage mothers: Pregnancy and sexual behaviors], *Journal of Korean Home Management* 20, no 4 (2002): 1–12; Seunghee Choi,"*Chanŏ lŭl ipyangponaen mihonmo ŭi sangsil,*" (Unwed mothers' grief after giving up a child to adoption) *Proceedings from the conference Mihonmo ŭi hyŏnsil kwa chalip chiwŏn pangan* [Reality of unwed mothers and support

for self-reliance], (Seoul: KWDI, 2010), 26–45; KWDI, *mihonmo silt'aee kwanhan yŏngu* [Study on the unwed mother with special reference to the analysis of factors relating her occurrence and welfare measures], (Seoul: KWDI, 1984); Shin Jung Kim, Soon Ok Yang and Keum Hee Jung, "*Sisŏl e ipsohan mihonmo ŭi silt'ae*" [Reality of unwed mothers at maternity facilities], *Journal of Korean Academy Child Health Nursing* 10, no. 4 (2004): 468–478; Choon Rae Noh and Won Hee Kim, "Predictive Factors of Baby Release for Adoption among Unmarried Mothers," Journal of Korea Studies of Child Welfare 17 (2004): 49–79; Kyung Ae Park et al., "Teenage Childbirth," *Korean Journal of Obstetrics and Gynecology* 18, no. 11 (1975): 923–928; and Mi Hyun Yoon& Jae Yeon Lee, "Characteristics of Teenaged Unwed Mothers in Korea," *Korean Journal of Child Studies* 23, no. 3 (2002): 149–167.

51. Since the early 1990s, adoption agencies and quasi-governmental organizations such as Overseas Koreans Foundation have organized motherland trips for Korea-born adoptees. Through the program, adoptees participate in a variety of cultural activities—such as visiting folk villages; attending a traditional Korean wedding; attending a cooking class; and participating in social service visits, such as to orphanages and maternity homes. Interested adoptees can search for their birth families.

52. The four books include Sara Dorow (ed), *I wish you a beautiful life* (St. Paul: Yeong & Yeong Publishing Company, 1999); *Dreaming a World* (St. Paul: Yeong & Yeong Publishing Company, 2010); Social Welfare Services, *Pitanhyang k'och'mu ŭi k'ochmal ch'ŏlŏm [Like a word of stock]*. (Seoul: Social Welfare Services, 2001); Social Welfare Services. *Pyŏl ŭl poneda [Send Away the Stars]*. (Seoul: Social Welfare Services, 2003).

53. Rupa Bagga-Raoulx, "Mothering Across Borders: South Korean Birthmothers' Perspectives," in *Mothering in East Asian Communities: Politics and Practices*, ed. Patti Duncan and Gina Wong (Bradford: Demeter Press, 2014), 181–215.

54. In "*pitanhyang kkoch'muŭi kkoch'chŏmch'ŏlŏm*" (Like a word of Stock) (2001), a letter collection from Hye Rim Won, one letter reads thus:

"I haven't been able to take care of you well. ... you will come into the light within a month. ... My heart is broken ... when you come out of me, you will be sent away to a better home. ... I am so sorry.

I should take care of you well inside. But I didn't and instead harmed you. The day of our separation is approaching. I will miss you very much even after I send you away" (Seoul: Social Welfare Services, 2001), 71.
55. "... what I also hope is that wherever you are, you understand that the Lord Jesus is with you and that you are a child of God. ... I will never forget you but I will always pray for you. My love for you will continually grow," In *I Wish You A Beautiful Life*, ed. Sara Dorow, 45.
56. Ibid, 37.
57. This adoption-first law was challenged both by adoptee activists and advocates supporting single-mothers' rights to family preservation, and was finally revised to include stipulations for oversight of the adoption process and to delay the adoption decision until one week after delivery (*Joong-Ang Daily,* 07/01/2011).
58. See Eleana Kim, *Adopted Territory*, Jodi Kim, "An 'Orphan' with Two Mothers: Transnational and Transracial Adoption, the Cold War, and Contemporary Asian American Cultural Politics," and Barbara Yngvesson, *Belonging in an Adopted World*.
59. This practice is in contrast to the common practice of reporting a baby's birth registration to a local government community center within a month.
60. Sook Bang, "*urinara mojabogŏnŭi hyŏnhwanggwa paljŏnbanghyang*" [The Current Affairs and Directions of Maternal and Child Health in South Korea] *han'guk moja pogŏnhakhoe ch'angnipkinyŏm haksuldaehoe charyojip*. (Seoul: The Korean Society of Maternal and Child Health, 1996), 31.
61. Ae Ran Won ed., *Ae Ran Won 50 nyŏnsa* [Seoul: The 50-years-History of Ae Ran Won, 2010], 106.
62. Seo Chae Rim (birth mother) in an interview with the author, January 2, 2012.
63. Due to major legal changes affecting their operation, maternity homes no longer underscore their explicit guideline to promote adoption as the "future plan." Rather, they support the birth mother's choice, whether it is to raise the child herself or to place the child in adoption.
64. "Introduction to Esther's Home," accessed on March 1, 2011, http://www.esther.or.kr (The original has disappeared).

65. "Introduction to the Welfare Center," accessed on March 1, 2011, http://swinaebokji.or.kr (The original has disappeared).
66. Jodi Kim, "An 'Orphan' with Two Mothers."
67. Orlando Patterson, *Slavery and Social Death: A Comparative Study* (Cambridge, MA: Harvard University Press, 1982).
68. Jodi Kim, "An 'Orphan' with Two Mothers," 857.

PART II

Reconnection: Virtual Mothering

CHAPTER 4

Television Mothers: Birth Mothers Lost and Found in the Search-and-Reunion Narrative

July 20, 2005, 8:30 AM
 Another summer visit, back home in Korea. I turned on the television, and my mother's favorite morning show—*Ach'im Madang* [Morning Forum]—was about to start. It was Wednesday, so its weekly feature, a family search show called "I Want to Meet This Person," was airing live. Everything about the show looked the same as it did a year ago—the same hosts, studio setting, and format. People came to the podium, one after another, with stories of separation, looking for their loved ones, naming all identifiable physical traits or information. Two Korean adoptees came to the podium, looking for their birth families. This week's program was nothing special! I could have fallen asleep to these unrelenting stories of separation and loss told in monotonous tones, with the hosts saying the same things they say every time. Watching this reality search program, I had no clue about the role that I was soon to perform for the show in the reunion of a Korean adoptee from the Netherlands, Nina de Bruijin, a.k.a. Lee Jung Soon, and her birth mother, Cho Soon Ok.[1]

Ach'im Madang's "I Want to Meet This Person"[2] is the longest-running, weekly search show embedded in a TV morning program, and has been on the air since 1996. This morning show is estimated to be the most watched of several family-search programs airing on Korean television.[3] Based on the show's website information, as of 2011, more than 470 Korean adoptees have appeared on the show; of those, 13.4 %, or 67

© The Editor(s) (if applicable) and The Author(s) 2016
H. Kim, *Birth Mothers and Transnational Adoption Practice in South Korea*, DOI 10.1057/978-1-137-53852-9_4

people, have been reunited with their birth families.⁴ This figure is much higher than the average reunion rate, which is estimated to be 2 % to 3 % of all adoptee-initiated searches in a year.⁵ Each Wednesday, about five or six people, including one or two Korean adoptees, come to the studio and, in hopes of a reunion, share their stories of loss with the live audience.

This chapter engages the post-1990s phenomenon of birth mothers appearing on popular television shows, and illuminates how birth mothers become reattached to their motherhood and mothering via a powerful homecoming narrative—that of search and reunion—to once again fulfill the South Korean state's neoliberal national security mandate. I examine the detailed processes by which birth mothers, who once lost their mothering to adoption, emerge as the ultimate mothers through the intersection of media technologies and the post-1990s neoliberal state apparatus. Recasting the televised narrative of search and reunion into three major tropes of motherhood, this chapter delineates how the motherhood of birth mothers, once expunged without any recognition, is revalued as the ultimate maternal figure suffering a life crisis. In so doing, I seek to disrupt the prevailing South Korean adoption discourse that normalizes the birth mothers' loss of mothering as inevitable.

The first appearance of adoptees on Korean television was in a 1989 television documentary entitled *urinŭn chigŭm – haeoe ibyanga*, "Where are we now?"⁶ on Korean adoptees living in the US and Western Europe. In the epilogue, an adoptee raised in Sweden, Susanne Brink, a.k.a. Shin Yu-Suk, then 26, was presented as a depressed, young, unwed mother. The melodramatic story of Brink's loss and sadness immediately arrested the public's attention and stirred up national sentiments of regret and shame over South Korea's involvement in transnational adoption; until then, adoption had largely been a silent part of Korea's history. Three months after the documentary aired, Brink came to Korea and reunited with her birth mother and her brother, all of which was broadcasted in a 1990 documentary entitled "Susanne Brink's *Arirang*."⁷

Since the 1990s, the number of adoptees visiting Korea has steadily grown to an estimated 2000 to 3000, annually. Not only did adoptees start visiting Korea in increasing numbers, but they also received more and more public attention. The media coverage of adoptees dubbed their visits as a "return," and ultimately rooted their cultural explorations as a search for the "birth family"; part of this narrative was due to the critical number of returning adoptees who wanted to find their birth families, and who used the mass media to publicize their searches. The returning adoptees and their search for their birth mothers became subsumed under the narrative of separated families, which was an ongoing legacy of the Korean War; and, by the mid-1990s, the stories of adoptees were incorporated into popular subjects for television broadcast, particularly the wildly popular, live, televised search shows. Over the past 20 years, South Korea's transnational adoption practice, once obscured in the national memory, has been constructed and memorialized as a shameful, but inevitable, fact of Korea's past, despite it still being unceasingly practiced today.

On the cusp of the new millennium, the national rhetoric of "eradicating past vices" and "reconciliation" was adopted to frame social issues that had their origins in South Korea's traumatic past. The multiple traumas of Japanese colonialism, the Korean War, and the postwar repressive military state were brought to the forefront by a then burgeoning civil society, as well as by progressive, civilian presidential administrations that pushed forward a politics of reconciliation. These efforts echoed similar processes taking place in other international contexts. It was during this time, and in this particular political landscape, that South Korea's history of transnational adoption came to be recognized as a shameful event.[8] Thus, Korean adoptees were transformed into a central political subject in the national discourse on reconciliation. A political resignification of adoptees was coupled with a rise in their economic valuation, as South Korea became increasingly entrenched in a neoliberal global order.[9] Under the rubric of this new, global economic imperative, that is, the neoliberal logic of capitalism, South Korea's state-led economic development model was restructured to promote free market practices. In the face of global economic restructuring, the Korean government revalorized "overseas Koreans" as potential bridges between the East and the West.[10] In 1998, the government established the Overseas Koreans Foundation (OKF), a government-funded, nonprofit organization that helped Koreans overseas to develop and maintain a national allegiance to South Korea.[11] Recognizing Korean-born adoptees as belonging to the category of overseas Koreans, the OKF offered them a consolidated network of motherland tours, culture camps, Korean language scholarships, and other fellowship programs. In other words, Korean adoptees, once viewed as "excess children," have, under the mandate of neoliberal global capitalism, been revalorized as valuable national assets. Under the demographic, political, and economic landscape of the 1990s, Korean adoptees—once viewed as wretched victims of war, poverty, and personal misfortune—have been resignified as competitive cosmopolitans with the cultural capital to advance the nation's political and economic agenda.[12] On these shifting terrains there has emerged the figure of the Korean birth mother.

This chapter examines the emergence of the Korean birth mother on television search shows. These shows are a key cultural institution that has shaped the adoption discourse, which is imbued with traumatic affects and narratives of overcoming great hardships. Neil Smelser describes cultural trauma as "a memory [that] must be made culturally relevant, that is represented as obliterating, damaging for an essential value of society [and] therefore, associated with a strong negative affect, usually, disgust, *shame*, or *guilt*."[13] Rendering South Korea's extensive involvement in transnational adoption as a cultural trauma, the televised search-and-reunion show deploys an affective panorama of pains, shame, and guilt over family losses, suggesting a fractured kinship in South Korea's normative patriarchal family ideology.

Another constituent of the Korean adoption discourse on television search shows is a suspiciously uniform story of adoption: the search-and-reunion narrative. Paul Connerton, in his influential book *How Societies Remember*, offers important insight into the role of a particular narrative in the formation of a social memory. He argues, "In the name of a particular narrative commitment, an attempt is being made to integrate isolated or alien phenomena into a single unified process."[14] In other words, a television search-and-reunion narrative is an utterly fabricated social memory that has been serialized into various elements and arranged in a certain order, so as to construct a social memory of transnational adoption. Thus, television search shows offer a crucial site in which the Korean adoption story is incorporated into the collective national trauma of separated families, and then resolved with a family reunion in the framework of a particular narrative commitment.

Over the past 20 years, numerous television search shows, with their faithful commitment to the search-and-reunion narrative, have brought forth Korean adoptees and their Korean mothers, both of whom were erased from South Korea's official history, and presented them as individual subjects of a national trauma. The story of the Korean adoptee's search for his or her birth mother and their eventual reunion is seen as a reconciliation of both personal trauma and collective cultural trauma. By reforging broken family ties, Korean adoptees and their Korean mothers become nationally recognized citizens who push forward the nation's reconciliation with its past, as well as who help to bring about reunification with Koreans overseas, so as to advance South Korea's current global agenda of neoliberal integration.

This chapter looks at how the birth mother, who has been erased from the nation's official history and adoption discourse, has become a central, newly significant figure appropriated as an allegory of South Korea through the search-and-reunion narrative, which is contingent upon television technology. Recognizing the temporal and technological apparatuses that express the figure of the birth mother, I examine the ways in which birth mothers join with technological apparatuses to activate maternal qualities, thus allowing them to be registered as virtual mothers. The virtual mother is not granted motherhood simply from the fact that she gave birth to a child who is now an adoptee; rather she emerges as a performative, technologically mediated, and enacted figure at the intersection of TV technology and a mother. Therefore, I examine the tele-technological processes involved in constructing a birth mother within the radical and fragmented temporality of a television show, so as to emphasize the performative aspects of virtual mothering.

As a critical and performative methodology, I inversely apply Connerton's insight of a particular narrative commitment. By applying an inverse approach to examine how the search-and-reunion narrative unfolds via television's spatiotemporality, I carefully disentangle the many heterogeneous elements conjoined through the configuration of virtual mothering. Then, I recast the virtual mother into three different, but interlaced, tropes: biogenetic motherhood, affective motherhood, and developmental motherhood. By staging this tripartite maternal figure displaced from the prevailing narrative construction, I interrupt and highlight how adoption, as a cultural trauma, instantiates the site of the maternal body, appropriating maternal affects and turning the birth mother's sense of shame and guilt into a sense of reconciliation and pride.

Ach'im Madang—I Want to Meet This Person

On a research trip to Korea in 2005, I visited Global Overseas Adoptees' Link (G.O.A.'L), an adoptee self-advocacy organization; one of their primary functions is helping Korean adoptees to reunite with their Korean families. I introduced myself as a researcher working on a project about Korean birth mothers. Not a week had passed after my visit to G.O.A.'L when I received a phone call from a staff member. She asked me whether I was available and interested in working on an upcoming reunion show episode. I agreed to do it. This is how I came to be a translator for a Korean adoptee, Nina de Bruijin, and her birth mother, Cho Soon Ok, on live, national TV.

My involvement in the show's production leaves me with a methodological dilemma. The rich backstage information has no place to be discussed when employing discourse analysis. Yet, if I organize my storyline in terms of my participant observation, then I risk diluting the processes by which the figure of the birth mother is virtually recognized. With an awareness of my particular involvement as a translator (both onstage and off) for the television search show, and based on three episodes which aired on July 20, August 3, and August 17, 2005,[15] I combine autoethnography and discourse analysis to highlight the ways in which the particular story of Cho Soon Ok and Nina de Bruijin[16] unfolds into a clichéd media story of search and reunion, with a focus on virtual mothering and the nationalistic discourse on adoption.

4.1 Studio A: Naturalized Motherhood

On these shows, Korean adoptees are instantly made into Korean subjects by reasserting their Korean names. Nina de Bruijin was no exception. On her first television appearance, Nina de Bruijin, a Korean-born Dutch adoptee, introduced herself in both Korean and English. She first said, *Annyonghaseyo, che ireumun ichongsoonimnida*; "Hi, my name is Lee, Jung Soon", in a fresh—a bit too fresh to be convincing— Korean.[17] She then translated herself into English, another foreign language to her; a more elaborate version of the introduction followed:

> Hello, my name is Nina. I was born in Seoul, on September 4th, 1978. I was born in Kang Nam Gu, Taepyung Midwife's Clinic. I was brought to Korea Social Service on September 5, 1978, and sent to the Netherlands when I was three months old.[18]

She performs her greetings in Korean, then jumps right back to her Dutch identity—Nina de Bruijin—which, along with her adoptive family, was never mentioned again. Throughout the entire show, she is referred to only by her Korean name, Lee Jung Soon.

The show's hostess mentions that this adoptee's name, Jung Soon, was allegedly given by a third party, presumably a social worker at the adoption agency, who might have constructed her name by taking one syllable from each of her biological parents' names.[19] In other words, "Lee Jung Soon" was an utterly fabricated identity, created to find her a home outside of South Korea; but this time, her Korean name admits Nina de Bruijin back into Korea. Her Korean name, Lee Jung Soon, however fabricated, was evidence that Nina de Bruijin had a connection to Korea, and thus lay the ground for suturing the broken family ties between this Korean adoptee and her Korean family, most of whom had no knowledge of Nina's birth and adoption until the show's production.

Shortly after Jung Soon's profile and pictures air, there is a phone call, allegedly from her birth mother. While watching the first episode of Nina and Cho Soon Ok's search-and-reunion as a regular viewer, I could only wonder at the amazing, mysterious timing of the phone call, I had to believe that it was a random accident, pure luck. "Maybe Nina is extremely lucky," I thought. The hostess unexpectedly interrupts herself, and urgently tells Jung Soon. "Jung Soon-ssi,[20] There is a phone call. M-o-t-h-e-r? From a mother." A translator's indistinct voice follows. The camera rests for a speechless moment on Nina's face. The hostess asks Jung Soon to take the call from her mother. Nina's face registers bewilderment. A sense of uncertainty fills the entire studio. The translator says something to Nina. Nina imitates the translator's "*um-ma*"—mother, in Korean—a word whose meaning she might not even understand. A woman on the phone says, *kurae, chongsonna, mianhada* "Hello, okay, Jung Soon; I am sorry." The show's hostess interrupts and verifies the caller's name, Cho Soon Ok; her husband's name; and, the fact that she has five daughters. This alleged birth mother affirms everything the hostess says. A round of applause follows. Their reunion, after DNA tests had been completed and a further cross-examination of background information had been made, was aired two weeks later.

Later, I learned from Nina's birth mother that she had not called the program. In fact, it was the show's producers who had first contacted her. Cho Soon Ok's close friend, apparently having no knowledge of the adoption, had seen the preview for *Ach'im Madang*, in which Cho Soon Ok and Lee Jung Hwan were named. She called Cho Soon Ok and told her, "There is a someone called Lee, Jung Soon, looking for you and your husband." At first, the mother replied, "I don't know what you are talking about." But soon Cho Soon Ok began to remember an unnamed baby she had left behind, a few hours after delivery. She was too nervous to call the television network to identify herself, so her friend called for her. Then, around 9 am, on the day that Nina's search aired live, the television crew called Cho Soon Ok, and told her to wait on the telephone line.

It was in this manner that Cho Soon Ok became part of the search-and-reunion narrative, which is inextricable from television technology. As she greeted her just-returned daughter on the phone, she became a virtual mother. Television technology and its particular storytelling techniques cannot be disentangled from the televised figure of the birth mother, for it is television technology that searches for and finds the birth mother—in this case, Cho Soon Ok—who, voluntarily or involuntarily, agrees to respond to her child's cry on television, thereby activating her virtual mothering.

In the show's narrative, Cho Soon Ok, instantly recognizes her daughter despite tens of thousands of days of separation; this recognition is supposed to indicate the irrevocable tie that exists between a mother and a daughter. Cho Soon Ok's call to the studio was made to appear as though it were spontaneous, suggesting that this alleged birth mother had been waiting all along for her daughter's impending return. She utters her daughter's virtual Korean name, Jungsoon, as if it were a name that she has held dear all along, and apologizes to the alleged daughter, all in the same breath, following the script of virtual mothering. Once basic information from the adoption file is acknowledged and the caller's familial information is put forth, the show forges the firm belief that they are related. The scripted acts that Cho Soon Ok performs establish the necessary conditions for this alleged birth mother to be perceived as a credible mother.

* * * * *

Today is the day that Nina de Bruijin and her Korean mother reunite. I am nervous about appearing as an interpreter on a national television show, although it should take only five to ten minutes. At 6 am, I arrive at KBS, the Korean national TV broadcasting company, and see three women sitting outside the building. One young Korean lady, smoking nervously, stands out. It is rare for women to publicly smoke in South Korea, and instantly I sense she must be the Dutch adoptee for whom I will be translating. I introduce myself to Nina de Bruijin and Imca, her childhood friend, who has accompanied Nina from the Netherlands, to this foreign country. Nina seems to have been informed that she is going to meet her birth mother today.

At 6:30 am, a woman, one of the show's writers, walks out of the building and takes us to a waiting room where the day's participants are practicing their presentations, and waiting for the show to begin. Among the participants, there is another Korean adoptee from Norway. One of the show's writers sits down with each participant and helps him or her to memorize the narrative to be delivered. They form the story of separation together. This scripter tells me, "You can speak English in a full voice; these days many audience members (referring to TV viewers) speak English. They prefer it that way." This comment makes me more nervous. Immediately, my focus shifts from Nina to my English. We enter the studio ten minutes before the 8:30 am show time.

"*Wow! The studio looks much smaller than it appears on television,*" I think to myself. "*Quite intimate. Hmm. Oh, these guys are the famous hosts.*" Across from me sits a familiar-looking actress, who often plays a grandmother in Korean films and television shows. She has a glamorous hairdo and is wearing makeup. She looks very young in person. I am trying not to get too fascinated and distracted by this new, cool experience. I turn to look at Nina. She looks very nervous. Her anxiety seeps into my body and doubles my anxiety level. I learn that the women sitting next to us are paid audience members. Some have handkerchiefs on their laps, ready to start crying at any moment. Today, in addition to Nina, there are five people scheduled to introduce themselves, each hoping for a reunion of their own.

After two participants present their stories of separation, Nina and I rise from our seats and walk to the center of the small studio, which will shortly become a site of reunion for Nina and Cho Soon Ok. In this space, one will turn into a daughter and the other into a mother, and their ties will be instantaneously, irrefutably woven through a narrative of DNA and physical resemblance. One of the show's hosts repeats that one can recognize one's mother or daughter, just by glancing at her face. According to the co-host, "We don't need to go on with the DNA test. I can automatically tell they are related, but just in case ...." As soon as Nina and her mother hug each other and shed tears, the ritual of reunion ends, and the narrative moves forward, as a professor of forensic science from a prestigious university informs them about the DNA test results over the phone: "I examined 17 non-sex chromosomes, as well as 5 sex chromosomes. A daughter inherits everything from her mother, so I can confirm that they are mother and daughter. Congratulations!" This invisible male figure serves as the voice of science and authority, and confirms that Nina and Cho Soon Ok are mother and daughter. Another round of applause follows from the audience.

Through the ritual of DNA testing, Nina de Bruijin is reborn as a Korean national, with no margin of error. This moment of connection, backed by scientific authority, epitomizes the patriarchal order that ultimately dictates the terms of kinship in the realm of the traditional family, even when the patriarch is absent. One of the hosts asks Nina sweetly, "I heard you were the one who really wanted to do the DNA test. Why did you ask for that? Couldn't you just believe that you have found your (birth) mother?" As I translated this offensive question, I subconsciously mimicked the host's soothing voice; only later was I embarrassed by what I had done. How could anyone identify a mother of whom one had no memory, merely by looking at her? How could any woman identify a child she had given birth to and immediately separated from nearly 30 years ago?

The inviolable bond between a mother and a daughter, corroborated by DNA, reconstructs the family via a compulsive narrative of identification; Eleana Kim might describe the process as one of integrating Korean adoptees into a model of homogenous Korean citizenship.[21] During the show, the well-known Korean actress, in her role as a commentator, asks whether the birth mother's other five daughters also have curly hair, and Cho Soon Ok responds affirmatively. Curly hair, a common feature shared among all family members, is evidence of familial ties and symbolic of an irrevocable identity that has been mapped out biologically. The Korean birth mother signifies not only the biological origins of this Korean adoptee, but also the biological hub through which Nina is connected to the rest of her family.

The final sequence of Nina's search-and-reunion show starts with the female host's narration. "This is the way home," she says, as images of Jung Soon's homecoming fill the screen. We see Nina, making her way to the home of her Korean family, a place where she has never been, and which she has never called home. The camera zooms in on a close-up shot of two clasped hands (Nina and her mother's), as the host comments: "Although there is no shared language, it must be really good to be with a mother. It must be really good." Witnessing Nina's devastating level of frustration over not being able to communicate with the just-met family, I found the host's comment to be a futile effort to make the experience of the reunion uncanny, by suggesting that a mother signifies "home." Home, in other words, refers to a place where one can find an ultimate sense of peace and comfort.

The final image of Nina's story shows the family, along with Nina's friend, Imca, and me, her translator, as we all gather together to share some fruit. What is not captured on camera is when one of the television cameramen suggests that the mother hand a piece of fruit to her daughter. Cho Soon Ok gives Nina a piece of watermelon, and Nina responds by giving a tangerine to her mother. The host once more congratulates Lee Jung Soon and her Korean family, and the scene concludes with Nina, smiling, as the host says, "Now, the whole family has come full circle with their found daughter filling her own empty spot."

Many feminist accounts have noted that women acquire their citizenship via their identity as a wife and mother in the process of nation building.[22] According to Seungsook Moon, Korea's official nationalistic discourse is based on the patrilineal family, by which a male-headed family structure is the basic unit of the nation. In her words, "...the Korean nation is essentially a familial community in which members have collective orientation...."[23] In this light, Cho Soon Ok's motherhood was presented to the audience through her husband's name, which affirmed her allegiance to a normative patrilineal family order. The very same normative family imaginary that once devalued and misrecognized a working-class, poor mother's reproduction, as examined in Chapters 2 and 3, reorders and integrates Cho Soon Ok's motherhood into the patrilineal family imaginary.

Women's gendered citizenship is often discussed in terms of their reproductive function. Nira Yuval-Davis argues in her book *Gender and Nation* that blood and a sense of belongingness constitute national identity.[24] Soon after Cho Soon Ok appears on television, positive DNA results corroborate this virtual mother's maternal citizenship. This strong assumption about blood and belongingness reinforces the myth that "blood is thicker than water," and underlies the fantasy that adoptees have inviolable ties to Korea and an irrevocable identity as Koreans, thereby explaining their ultimate journey back to Korea as the motherland. The figure of the birth mother, as a repository of shared blood, functions as an affective pull toward the homeland.

The motherhood of this virtual mother is contingent upon an adoptee's return to Korea and a search for family members, premised on the narrative of redemption. I argue that Cho Soon Ok, as a site of origin and destination, through the myth of home/land, suggests the conditions of possibility for the maternal citizenship of South Korean birth mothers. Cho Soon Ok becomes visible and recognizable as a mother of this newly-made South Korean subject, only within the national sphere. She is realized as a virtual mother who embodies the adoptee's lost origins, roots, and home; meanwhile, Nina de Bruijin is able to claim her Koreanness upon her reunion, sited within the television studio and its particular temporality. Television's particular temporality freezes and linearizes the loss of time experienced by both parties, that is, the birth mother and the child. It flattens the complexities of loss, and, instead, spatializes the loss to be cast onto the body of this virtual mother, as is actualized in each transmitted scene.

A critique of the trope of a biogenetic, naturalized motherhood is found in Tobias Hübinette's analysis of cultural representations of Korean adoptees and birth mothers. He poignantly discusses a blurred merging of the birth mother with South Korea, and the political implications of that merging. Korea becomes a motherland when a birth mother's maternal citizenship is claimed though the symbols of origins, roots, and home. Upon reunion, a Korean adoptee claims her Koreanness. The slippage between mother as nation and nation as mother fosters naturalized and nationalized, maternal images of birth mothers, whose losses are also recuperated through the adoptees' homecoming. I argue that the naturalized discourse of motherhood in "origins," "roots," and "home" allows birth mothers to be recognizable as virtual mothers, and yet forecloses a critical analysis of the structural constraints promoting transnational adoption. This discourse tends to appropriate the body of the birth mother, once more, in the service of national reconciliation, as part of South Korea's nation-building project in the global era.

4.2   Studio B: Affective Motherhood

While watching the first part of Nina de Bruijin's search show, a Korean woman calls the studio three minutes after Nina's appearance. Her first words, over the phone, are "Jungsoon-ah, I am sorry." I find this apology directed to her alleged daughter to be disturbing rather than heartbreaking. Her voice is too dry, too flat, too lacking in emotion, shattering my own expectation of a mother who has been separated from her baby for 28 years. I think to myself, "She is a mother who should have more feelings." Yet, this act of apology, despite its lack of emotion, is integral to the progression of the search-and-reunion narrative. By apologizing, she admits her own guilt in not raising her child. It is through this apology that Cho Soon Ok is re-territorialized into a virtual mother who performs the role of a legitimate birth mother.

For the following two weeks after Nina's initial appearance on *Ach'im Madang,* Cho Soon Ok cried in public and in private. Once unleashed, tears belatedly, but unceasingly, took over this woman. In the meantime, she tried to find out where Nina was staying in Seoul, so she could arrange a meeting as soon as she could, even earlier than the scheduled television show. But the show's crew and producers would not give her any detailed information about Nina's whereabouts. Nina was travelling in Korea, they said. She had to wait for the television production schedule. Two weeks passed. The two women were permitted to meet only during the show's production.

* * * * *

I find myself worrying whether I will cry in the middle of Nina's reunion, as I rise from my seat and walk toward the center of the television studio. Nina is facing a gate at the back of the studio set. The moment of the meeting between Nina and her alleged Korean mother, after 28 years of separation, approaches. The host urges Nina to call out "*umma*." "*Umma*," Nina says. Her Korean *umma* does not show up immediately. "*Umma*," Nina calls out again. As Nina's translator, I whisper to her, "A bit louder." "*Umma*," she calls again. This calling enacts Nina's search for her mother. Nina's repetition of the word builds suspense, shaking up the well-worn, scripted scenario of the reunion, by creating some doubt about whether or not she will actually come forward. After Nina calls out a third time, a woman neatly dressed in a blue striped shirt and a navy blue pair of pants walks toward the stage, entering through a separate entrance in the back of the studio.

As Cho Soon Ok walks through the studio, she pauses briefly to greet the audience. She does not take any time to examine her daughter's face, a face that she has not seen in more than 28 years. Instead, this Korean *umma* immediately proceeds toward Nina and embraces her. Nina hugs her back. I have no memory of what I was feeling or seeing. But the television screen tells me that there are a few seconds of indistinct voices and sobs from Nina's Korean mother. The scene is accompanied by melodramatic background music, not played inside the studio, and added afterward. The camera zooms in to get a close-up shot of the birth mother's sobbing face, which is already hidden in Nina's shoulder. Instead, Nina's face is framed. She is smiling, but not crying (Fig. 4.1).

Thus Cho Soon Ok emerges from secrecy and shadows. She instantly becomes a mother to her adopted daughter when this Korean adoptee utters "*umma*." The reunion scene is a visual affirmation of the prevailing belief that this birth mother has been waiting all along for her daughter to utter '*umma*,' so that she could come out of the shadows and mother her long-lost daughter. Once more, the birth mother murmurs, "I am so sorry." Her apology delivered, with sobbing and tears, suggests the great

Fig. 4.1 A photo taken at the reunion between Cho Soon Ok and her daughter (courtesy of Nina de Bruijin)

suffering and pain that Cho Soon Ok must have lived with, all these years. Furthermore, her emotional display, fraught with guilt and shame, echoes the Korean nation's emotions toward Korean adoptees, one all-too-well manifested in the following speech by President Kim Dae Jung at a reception for 29 adult adoptees, raised in the US and Western Europe, who were invited to the presidential residence in 1998.

> (…) Looking at you, I am *proud* of such accomplished adults, but I am also overwhelmed with an enormous *sense of regret* and all *the pain* you must have been subjected to. Some 200,000 Korean children have been adopted to the United States, Canada, and many European countries over the years. I am *pained* to think that we could not raise you ourselves, and had to give you away for foreign adoption. The reason for the adoption was primarily economic difficulty. But there were other reasons. Koreans traditionally have a habit-of-the-heart that placed too much importance on blood-ties. And when you don't have that, people rarely adopt children. So, we sent you

away. Imagining all the *pain* and psychological conflicts that you must have gone through, we are *shamed*. We are *grateful* to your adopted parents, who have loved you and raised you, but we are also filled with *shame*.[25] (my italics)

Thus, Kim acknowledged the pain and loss suffered by Korean adoptees. This unprecedented official apology is indicative of how the adoption discourse in South Korea is often deeply associated with negative affects, such as shame and guilt.

Given this as a backdrop, I posit that the affective narrative of shame in which the figure of the birth mother engages with the configuration of a virtual mother, as in Nina's search and reunion, grounds the maternal citizenship of the birth mother, Cho Soon Ok. The rhetoric of mother-as-nation vis-à-vis nation-as-mother once again juxtaposes a mother's shame and guilt with South Korea's emotional state in the context of the more than 60-year-long history of the transnational adoption practice, and, further, develops into a politics of reconciliation.

Sara Ahmed discusses the politics of shame and reconciliation, arguing that shame involves a double play of "exposure and concealment."[26] She writes, "…[S]hame exposes that which has been covered…shame covers that which is exposed (we turn away, we lower our face, we avert our gaze)….."[27] In the process of Cho Soon Ok's involvement in virtual mothering, these dual qualities of shame clearly emerge. Cho Soon Ok, despite her flat delivery, engages an affective narrative by acknowledging her guilt as soon as she becomes a virtual mother on the phone. The sense of shame and guilt becomes more poignantly palpable when she enters the studio for the reunion. As she walks out of secrecy and shadow, she immediately covers herself by averting her eyes and looking down, her mask throughout the show. The birth mother's downcast gaze exposes that she is ashamed, as does the hurried burying of her face in Nina's shoulder. The series of actions attempting to cover herself indicates her state of being burdened with shame. Cho Soon Ok becomes a virtual mother by displaying the shame of not having fulfilled her motherhood.

How is her shame then articulated into her worthiness of being a mother, thus inscribing her as a birth mother? Ahmed discusses how shame can reconstitute subjects into a social ideal, thus aligning the ashamed with affective citizenship. She writes:

> Shame can reintegrate subjects in their moment of failure to live up to a social ideal. Such an argument suggests that the failure to live up to an ideal

is a way of taking up that ideal and confirming its necessity; despite the negation of shame experiences, my shame confirms my love, and my commitment to such ideals in the first place. [28]

The exposure of her shame is a critical moment for the birth mother, Cho Soon Ok. As she confesses her failure at living up to the ideal of motherhood, simultaneously, through her shame, she affirms her aspirations for and commitment to motherhood. Her motherhood is fleshed out in terms of her exposure and display of shame, an integral part of virtual mothering in the search-and-reunion narrative. For a birth mother whose motherhood had not been acknowledged nor valued in the national sphere, whose maternal citizenship had been revoked, it is restored through the televised performance of shame. The figure of the birth mother is, once again, made to reassert a source of national disgrace in a ritualistic media spectacle, thus the unrelenting practice of transnational adoption from South Korea turns into a personal misfortune; in return, the birth mother acquires her maternal citizenship to South Korea.

Aside from the symbolic qualities of motherhood—of home, origins, and roots—feminist accounts point out that affective qualities of motherhood play a crucial part in the production of citizenship and the nation-state.[29] Affective qualities are not less important than "blood" in the construction of the nation-state. For example, Hübinette explains how Korean nationalism is based on not just a biological genealogy of family but also a particular emotional state, such as *han*. The term *han*, according to Hübinette, is generally defined "as a long accumulated, suppressed pent-up mixture of sorrow and anger caused by the injustices and hardship of Korean history."[30] In other words, Cho Soon Ok's affective quality of shame and pains are interpreted as a uniquely Korean cultural aspect of suffering shared by Korean people throughout their long history.

The shame does not just apply to Cho Soon Ok's maternal citizenship; it also pushes Korea's reconciliation process. As Ahmed points out, "shame becomes crucial to the process of reconciliation or the healing of past wounds."[31] Applying her insights on shame and reconciliation, along with feminist accounts of gendered citizenship, to the configuration of the virtual mother, I recognize parallels between South Korea's emotional position toward transnational adoption and its movement toward reconciliation. As the shame redeems her failed motherhood, it also renders South Korea as a nation that deplores the losses involved in transnational adoption, and thus ready to begin the process of reconciliation. Through the affective figure of the birth mother who is epitomized as a figure of shame and guilt in the search-and-reunion narrative, South Korea brackets its loss and recovers from its shameful past.

As the search-and-reunion narrative progresses, affective qualities of the show transition from a sense of shame and guilt to a sense of reconciliation and pride. Via the diffraction of shame onto the bodies of women who have been absolved of their failure in carrying out their duties as mother-citizens, virtual mothering paves the way for South Korea to move from feeling shame about its past to feeling proud about Korea's new era of globalization. This progression in the narrative might be characterized in terms of Ahmed's idea about the "re-covering of shame" as a move toward reconciliation.[32] The ways in which adoption storytelling recovers from its shameful stage is built into the following discourse of motherhood in development.

4.3 Studio C: Motherhood in Development

Nina, Imca, and I follow the female scripter. As soon as we enter the waiting room, we see a dozen Korean participants getting ready for the show. The majority are working class, and had been separated from their family members, primarily due to economic reasons, and predominantly during the 1960s and 1970s. Under Korea's national development slogan, "Sŏn sŏngchang hu punpae", (First, Growth; Second, Redistribution), low wages and long hours were believed to be a legitimate labor practice. Needless to say, little public assistance was available for working-class families in dire economic straits. In extreme cases, these difficult circumstances led to the disintegration of the family. After being separated from their families, many of the show's participants grew up in orphanages. Nina, through her attentive gaze, seemed to be trying to figure out what kind of life she might have led if she had remained in Korea.

On *Ach'im Madang*, the Korean adoptee's search for the birth family is placed in the landscape of generalized family separation, which occurred primarily due to the war and poverty, thus creating a very specific context within which the adoption narrative of search and reunion is coordinated. Aligning adoptees with other Korean national participants points out a shared experience of economic struggles that were widespread during the national developmental period.[33] This national memory of poverty and the family disintegration that resulted naturalizes economic struggles as the condition and circumstances surrounding the adoption decision, thereby always prefacing Korea's adoption discourse with the following: "Poverty leads to adoption from Korea." Assigning poverty as the sole background of the adoption decision forecloses any critical inquiry of structural forces, such as gendered violence, and other injustices, implicated in adoption circumstances, as detailed in the previous two chapters. The poverty which encroached on Cho Soon Ok's motherhood is now integral to the search-and-reunion narrative by which she is re-territorialized into a virtual mother.

During the initial contact over the phone, Cho Soon Ok, the alleged birth mother, is asked to confirm family information, including the names of her husband and daughters, as well as to rationalize the circumstances surrounding Nina's placement into adoption. "You were economically devastated at that time, weren't you?" the host says, prompting poverty as the primary motivation for adoption. The co-host tells the alleged birth mother and audience, "At that time, [the economic] situation [was bad], right?" Cho Soon Ok answers: "...[T]he [economic] situation was pretty bleak and my leg was in pain." This answer folds nicely into a scenario in which she could not raise her own child due to bad health and poverty. No comments or further questions follow up on her simple explanation on why Nina had to be given away, to live her life without knowing that her Korean family existed.

No one dared to ask why Cho Soon Ok, like so many others, had experienced such extreme economic hardship that she was forced to choose adoption for her just-born baby. The answer tacitly lies in the total absence of Nina's birth father from the show. While Cho Soon Ok's sexuality was on display for the public's purview, and tightly scripted within the domain of the family imaginary, the figure of the missing birth father was never brought to light. However, as soon as the adopted child was situated in a web of a legitimate family, the figure of the birth father slipped into the background. Regardless of Cho Soon Ok's current marital status (she was married), the figure of the birth father is the constitutive outside to the search-and-reunion narrative, made into a palpable absence, so that Nina's adoption story can fall neatly into a generic origin narrative, one of absolute poverty. Thus, Cho Soon Ok could just as well be portrayed as a legitimate single mother in extreme poverty, who, at the time of the birth, was considered incapable of parenting a child, without a husband.

The absence of the birth father, along with the patriarchal belief that the father should be the primary provider, naturalizes Cho Soon Ok's economic struggles. In this script, her poverty is considered to be the misfortune of an individual birth mother, rather than the responsibility of anyone else, especially not the Korean government. Poverty serves not only as the viscerally painful backdrop of adoption but also as a familiar reality for many working-class people in the past. This shared history of poverty renders a poverty-induced family separation as a traumatic but mundane event, which thus inscribes the figure of the birth mother as a victim of poverty, rather than as a mercilessly cruel mother who abandoned her child. Through this narrative, the face of the Korean normative patriarchal family and the nation's inadequate state welfare policy goes unquestioned.

On the day of reunion, as soon as their precarious relationship is confirmed as that of a mother and a daughter, the show's host starts to weave a narrative of adoption circumstances for Nina's case. The hostess insinuates the possible reasons for adoption: poverty and too many daughters, as if they are all self-evident reasons. Cho Soon Ok, in turn, reaffirms the circumstances of Jungsoon's adoption to be economic difficulties and five daughters, as if repeating after the host. Cho goes on: "Kuttae tangsienun chounbumo mannaso chal sarurago kurraeso ponaen kot," (I wished she [Nina] could find good parents and live well. That was my hope for her at that time).

This narrative of dire economic conditions, in coordination with Cho Soon Ok's good intentions, turns the act of relinquishing the baby into a wise, motherly choice intended to enhance the baby's future. Cho Soon Ok becomes a virtual mother reuniting with her daughter, a newly made Korean subject; by articulating her well-meaning intentions to continue being a good mother, her mothering is radically redefined. Therefore, this virtual mother is not seen as just a passive victim; rather, situated in the national narrative of progress and development, she is rendered into a heroic figure who has demonstrated courage and sacrifice.

In the logic of this narrative, for a poor mother to have entrusted her beloved child to adoption, there must have been a firm belief that adoption would offer better life opportunities for the child than any she herself could have provided. Cho Soon Ok affirms this logic, with her silence. The sequence of scenes, interwoven into the show's very fabric, suggests a shared consensus regarding the "better future" that adoption ensures. What explains this shared cultural belief that transnational adoption offers a better life?

Many Korean diasporic cultural theorists, such as Chungmoo Choi, Kyeyoung Park, and Ji-Yeon Yuh point out the enduring and widespread cultural belief of the "American Dream."[34] The American Dream encompasses a set of ideals and a perceived future that is associated with the US, a nation which is viewed as an expressway to modernity and personal prosperity as well as fairness and equality. This fantasy reflects the history of South Korea's postwar economic and military dependence on the US, and the US military's occupation of the country, persisting to this day. The hold of the American Dream is also reflected in the US's long history of being the largest and earliest recipient of Korean babies via transnational adoption. I extend the notion of the American Dream to a birth mother's idealization of adoptive parents and life, generally, in the West. Although Cho Soon Ok's daughter, Lee Jung Soon, had been adopted by a family in a country other than the US, I speculate that a mother's wish upon choosing adoption dwells in her belief that her daughter will be sent to a better place, *like* the US, where her daughter's development will be provisioned for.

The show's host asks me to ask Nina what she does in the Netherlands. Nina, with her usual bright smile, answers, "I am still in school, but almost graduating. I am writing my thesis in social science." After my translation of Nina's answer into Korean, the host adds, "Like the mother wished, her daughter turned out great. She is almost graduated from school, so she will be able to become a successful career woman in the near future." A TV personality sitting at the edge of the stage intervenes: "I, sort of, knew that Lee Jung Soon would turn out really well, due to her absolutely positive attitude." Cho Soon Ok becomes a virtual mother, having proved that the investment in adoption successfully resulted in the production of Nina's resilient personality, and her bright, prospective life as a young professional, and, perhaps most importantly, by her (inevitable) return to her home/land, South Korea.

The figure of the birth mother, originally disclosed only as an emblem of shame and guilt, is re-territorialized into a figure who privileges the child's development, by sacrificing her own mothering. Through the choice of adoption, Cho Soon Ok renunciates her own mothering, thus performing the ultimate act of motherly love, an act grounded in the American Dream, that is, the promise of a better life for the beloved baby. In the face of dire circumstances—in her case, bad health and poverty—she, as a mother, made the most difficult, but ultimately rational, choice for her child's development. Nina's return to the homeland (and her apparent success) reinscribes Cho Soon Ok—previously considered an absent, negligent mother—into a responsible mother. No longer a victim of her personal misfortunes, she becomes a proud, successful mother.

A closer examination of the process by which a virtual mother is articulated in the nation's developmental discourse reveals the state's appropriation of mothers who gave up their children to adoption. A juxtaposition of South Korea, the nation-state, with the figure of the birth mother unfurls a story of adoption that goes like this: Due solely to poverty, Koreans had to send numerous children away, but it was a well-meaning act, intended to provide better life opportunities in more prosperous countries. As Korean adoptees began returning to their homeland, this narrative allowed South Korea to acknowledge its sad and shameful role in transnational adoption, and then to step forward and proudly reclaim the individual adoptees' transformation from a poor orphan to a competitive, successful cosmopolitan.

* * * *

My TV role as translator ended when I left the television studio. Yet the real job of translating had just begun, and would span from several hours to entire days filled with conversations in which the family tried to fill in that which had been lost and obscured. In sharp contrast to the congratulatory tone with which the television show ended, and despite my mother's excitement about me appearing on her favorite morning show, the reunion that I witnessed that day was accompanied more by tears, than laughter. Days of limited and disrupted conversations, riddled with holes of memory, language, and a family's fractured past, were confusing, frustrating, and unsatisfying.

After the television show, I continued to translate for the family, as they sought to get to know each other. I ended up meeting Nina's four older sisters, and her biological father, all of whom were deeply affected by Nina's sudden appearance in their lives. No one knew there had been another member of the family. Nina's ambivalence and anxiety about her unknown past did not dissipate, but instead became more volatile after meeting her lost family. She repeatedly asked questions about the circumstances of her adoption, as if she could recapture her life—from her birth to the first 100 days of her life in Korea—by collecting and arranging such accounts, into some order. But her Korean mother barely remembered anything. Her Korean father does not—did not—even remember his wife's pregnancy. Nina's appearance seemed to exacerbate tensions among the family members, and Nina wondered whether her search had been the right decision for her, and her families, both adoptive and birth.

My invasive journey into this family's past overwhelmed me. The intensity seemed a betrayal of my initial enthusiasm. I felt like I had become caught up in the personal drama and dilemmas of a stranger, who found my role vital. Nina and her Korean relatives constantly, day and night, needed a translator to communicate with each other, a need I found to be beyond my capacity to fulfill. At the same time, leaving them together without me also left me with a sense of guilt and uneasiness. Before returning to the US, I had several conversations with a frustrated, tearful Nina. I also received a few angry phone calls from her birth father, and many more calls from her elder sister.

Time passed. Despite my critical stance toward the search show, I also found myself faithfully following the invisible, yet clearly demarcated, narrative lines and actions, each and every step which moved toward a resolution of loss and sadness. Listening to myself, over and over again, on the television screen gave—gives—me an eerie feeling. It was me, but not me. There was nothing much that I could have done differently, given the role I had been assigned. I wonder whether Nina de Bruijin and her Korean birth mother might have felt—feel—similarly about their own roles as had I, in my role as a translator on a television search-and-reunion show.

4.4 The Hidden Logic of the Search-and-Reunion Narrative

The story of Nina de Bruijin follows a formulaic narrative of a Korean adoptee's search for and reunion with her birth mother. Troubling the narrative circumscription of the birth-mothers' motherhood, this chapter has examined the heterogeneous elements and processes involved in the configuration of a virtual mother, who is uniformly, repetitively, and compulsively actualized, through a particular, televised storytelling technique of search and reunion. Cho Soon Ok is articulated into a virtual mother who deploys selective nodal features of motherhood—"naturalized" motherly qualities (e.g., origins, roots, and homeland), affective qualities (a shameful, pained mother, a failed, but reclaimed, ideal motherhood), and nurturing qualities related to the child's development (i.e., disavowal and the restitution of motherhood).

By treating the technological mediations and processes involved in the configuration of the birth mothers' maternal qualities as a focus of analysis, this chapter has offered a critique of the nationalistic rendering of motherhood in the transnational adoption discourse. From this vantage point, the birth mothers' motherhood is neither "nature" nor "nurture," but rather, a "machinic assemblage"[35] of birth mothers' organic bodies, discursive constructions and technological apparatuses. Furthermore, this approach informs us about the radical finitude of virtual mothering, which disrupts the tendency to presume the motherhood of a birth mother existing outside of the television studio or beyond television time. In other words, virtual mothering does not grant an immediate maternal relationship to the adopted person, who has just met his or her Korean mother after a one-time "reunion." Rather, as Anagnost noted in her discussion of technological mediation and the production of kinship, virtual mothering, as a technologically enactive form of mothering, disturbs the overwhelmingly biogenetic basis of the family vis-à-vis the nation narrative.[36]

The virtual mothering that emerges in the TV search-and-reunion narrative helps to build a critical genealogy of the systemic appropriation of South Korean women's reproductive rights throughout the more than 60-year-long development of transnational adoption. In other words, 28 years earlier, a Korean birth mother, Cho Soon Ok, by disowning her child, participated in the Korean government's national family planning policy, thereby, securing the nation's economic well-being. Now, under the neoliberal mandate of "Global Korea,"[37] Cho Soon Ok's earlier disavowal of her motherhood is re-articulated into a mother's willful sacrifice of her own mothering, paradoxically, in the name of providing the child with the best possible opportunities. Aligned with the neoliberal ethos of maternal citizenship, she appears to invest her child into promised, future outcomes of global competitiveness. Her reclamation of motherhood serves as a vehicle to expand "Global Korea," by embracing Korean adoptees, who have recently been recognized as potential assets for South Korea's global neoliberal project. Following the meta-narrative of separated families, the adoptees' search-and-reunion narrative incorporates contemporary Korean adoptees into the nation's postwar past, a past fraught with poverty and helplessness; and through the return and subsequent reclaiming of their Koreanness, the adoptee narrative highlights the Korean adoptee as a harbinger of a competitive global Korea.

This nationalized narrative is interlaced with the redemptive logic of loss. Casting South Korea's long history of transnational adoption within the search-and-reunion narrative entails a particular assumption about the cultural politics of loss: the belief that loss is retrievable and recoverable. In order for a loss to be recovered, the loss has to be containable—occurring at a certain time and locatable in a certain place. The search-and-reunion narrative arrests spatiotemporal movements within televised time-space, thereby confining the losses involved in the history of transnational adoption practice onto the body of the birth mother. Hence, the reunion between an adult adoptee and the birth mother becomes a moment during which her virtual mothering is acknowledged and activated, and serves as the show's climax, suggesting a recovery of the losses that were incurred by the adoption practice decades earlier.

What are the implications of this understanding of loss for the national memory of transnational adoption? In her poignant analysis of family as a metaphor for the nation, Anne McClintock contends, "Since children 'naturally' progress into adults, projecting the family image onto national 'progress' enabled what was often murderously violent change to be legitimatized as the progressive unfolding of natural decree."[38] By casting the Korean adoptees' search and reunion as "the progressive unfolding of natural decree," the search-and-reunion narrative works to normalize Korea's more than 60-year-long practice of transnational adoption, and, in turn, fails to recognize the subsequent traumatic effects of adoption for birth mothers, as well as for adoptees; thereby, it reduces the history of transnational adoption to a shameful, but inevitable, side effect of Korea's rapid economic development.

Earlier I discussed the ways in which the figure of the birth mother is elided. This chapter has explored the ways in which this discourse brings the figure of the birth mother out of the shadows; and yet, troublingly, this now-visible birth mother figure is manipulated to serve a nationalistic rendering of loss, within an intricate dynamic of fantasy and exclusion in the adoption narrative. South Korea's seemingly forthright adoption discourse embeds the fantasy of the successful adoptee's return, and his or her willingness to participate in a "Global Korea." The sequential, search-and-reunion narrative relies on a succession of fantasized events: poverty-induced adoption, a successful Korean adoptee's inevitable return, a joyous, redemptive reunion with the birth mother, and the rebuilding of the family. However, this fantasized narrative, presented as an instant resolution of national losses, is inevitably built upon the exclusion of the varied circumstances under which adoption can occur; it also ignores South Korea's ongoing, uninterrupted engagement in transnational adoption.

The history of adoption is implicated with multilayered violence against women and children. The search-and-reunion narrative whitewashes that history, obscuring South Korea's long-term deployment of the transnational adoption practice as a biopolitical apparatus for managing an excess population. In the dominant adoption discourse, the struggles that *kijich'on* mothers, single mothers, and poor, working-class mothers, have faced, such as domestic violence, poverty, and spousal neglect, are never mentioned. Meanwhile, South Korea continues to not acknowledge its current involvement in transnational adoption. As a result, the search-and-reunion narrative serves as another mechanism to overshadow single, working-class women who became birth mothers after 1990.

This chapter critiqued South Korea's transnational adoption discourse, and the nationalistic appropriation of the birth mothers' lost-and-found motherhood. The next two chapters examine two other sites of virtual mothering: Internet technologies and an oral history collection. By engaging with what has been excluded from this powerfully crafted search-and-reunion narrative, I examine the post-adoption and post-reunion accounts of birth mothers, and further analyze the ways in which other sites of mothering produce different kinds of mothering. In the next chapter, I examine a birth mothers' Internet café, called *A Sad Love Story of Mothers Who Sent Their Children Away for Adoption*, where younger birth mothers who separated from their children after the mid-1990s, perform and experience their losses and sadness through Internet technologies, thereby performing and enacting virtual mothering.

Notes

1. I changed both names to protect their anonymity. The adoptee offered her own pseudonym, and I selected the birth mother's name. As for the adoptee's name, I interchangeably refer to her both by just her first name and her full name.
2. The origins of this show can be traced back to 1983, when KBS (Korean Broadcasting Systems, Inc.) aired a live, unprecedented television special for families who had been separated during the Korean War and its chaotic aftermath. More than 100,000 people appeared on the show, which aired for 453 hours and 45 minutes over 138 consecutive days, from June 30 to November 14. Slightly over 10 % (10,180) of all individuals who appeared on the show were reunited with their separated family members. This moment left a profound cultural and political imprint on South Korea, as it was the first national acknowledgment of the painful, repressed memory of separated families as a legacy of the Korean War. Since then, separated families and the imperative of family reunions have been built into the cultural tissue and affective fabric of postwar Korean society.

3. The theme of "search and reunion with family" is of powerful and unyielding interest for Korean people. According to Yi, Jae Oh, a KBS producer, "…Adoption, separation because of war, it doesn't matter. The idea of reuniting families has universal appeal in Korea. The reunion of a family is very important." Martha Vickery, "Reunions: The Task of Finding." *Korean Quarterly* 8, no. 2. (2004): 19.
4. Based on the show's website, the 1997 and 1998 records do not include adoptee information. I suspect the show began including adoptees in 1999.
5. Jeannie Hong, *Guide to Korea for Korean Adoptee: International Korean Adoptee Resource Book* (Seoul: Overseas Koreans Foundation, 2006), 624.
6. This award-winning documentary aired in 1989, a year after the Western media's moral criticism drew negative attention to South Korea. Susanne Brink was the first Korean-born adoptee whose search and subsequent reunion was made into a documentary. The documentary became enormously popular and was made into a film the following year. In MBC *In'gansidae*, "urinŭn chigŭm – haeoe ibyanga." Directed by Jang Suk Ko, (Seoul: Munhwa Broadcasting Corporation, 09/09/1989).
7. *Arirang* is a Korean folk song more than 600 years old, without a clear history of its origins. The song is about the travails encountered by the subject of the song, while crossing a mountain pass. There are several regional versions, with different lyrics. One of the most frequently sung folk songs, it is regarded as expressing the painful struggles of the Korean people.
8. Tobias Hübinette, "Comforting an Orphaned Nation: Representations of International Adoption and Adopted Koreans in Korean Popular Culture" (Ph.D. diss., Stockholm University, 2005), 103.
9. The South Korean government's efforts to incorporate Korean adoptees into the Korean national sphere culminated in a 2011 law that allowed Korean adoptees to have dual citizenship.
10. Eleana Kim, "Wedding Citizenship and Culture: Korean Adoptees and the Global Family of Korea," in *Cultures of Transnational Adoption*, ed. by Toby A. Volkman (Durham: Duke University Press, 2005), 50.
11. http://www.okf.or.kr/, accessed on October 10, 2014.

12. After Susanne Brink, Korean adoptees' stories have grown steadily visible in Korea. In January 1996, another television documentary, entitled 'Sungduk Bauman, Who will Save This Child?', aired; it featured Brian Sungduk Bauman, a 22-year-old West Point cadet, a Korean adoptee struggling with leukemia, and his journey to Korea to find a compatible bone marrow donor. In response to his story, a nationwide drive for bone marrow was organized and a Korean donor, Seo Han Kook, was found in 1996. As encapsulated in the title of the documentary on Sungduk Bauman, earlier portrayals of Korea-born adoptees on Korean television treated adoptees as still-orphaned children and focused on their struggles and misfortunes. Today, however, Korean adoptees are no longer seen as wretched victims of poverty and personal misfortune, and are instead featured as resilient and successful global citizens. In 1999, when South Korea was still struggling with the aftermath of the Asian financial crisis, another Korean adoptee, Shin Ho Bum, became a national icon. He had become a war orphan during the Korean War and was adopted at the age of 16 by a military dentist, Ray Paull, who had been working in Korea at the time. Shin made his way up to become a US senator in the state of Washington. Paralleling South Korea's modern history, his successful story moving from a war orphan to a prominent US politician became emblematic of the Korean adoptee's newly signified status as a competitive global citizen, and was followed by others, such as Toby Dawson, a US Olympic bronze medalist in Torino 2006, and Fleur Pellerin, a.k.a. Kim Chong Sook, serving as the top official in the Ministry of Culture and Communication in President Francois Hollande's cabinet.
13. Neil Smelser, "Psychological Trauma and Cultural Trauma," In *Cultural Trauma and Collective Identity*, edited by Jeffrey C. Alexander, Ron Eyerman, Bernhard Giesen, Neil J. Smelser, Piotr Sztompka, (Berkeley: University of California Press, 2004), 36.
14. Paul Connerton, *How Societies Remember* (Cambridge: Cambridge University Press, 1989), 26.
15. The first segment of the show on July 20 had a different translator.
16. Nina de Bruijin returned to Korea for the first time in 2005 after being sent to the Netherlands in 1978. Though her adoption file marked her as an abandoned baby, she had always wanted to find her Korean birth family. So she waited. Waited for twenty-eight

years. Until the time she felt ready and strong enough to handle any news. Finally, before making her trip to Korea, she contacted the Korean Social Services (KSS), her Korean adoption agency. A month or two passed. She called. Then she got a call from Korea. They had information about her family in Korea but were unable to track them down. So Nina came to Korea and went to the adoption agency, accompanied by her adoptee friend who was then working for G.O.A.'L. There were two files—one in Dutch, the other in Korean. The Korean file indicated she had an entire family—a mother, a father, and five sisters. But the Dutch file said that she had been an abandoned baby. She was not sure what to do next, and a friend suggested that a television search show might be her best option. So she said yes. She was interviewed and screened for her suitability to appear on the show. There was another selection process to find her family, but this time, to find her family in Korea. They shot a trailer in advance of her live appearance, which was aired in the week preceding the television broadcast.

17. Excepting Nina's introduction and my translations for Nina, which were in English, this show was conducted in Korean. Material quoted from the show is therefore the author's own translation.
18. Cho, Yeon Dong. *Ach'im madang*. Television Broadcasting. Seoul: Korean Broadcasting Systems, Inc. July 20, 2005.
19. A Korean name typically consists of two syllables, so "Jung Soon" is supposedly a combination of her Korean father's name "Jung" and her Korean mother's name "Soon."
20. "*Ssi-*" is a gender neutral suffix for adult, similar to "ma'am" for women and "sir" for men.
21. Kim, "Wedding Citizenship and Culture," 55.
22. Sungsook Cho, *Omoniranun Ideolloki* [The Ideology of Motherhood] (Seoul: Hanool Academy, 2001); Hübinette, "Comforting an Orphaned Nation"; Anne McClintock, "Family Feuds: Gender, Nationalism and the Family," in *Feminist Review* 44, no. 1 (1993): 61–80; Seungsook Moon, "Begetting the Nation: The Androcentric Discourse of National History and Tradition in South Korea," in *Dangerous Women: Gender and Korean Nationalism*, ed. Elaine H. Kim and Chungmoo Choi (New York: Routledge, 1998); Nira Yuval-Davis, *Gender and Nation* (London: Sage Publication, Inc., 1997).
23. Moon, "Begetting the Nation," 54.

24. Yuval-Davis, *Gender and Nation*, 26.
25. Translated from Korean into English , "President Kim Dae Jung's Speech: October 23, 1998 at the Blue House." *Chosen Child* 1, no 5 (1999): 15–6.; emphasis added.
26. Sara Ahmed, *The Cultural Politics of Emotion* (New York: Routledge, 2004), 104.
27. Ibid.
28. Ibid., 106.
29. See Sara Ahmed, *The Cultural Politics of Emotion*, Ann Anagnost, "Scenes of Misrecognition: Maternal Citizenship in the Age of Transnational Adoption," in *Positions: East Asia Cultures Critique* 8, no. 2 (2000): 389–421, Sungsook Cho, *Omoniranun Ideolloki*, Hübinette "Comforting an Orphaned Nation," and Yuval-Davis, *Gender and Nation*.
30. Hübinette, "Comforting an Orphaned Nation", 140.
31. Ahmed, *The Cultural Politics of Emotion*, 101.
32. Ibid., 104.
33. Yang Myung Ji, "The Making of the Urban Middle Class in South Korea (1961–1979): Nation-Building, Discipline, and the Birth of the Ideal National Subjects," *Sociological Inquiry* 82, no 3. (2012): 424–445. Yang indicates that the emergence of a sizable middle class in South Korea did not occur until the mid-1970s. Before then, most people were struggling just to meet the basic necessities of daily life.
34. See Chungmoo Choi, "Transnational Capitalism, National Imaginary, the Protest Theater in South Korea," in *Boundary* 2, no. 1 (1995): 235– 261, Kyeyoung Park, *The Korean American Dream: Immigrants and Small Business in New York City* (Ithaca: Cornell University Press, 1997), and Ji-Yeon Yuh, *Beyond the Shadow of Camptown: Korean Military Brides in America* (New York: NYU Press, 2002).
35. Gilles Deleuze and Felix Guattari. *A Thousand Plateaus: Capitalism and Schizophrenia*. Trans. Brian Massumi. (Minneapolis: University of Minnesota Press, 1987), 79.
36. Anagnost, "Scenes of Misrecognition," 390.
37. The term "Global Korea" is the most commonly used slogan, indicating the direction and desire embedded in the South Korean government's neoliberal capitalistic agenda.
38. McClintock, "Family Feuds," 63.

CHAPTER 5

Performing Virtual Mothering and Forging Virtual Kinship

The televised search-and-reunion narrative originating in the mid-1990s, with its emphasis on "irrevocable ties" between mothers and their children, and on the "reconciliation" and "regeneration" of the family, illuminated the figure of the hitherto unknown birth mother, challenging the then-prevailing myth of birth mothers who mercilessly, selfishly abandoned their children. Yet, the revelations of older birth mothers who experienced dire circumstances compelling them to relinquish their babies failed to acknowledge South Korea's ongoing involvement, even today, in transnational adoption, and also perpetuated the social stigma and material deprivations of single motherhood that drive so many young, unmarried, poor, working-class women to surrender their child into adoption, as discussed in Chapter 3. Here I focus on the younger cohort of Korean birth mothers, originating in the 1990s, who are veiled from the public consciousness and obscured by the emergent, televised figure of the middle-aged, poor, waiting-and-sacrificing birth mother, by examining traces of their performances in an Internet café[1] entitled *A Sad Love Story of Mothers Who Sent Their Children Away for Adoption* (café.daum.net/adopteemam, called *A Sad Love Story of Mothers*, hereafter).

From 2001 to 2005, this Internet café witnessed and accumulated the sadness, pains, regrets, ambivalence, shame, and guilt of birth mothers, thus rendering a rare archive of the birth mothers' intimate feelings and affects over adoption losses. By engaging this collection of birth moth-

© The Editor(s) (if applicable) and The Author(s) 2016
H. Kim, *Birth Mothers and Transnational Adoption Practice in South Korea*, DOI 10.1057/978-1-137-53852-9_5

ers' affectively charged, personal accounts, repetitive within an individual, and reverberating across the website over time, this chapter aims to flesh out the birth mothers' performative trails of virtual mothering and to acknowledge their bygone presences and bygone children. In so doing, this chapter aims to recast this website, not only as a rare public forum where birth mothers could share feelings and thoughts after adoption, and receive care and support from others, but also as a counterpublic, in opposition to the social governance of birth mothers, which tends to be managed through silence and secrecy. As reflected in the website entries, *A Sad Love Story of Mothers* has served as an ephemeral, but enduring experience—for birth mothers and their bygone children, as well as for other birth mothers.

A pivotal finding in my analysis is the observation that while virtual mothering may be initiated by an individual who wishes to express her adoption losses on the Internet, those efforts must be collaboratively acknowledged and mediated on the Web through a shared recognition of losses, for virtual mothering to be activated. As birth mothers transmit intensities and affectivities through the Internet, a sense of intimacy is fostered, producing a kind of relatedness and a sense of affinities beyond those of a more traditional, blood-related kinship, thus presenting a new terrain of politics on which to build intelligibility and solidarity. This website serves not only as a site of virtual mothering, but, more importantly, as a site of resistance against the social death of birth mothers and their "orphaned" children, by fostering a virtual kinship through which birth mothers transform into a critical population of virtual mothers.

The Internet café was established by "Jaewon",[2] then a 25-year-old birth mother, on August 20, 2001. She, like so many birth mothers whom she later interacted with, knew little about adoption when she relinquished her daughter in 1999. Since then, Jaewon had educated herself by clipping newspaper articles on adoption and constructing an adoption scrapbook; by volunteering at the Global Overseas Adoptees' Link (G.O.A.'L), an adoptee advocacy organization; and by seeking opportunities to meet Korean adoptive parents' groups. At a domestic adoptive parents' retreat in Naju, a city in South Jeolla province, in the summer of 2001, she met another birth mother for the first time, and subsequently, felt driven to create a space where birth mothers could share their adoption experiences and information with other birth mothers. Since then, the website, albeit open to (prospective) adoptive parents, adoptees, and all others, has been primarily operated by, and for the benefit of, birth mothers,[3] who play key roles in managing the site, from handling administrative responsibilities for the membership (e.g., giving greetings and encouraging the members to provide a self-introduction) to active participation in the public forum.[4]

As soon as the website was launched, the membership[5] grew rapidly, reaching more than 100 birth mothers by the end of 2001. The first two years (2001–2002) observed the heaviest volume of posts and replies, averaging about ten postings a day; at least four off-line meetings in person occurred, and there were many regular, online chats. The birth mothers' instant response and participation is noteworthy, suggesting their urgent desire to speak about their adoption experiences and to share them with one another. In subsequent years, the membership multiplied incrementally; eventually, the volume of daily traffic slowly decreased, and trickled to a few posts a year, nearing the end of 2005. During those years 2001 to 2005, 95 % of the website postings were created, and 80 % of all birth mother users came and left.

The individual birth mothers' online activity resembled the website's own life cycle, explosive at the initial stage, gradually reduced over time, and then finally fading from the website.[6] The majority of birth mothers who regularly attended the forum were in their late teens or early twenties.[7] Newcomers generally entered and posted an introduction, describing their relationship to adoption, most often, soon after their baby was transferred to the adoption agency, or, in several cases, several years after the adoption placement. Upon the birth mother's self-introduction, key figures—either a webmaster or a frequent user—greeted and granted the new inductee full access to the website.

Members of the Internet café can browse and respond to existing posts or create their own entries; the option to upload photographs is available, and exercised by many. The birth mothers' involvement with the site lasts from a day to years, but all eventually leave, even the most active bloggers; ten members remained members for one to two years. As they drifted away, birth mothers typically terminated their membership status, and, at times, took their own postings with them.[8] This cycle was repeated by new birth mothers who joined, until the end of 2005. As of this writing, *A Sad Love Story of Mothers* is a technically active, but inert, website.[9]

At the website, the birth mothers' personal narratives primarily articulate adoption losses—the loss of the child, the loss of mothering, and the loss of the mother–child relationship. I consider the personal narratives of adoption losses to be a cultural performance, or as Kristin Langellier might argue, an event that imparts "transformative power to assert self-definitions about ... the existence, worth, and validity of a person or group as meanings not otherwise available to an audience."[10] The most often self-asserted definition that emerges out of the birth mothers' personal narratives is that they are mothers, thus informing the hermeneutic lens with which I render the café posts as maternal acts, or performances.

However, it would be problematic to analyze the birth mothers' maternal acts without considering the website's once effervescent, but now dissipated state, a quality comparable to José Esteban Muñoz's concept of "ephemera," which he describes as an "alternate mode of textuality and narrativity like memory and performance."[11] Ephemera are, as Muñoz states, "remains after a performance, a kind of evidence of what has transpired but certainly not the thing itself."[12] Muñoz's idea of ephemera frames the birth mothers' personal narratives in "traces, glimmers, residues" of maternal acts that have transpired and been etched onto the Internet, long after the birth mothers' performance has ceased to be actively present. With this in mind, I engage the personal narratives of adoption losses as ephemeral maternal acts that the birth mothers have performed on the stage of *A Sad Love Story of Mothers*, in response to the social, political, cultural depreciation of their value and their labor as mothers.

5.1　An "Ephemeral, but Enduring"[13] Site of Mothering

What is it about Internet technologies that enable numerous birth mothers to disclose their stigmatized experiences and to share adoption losses with one another? A key difference is the time-space configuration that exists on the Internet, especially compared to the normative time-space organization of everyday life. To emphasize the alterity of Internet time-space, I analyze the website, applying Michel Foucault's notion of heterotopia, which identifies countersites characterized with "the curious property of being in relation with all the other sites, but in such a way to suspect, neutralize, or invert the set of relations that they happen to designate, mirror, or reflect."[14] Operating along mutually exclusive, yet parallel forces that resemble, but invert, the social order, the Internet constitutes an alternative time-space for birth mothers onto which they can enact virtual mothering.

First, let us consider the *spatial* organization of the virtual mothers. Media theorist Wendy H. Chun, theorizing cyberspace as a heterotopia, describes the Internet's unconventional organization of space and its potentiality for new formations of identity: "Cyberspace absents oneself from one's actual physical location. ... This disappearing body supposedly enables infinite self-re-creation and/or disengagement ...."[15] Applying Chun's astute observation to the birth mothers' Internet café elucidates how the identity of a birth mother is enabled by her physical displacement. In the face of the abject social stigmatization of single motherhood, and the moral persecution for not carrying out one's normative maternal responsibilities, the spatial order of the Internet allows the absence of mothering "over here" to transform to a kind of mothering "over there." As Chun notes, the configuration of mothering emergent "over there" is not indexical, but refractory, fragmentary, and incoherent from the birth mothers "over here." Thus, virtual mothering is performed by birth mothers on the Internet "over there", but not by a representative birth mother "over here." The spatial displacement of the birth mother enigmatically leads to the activation of "the virtual mother-self" on the Internet.

Now, let us consider the *temporal* nature of virtual mothers. The Internet operates in two opposite, but interlacing, temporal structures, evocative of Foucault's concept of time in heterotopia. The two time orders are simultaneous: on the one hand, the time of museums or libraries refers to "indefinitely accumulating time," and, on the other hand, the time of festival highlights "its most fleeting, transitory, precarious aspect."[16] Simply put, the Internet's temporality adds—and freezes—each entry, casting temporal environments that accumulate the birth mothers' adoption losses over time, capturing the moments of adoption losses in the "here and now." Within the heterotopic, spatiotemporal logic of Internet technologies, the café serves as a venue wherein birth mothers enact their mothering "over there" on the Internet, yet always in the "here and now" via absenting herself from "over here." This chapter emphasizes how virtual mothering takes place only within the time/space continuum of Internet technologies, as opposed to the heteronormative time/space for mothering within the domain of the family. In this way, I understand the birth mothers' Internet café as a site of mothering, or what I call *virtual mothering*.

The virtual mothering that birth mothers perform on the Internet entails several "otherly" traits. It is always belated, affective, performative, short-lived, and collaborative, yet not entirely volitional. Virtual mothering on the Web always begins after the separation from the child. This belatedness is often manifested clearly in a birth mother's screen name, for example, "It is too late" (*nŏmu nŭ˘cho pŏlyŏssŏ*); the screen name also establishes the affective texture of her virtual mothering, as in "Sad Heart"(*sŭl'p˘n mamŭlo*). Directed toward the bygone child, virtual mothering attends to individual and collective adoption losses that are often engulfed in volatile emotions, often beyond one's capacity to contain for long; thus, most birth mothers eventually leave the site. However, even though they leave, their performative traces have been disseminated instantly, and are circulated permanently. These transient, but gripping affects of mothering are registered as the remains of a performance, drawing in anonymous birth mothers and non-birth mothers, who upon following the traces, create new traces of virtual mothering over time. Therefore, as long as the website is active, the virtual mothering is technically incomplete and always already in formation.

The most powerful traces of virtual mothering left on the Internet café are birth mothers who enact their lost mothering by telling about and showing pictures of their bygone child. I argue that these maternal performances invocate their stigmatized losses, but, more importantly, in doing so, generate a renewed identity and new socialities of being a birth mother. As Stacy H. Jones claims, telling is a powerful mode of mothering, and one that is particularly significant in the absence of a "naturalized connection" with a baby.[17] Jones, writing from an adoptive mother's point of view, delineates the significance of storytelling in performing (adoptive) motherhood.

> While such [adoption] stories might begin with loss and are flushed with shame, they unfold in the tripled movements that loss and shame make: toward painful decision-making, toward the impossibility of any simple or natural maternal connection, toward a refigured and renewing relationality.[18]

Applying Jones' insights on telling and performative mothering to the birth mothers' Internet entries casts them as brief, but repetitive, episodes of storytelling. In the physical absence of her baby, who has been relinquished via adoption, and thus can no longer provide a "natural" maternal connection with the baby, a birth mother instead engages in acts of telling online. By telling online, she reflects on her decision-making process, and inevitably laments the separation, thus re-enacting her mothering, and virtually refiguring her relations with her child.

Telling on the Internet means being perpetually on display. A crucial quality of this performance is the refiguring of the renewed relationship between a mother and a child, which is enacted and mediated through the act of telling via Internet technologies; this refiguration is immediately shown, and always on display. Through this process, the birth mother's relationship to her own bygone child is no longer private. Instead, the relationship infinitely expands the scope of potential relationalities, carving out a foundation for a sense of affinity or belongingness to develop beyond the re-suturing of what had been broken or lost. Thus, maternal acts of telling are not delimited to the acknowledgment of the lost child, the lost relationship to the bygone child, and/or its renewal; rather, they are always accompanied by a new kind of sociality that extends beyond the imaginary, biological mother–child relationship.

Building on this show-and-tell framework, this chapter identifies virtual mothering as the traces left after a performance of mothering,[19] and organizes it into three dimensions. The first dimension is the construction of the birth mothers' accounts of the loss, stated as if speaking directly to the child. My analysis dwells on and explores the affective textures through which the birth mothers' losses are rendered legible through the enactment of performative speech acts. Hailed by painful sensations, the virtual mother enters the site (1) to deliver an apology and express her regrets about the adoption decision; (2) to wish for the child's happiness; and (3) to incant a promise for a future reunion.

Virtual mothering is marked by scurrying away from the pain and moving toward happiness, that is, the moment of reunion. These performances might well be expressed in terms of simultaneous attempts, both to remember and to forget, and to connect to and disconnect from, the relinquished baby. Analyzing the birth mothers' posts in terms of affective trails of performative speech acts highlights the birth mothers' adoption losses, and also helps to delineate the flickering life of virtual mothers, as birth mothers enter and exit the website, leaving traces of the pains and losses to be archived in the website after their departure.

The second dimension of virtual mothering attends to the photographic evidences of virtual mothering. Three key aspects about the photos became evident, when juxtaposing the birth mothers' accounts with the baby photos in the café's photo room: (1) the photos materialize the birth mother's dilemma of simultaneously attempting both to remember and to forget the relinquished child; (2) the photos are evidence of the birth mother's persistent, active labor necessary to procure and post the photographs, amidst multiple social stigmas and personal fears; and (3) the photos reflect the birth mother's anxieties and ambivalence about being publicly identified.

Additionally, the act of displaying the photographs on the global circuitry of the Internet demands a consideration for the intermedial processes and possibilities implicated and embedded in virtual mothering.

Based on this observation about intermedial processes, I develop the concept of *virtual kinship* as the third dimension of virtual mothering. It is a new type of sociality characterized by affinities and affiliations over adoption losses, and emerges in the birth mothers' Internet community, especially around moments or occasions heavily invested in by multiple birth mothers. By highlighting the co-evolving dimensions of virtual mothering and the new sociality forged through the website, I examine the ways in which *A Sad Love Story of Mothers* facilitates the care and support of its members by serving as an informal ombudsman, as well as an alternative, independent source of adoption knowledge and information. Thereby, I argue that the birth mothers' Internet café serves as a counterpublic through which birth mothers foster self-advocacy and construct a self-empowering community worthy of public recognition.

5.2 Painful Delivery to Virtual Baby: From Apology to Promise of Happiness

The most powerful affect driving birth mothers to tell about their bygone child is the pain associated with giving up their child to adoption. This pain encompasses the emotional devastations and physical effects of adoption losses, yet it should not be interpreted as an instinctual, maternal response or as a desperate desire to actually raise the child. Rather, the birth mothers' painful accounts point to their complex and ambivalent relationship with the adoption losses, as captured in this December 9th post:

> ID: December 9th   Date: 2005. 07.19 23:26
> Subject: My baby
>
> > My lovely baby,
> > I miss you so much that I might go crazy.
> > My heart feels like exploding.
> > I would rather go crazy; then I wouldn't have any memory of you.
> > I wish I had no thought of you.
> > Tears come along, whenever I think of you, several times a day.
> > My heart aches.

At witnessing her heart-wrenching moment of pain, the birth mother expresses a desire to see her bygone child; and yet, in the very same breath, she invites amnesia to obliterate her emotional devastation. The intensity of her pain fuels the desire to connect with the child, yet ironically precipitates the desire to disconnect from the child. Her ambivalence and tension toward the losses express that she yearns to be free from (the memory of) her child, as much as she wants to retain (the memory of) her child.[20] As epitomized in this post, the affectivity of various pains drives birth mothers toward—and away from—the Internet, thus characterizing the intense, intermittent, discontinuous texture of virtual mothering, and its rather convoluted and ambivalent desire to connect and to disconnect with the child through the Web.

Hailed by the pains, each birth mother enters the Internet café and encounters a gateway through which she reconnects with her bygone child; there, she attends to and delivers a form of care and love to her bygone child. The first step upon entering the café is to create a screen name. The most common style combines a baby's intended name with a mother, such as in the following: "Minyoung's mommy"; "Dahbin's mommy"; and "Minee's mom". Other names express the woman's feelings of sadness, guilt, shame and love that she feels toward her baby: "bad mother"; "sad mother"; "sad self"; "shameful mommy"; "I am sorry, Haesol"; "love for Hosuk"; "love for Jinsung"; "Unseen Love"; "it is too late"; "A smoldering knot in her chest". Some adopt random nouns, such as "nickname,"[21] or the transposition of a Korean word, such as a child's name, by typing the Korean word on an English- language keyboard to arrive at a string of English letters that lack any concrete meaning in English. For example, "gywjd" typed on an English-language keyboard becomes *hyo-jung* when typed on a Korean-language keyboard.[22]

Screen names serve as an entry into virtual mothering by having birth mothers enact their lost mothering through the evocation of the forbidden child's secret name and the expression of her emotions toward the child. They serve to reconnect the birth mother with her bygone child, but simultaneously serve as a protective layer that shields her off-line identity.[23] The dual functions of screen names establish an environment where the bygone child is acknowledged by the birth mother and turned into a virtual baby toward whom her virtual mothering is both directed and delivered.

Beholding the bygone child as the main addressee in the postings, the virtual mother performs maternal acts of telling. Certain topics reoccur frequently in the birth mothers' postings. These include a simple greeting to the child; a query about the child's well-being; the voicing of the child as the birth mother's secret love; and wishes for the child's happy, healthy life. However, first and foremost, the postings express regret over the adoption decision, and deliver a sincere apology for the act.

The following posting illustrates a typical correspondence between a virtual mother and the bygone child.

> ID: Bad Mother   Date: 2003.04.04
> Subject: I am worried
>
> ... Seung Ah ya
> I have been in deep regret about sending you away,
> Abandoning you, to be exact.
> Are you thinking badly of your mother?
> I want to change my decision of adoption four months ago.
> [I can't fathom myself] having signed the relinquishment paper handed to me by the adoption agency worker, while you were smiling right next to me
> Aren't I too immature?
> I belatedly have so much regret
> I should have raised you myself, even if it is very difficult
> ... I am so sorry.
> I miss you so much, my daughter, dearly.
> Before my death, I would like to see you, even once.

In this entry, "Bad Mother" calls out her child's name, Seung Ah, and simultaneously acknowledges herself as a mother. Vividly conjuring up the moment of relinquishment, she characterizes the adoption decision as an act of child abandonment, and expresses a deep sense of regret about having done it. In providing the background for her regrettable decision, she attributes it to her incapacity to raise a child, and, as a result, calls herself a "bad mother," as echoed in the postings of numerous birth mothers. In a similar vein, "I love you Jaehwan" describes how she did not have the courage to raise a child by herself.[24] Another birth mother, "A Real Pooh," apologizes for her lack of persistence and confidence about keeping the baby, having felt cowed by her parents' disapproval, and the social stigmas against single motherhood.

In telling online about the adoption decision, the birth mothers' accounts are filled with regrets about their incapacity to retain the baby, whether due to a lack of courage, persistence, maturity, financial independence, or any of their combinations. Taking full and sole responsibility for the decision, birth mothers apologize to the bygone child, expressing their regrets for not being able to mother him or her. The birth mothers' adoption narratives echo the societal view of the adoption decision as an individual woman's failure, largely stemming from her lack of various resources, which I argue absolves birth fathers from having any parental or social responsibility for the child, thus reinforcing the dominant ideology of a motherhood that requires crippling maternal sacrifices.

The sense of regret usually jumps from the time of the adoption decision to the time of the pregnancy, and then to the subsequent brief period, pending separation, during which the birth mother and the child are apart, yet still together. In accounts of their pregnancies, many birth mothers confess that adequate self-care and prenatal care were beyond their means, largely due to their marginalized position as a single, pregnant woman. Among birth mothers who had unplanned and unwelcomed pregnancies, many tried to cover up their condition under layers of clothes and belts, and/or engaged in reckless, self-harming behaviors, rather than trying to take good care of themselves.

The following post illuminates a birth mother's belated sense of appreciation for her baby, and her subsequent sadness:

ID: Eunbi's Mother   Date: 2002.04.01 05:39
Subject: I miss you dearly.

> When I had you inside my body, I wanted you to come out quickly. … My happiest moment was when you kicked in my stomach, as if you were saying "Mommy, I am here". When you moved inside me, you always tried to inform me of your presence. [But now] I do not have the sense of movement from you any more. … When I heard that you left the agency because you were placed for adoption, I felt like a stranger took the candy that I was licking. I think the time when you were inside me was a good one. You were my first and secret one, so I could not take good care of you. I could not talk to you much, either. That made me really sad…

The relief anticipated upon the delivery of her baby, as "Eunbi's mother" writes, was instead replaced with a sense of emptiness and loss, which grew even deeper after the adoption took place. By telling her baby that being pregnant was the happiest time in her life, "Eunbi's mother" offers her a memory of their shared past, and affirms her love and care for the child. Albeit she acknowledges the time as precious, she explains she could not offer "good care." Her inability to take care of the pregnancy leaves her with another layer of regret; she was unable to take care of the baby not only upon birth but also during the pregnancy itself.

The birth mothers' bodies, separated from their babies, constantly evoke the lost child, and birth mothers are often overwhelmed by feelings of belatedness and helplessness, as exemplified in the post below:

> ID: Byori   Date: 2001.10.05 23:25
> Subject: Crying myself to sleep
>
>> What if I could have nursed you even once,
>> I wish I could have hugged you even once ...
>> After delivery, my breasts were filled with flowing milk.
>> They looked swollen. What if I held your hand that you stretched out to me while I cut the umbilical cord ...I would not be as devastated as I am right now. ...

The account of "Byori," along with those of numerous other birth mothers on the site, tell of swollen breasts, suffering from inflammation due to a lack of nursing. Embodying the loss of the baby in her bodily pain, "Byori" writes that her own skin was smoldering with the emptiness. In doing so, she elaborates her deferred love and regret for what she could have offered—nursing, hugging, even just holding the baby's hand before separation. Yet, delivering a baby alone, as suggested in her own severing of the umbilical cord, must have been so overwhelming that she could not afford to engage with her baby, at that time. Tragically, the medical staff, overseeing her delivery, did not let her hold the newborn baby. Thus, her last glimpse of the baby is of her child's extended hand. Meanwhile, the entries of numerous birth mothers indicate that they never even saw their babies, thus creating an even greater sense of emptiness, in the lack of not even having an image to hold on to. The time period from the adoption decision to the baby's delivery, especially their brief time after the child's birth, are filled with a sense of regret, clustered around feelings of shame and guilt; such affects reverberate through innumerable entries, forming the website's affective foundation.

Eventually, the regrets expressed in the birth mothers' accounts subside, and yield to happiness, reflecting validation that adoption will secure the best possible future happiness for the child. For example, both "Choi Min Joo" and "Sun Hyungi" acknowledged how her baby's existence under the sky was the source of her own happiness. As an act of love, birth mothers offer their happiness to the child, offering to take on the child's unhappiness as if they, in doing so, could protect the child from unhappiness, and secure the child's future happiness ("Sungwon's Mother", 2005.04.23). By an overwhelming majority, the birth mothers cited the child's future happiness as the predominant motive for deciding upon adoption, thus reinforcing long-standing social governance that deploys adoption as the best available, motherly choice for unmarried women.

While rationalizing adoption as the best decision to secure the child's happiness, the birth mothers' conception of what constitutes that future happiness remains abstract and imaginary, and was most often associated with material abundance, a good education, and a life free from discrimination. In *The Promise of Happiness*, Sara Ahmed offers a luminous analysis of happiness and its directionality to the normative, and thus its regulatory force over life.[25] Ahmed argues that the future-oriented promise of happiness directs one toward the future, mandating one's life to move forward toward "happy objects". These objects are not random, but rather heavily invested with social ideals, which one can attain only by incorporating oneself to normative life choices. By drawing upon Ahmed's insight on happiness as "a technology of cultivation," I interpret the happiness expressed by birth mothers in the adoption discourse as a regulatory technology, governing the reproductive choices of single birth mothers, and, as a regulatory technology of life management, even after the baby is placed in adoption.[26]

The birth mothers' accounts of happiness indicate that happiness in the adoption discourse is not just on behalf of the child but also for the birth mother, thus further justifying the decision to place the child into adoption. In contrast, the life prospects or happiness of birth mothers were never part of the adoption equation for earlier generations of birth mothers, who were married, much older, and impoverished. Clearly, the contemporary birth mothers' decision to give up their child, as discussed in Chapter 3, is steered by, and conflated with, a prioritization of the mother's own life development before her mothering. By choosing adoption, namely, to give up mothering a child, it is presumed that the birth mother will be able to resume her otherwise crushed life. In the face of an unexpected pregnancy outside of marriage, the birth mother relinquishes the child not only for the baby's future happiness but also for her own future prospects. Both parties are re-affiliated with the potentiality of being good, virtuous, and deserving of happy objects, that is, a career, marriage, and legitimate motherhood, representing prospective life choices occurring in the correct sequence. In turn, for following such a prescription, they are deemed good, virtuous, and deserving mothers. Or as I describe them, as virtual mothers.

Yet, despite the promise of happiness, the birth mothers explicitly display excruciating pains, regrets, and disappointments about the adoption decision. Furthermore, the very promise of the birth mothers' future happiness exacerbates their shame and guilt about their incapacity and failure to raise the child. "I hate this" expresses self-disgust over the adoption choice. Rather than feeling like a noble, selfless mother, as branded in the adoption discourse, she posts that she feels like a "bad mother" about abandoning her child, and describes the act as an extreme form of selfishness. Aligned with this critical view of happiness, "Hoya," a birth mother, redefines happiness, accordingly: "I can't stand the fact that I sent my child away for adoption for my own happiness. ... [Belatedly] I still wanted my own happiness back. To me, living together with the child would be happiness. I would like to get that happiness back" (Hoya, 2000.08.15). These critical observations and articulations defy the dominant adoption discourse's promise that adoption will reinstate the birth mother's happiness and remedy her life crisis.

For birth mothers, their own promise of happiness is linked with the generalized fantasy of a future reunion with the child, at which point her happiness would materialize.[27] The common scenario of reunion depends on the adoptee's search-and-reunion narrative, as discussed in detail in the previous chapter. In the late 1990s and early 2000s, as stories of adoptees "returning home" saturated the news and pop culture in South Korea, these young birth mothers imagined the reunion as a highly likely, future event for mothers who placed their child into transnational adoption.

Yet, the fantasy of the reunion requires a great deal of endurance and patience, for the child must first grow up and reach an adult age before they can return, as cited in innumerable postings. Typically, 20 years is often cited as the necessary waiting period, as in the following example:

> ID: Hwanhee' mother　　　　Date: 2001. 09. 03. 00:44
> Subject: Our Hwanhee
>
> > Dear my baby, Hwanhee,
> > I am wondering how you are doing, in an unfamiliar country far away.
> > Unsure of the adoption decision, but it is too late to regret.
> > I hope you don't think that I sent you away because I don't love you.
> > I am always worried about you, what if you should have a difficult time growing up.

I hope you do well in mind, body, and thought.
... As time goes by, my heart for you grows bigger and bigger. I miss you, dear, my love.
I love you ... forever.
I will always pray for you and wait for the day when we meet again. I hope 20 years go quickly.
Please be well. I will look out for you in my heart. From a bad mother who loves you.

Although she is unsure about her adoption choice, "Hwanhee's mother" is able to imagine the reunion because of it. She delivers unceasing wishes for the baby's well-being and repetitively enunciates her love toward the child, emphasizing that her adoption choice was not due to a dearth of love.

Often, the wish for a reunion is stated as if it were a matter of impending fact: "I am sorry. I think of you. I live my life for the brief moment when we will see each other again after twenty years."[28] At other times, birth mothers speak of the reunion as if they could elicit a promise from the child. For example, "Heebom's mom" writes, "Today is your first birthday. On your twentieth birthday, let's celebrate together"[29]; and "Fashionable Ms. Lee" wrote, "... I buried you in my heart and will wait for the day of reunion with you. Please promise."[30]

Holding the fantasy of a future reunion with the child close to her heart, the birth mother's aim is to become "an unashamed mother" (the most frequently used phrase), and to construct a future self that her child would not feel ashamed of.[31] The work of becoming an unashamed mother requires self-advancement and self-betterment. For example, "*MazingGa Z*" writes, "... I will live wholeheartedly and be successful, so that I can be an unashamed mother when I reunite with Jaesang."[32]

Meanwhile, "*Hanŭl palaki*" proposes a very specific, normative life development plan: "I want to make a lot of money ... I am going to marry your father, and have another child, and wait for you, and later give you a gift when we meet again ..."[33] Through the articulation of the figure of an unashamed mother commanding a good life, birth mothers implicitly acquiesce to the social indictment against single mothers that they are too young, too poor, and too unmarried to raise their child, and that it is best to defer their mothering and motherhood until they are "ready."

Triangulated by the figure of the unashamed mother, the birth mother's fantasy of an inevitable reunion orients her present to the future, resignifying the traumatic moment now, as a crucial life stage necessary for self-transformation, and for moving toward the future. "Hwanhee's mom" says that she will work toward becoming a confident mother by preparing for and passing the high school graduation equivalence exam.[34] Meanwhile, "Unseen Love" tells her child that she will diligently study English, so that she will be able to communicate with him in the future.[35] "Hyuni," another birth mother, says she will write a daily letter to her child in a journal and give it to her on the day they meet again.[36]

As part of their life-transformation project, birth mothers try to engage and to amend their ordinary, mundane everyday life practices, as a central site to interrupt the present and to invest toward a future reunion. For example, "Our Eunbi" posts:

> Subject: Dear Baby   Date: 2003.11.23 07:18
>
> Dear Baby.
> I don't like living these days.
> I hate going to school and eating everyday.
> It takes a lot just to live. I want to give up everything, but do think, 'What if I see you after sometime, like 20 years'.
> Then, I want to meet you, as a mother whom you would not be ashamed of. So, I tell myself not to give up, and to live earnestly.
> You would feel ashamed of your mother if I dropped out of school?

For the sake of a potential reunion, "Eunbi's mother," who appears to wrestle with depression and hopelessness, makes a firm decision to resume a normal life. The key to the successful regeneration of her life is to attend to her emotional devastations and helplessness, as well as to prioritize concrete life tasks and a future-oriented agenda. As "Eunbi's mother" relegates her mothering toward a future reunion, she forces herself to focus on living on and living well, by controlling and overcoming the heart-wrenching moments now. The fantasy of reunion not only attends to the birth mothers' pains, regrets, shame, and ambivalence, by promising eventual happiness at the reunion; it also facilitates self-management of the intense affects, following the adoption losses.

A regulatory logic of happiness via the generalized fantasy of an inevitable reunion establishes a new goal for the birth mother's life, and requires that she take care of her daily life, by managing her feelings and emotions, especially around the adoption losses. Given the ordinary, normative field of life management, the birth mother's efforts to become an unashamed mother is at odds with her efforts to cherish memories of the child on the website. The following post reflects the tensions, dilemmas, and apprehensions about forgetting the child in order to reunite with him or her in future.

> ID: *Hanŭl palaki*   Date: 2003.06.08 02:48
> Subject: Hanul, I am living for you.
>
> Hanul. I am sorry. It's been a while.
> I have been busy lately…
> What I feel very sorry about for you these days is … that I do not think of you, as often as I used to.
> Lately, I have been busy with job interviews and couldn't think of you much.
> I wanted to live my life with the first thoughts just [after you left].
> I wanted to live as diligently as I could in apology for you.
> It seems that my mind has been small. I am so sorry. I shouldn't.
> If so, I have abandoned my Hanul twice …

In the post, "*Hanŭl palaki*" apologizes for her infrequent visits to the café, and for not providing enough attention to the child; to explain her absence, she cites her efforts to live well, that is, looking for a job and having job interviews. She nervously acknowledges that her initial thoughts to forever remember and think about the baby have faded, with the diligent efforts to manage her life. She apologizes for forgetting about the child, due to her anxieties, even as she has not yet forgotten the child, and insists that she will not. Her account uncovers the birth mother's painful dilemma, of both remembering and trying to forget the child, an affective trajectory which birth mothers experience as they embark upon becoming a virtual mother.

Undergirding the wide spectrum of affects generated by virtual mothering is ambivalence. Generally, the ambivalence emanates from the decision to place the baby in adoption. The birth mothers also express doubts about whether transnational or domestic placement was better. These complex feelings encroach upon the birth mothers' convoluted and complex relationship to the child, or more accurately speaking, her memory of the child. Holding the baby as a secret love object, birth mothers are deeply committed to remembering every single detail about the child, almost as if remembering were the only maternal act possible. Simultaneously, however, as much as they want to remember the child, they also employ forgetting as a technology of self-management in their avid belief in and commitment to a future reunion with their child.

5.3 Off and On the Stage of Virtual Mothering: Baby Photo Room to Virtual Family Album[37]

Other maternal traces that birth mothers leave in the Internet café are baby photographs, and traces of displaying those photographs. In the "photo room" of *A Sad Love Story of Mothers*, 72 photographs of 20 children are displayed.[38] 12 babies in the pre-adoption stage are presented in 21 photographs, while eight children in the post-adoption period are represented in the rest. Except for five photographs uploaded by a Korean domestic adoptive mother[39] and a Korean foster mother,[40] the vast majority of these photographs were uploaded by birth mothers.

My examination of the pre-adoption photos, along with the respective birth mothers' postings, indicates that four babies went overseas and that three were placed in domestic adoption; the fate of two is unknown. Meanwhile, two-thirds of the baby photos are post-adoption photographs of children, ranging in age from six months to pre-teens, and were posted by six birth mothers, all of whom chose transnational adoption. Reflecting South Korean adoption trends, five children lived in the US, and one in Sweden. The photos appear to have been taken and selected by the adoptive parents, and sent to the agency in the receiving country that had arranged and completed the child's adoption; from there, the photographs were sent to the adoption agency in South Korea for their records,[41] and/or for communications with the birth mother. The backgrounds of the photographs include a kitchen, a living room, a bathroom, a backyard, and a playground. Photos capture a moment in a child's ordinary round of daily activities. The children in the photos were shown taking a bath; waiting for a meal; riding a bicycle; and sitting, posed with a sibling, a family dog, and Winnie the Pooh. The backgrounds of the post-adoption photographs represent ordinary, mundane family time, marking a stark contrast with the institutional backgrounds of pre-adoption photographs. Additionally, the post-adoption photographs mark special occasions, such as a child's baptism or a birthday party, and show the child wearing Korean traditional clothes, suggesting the adoptive parents' acceptance of the bygone child into their family, as well as an appreciation and acknowledgement of the child's cultural heritage.

The pre-adoption photographs displayed online appear to be part of the birth mothers' personal records of their secret children, and are seemingly taken by the birth mothers with a digital camera, or a phone camera, right after the delivery. The images display infants, with their eyes closed or unfocused on the camera, wrapped in a blanket, and lying down alone, or held by a nurse. The backgrounds of the baby portraits, albeit not very clear, include the baby ward at a hospital, a waiting room at the adoption agency, and an Internet game room, all of which are striking, due to the baby's unfamiliar placement outside the home and the absence of the mother. The baby photos corroborate the baby's birth and existence, and seize upon a brief moment before the adoption placement is closed.

By uploading the photographs online, birth mothers share their secret child with other fellow birth mothers, as well as with anonymous users. The baby photographs are usually contextualized with a birth mother's annotation, identifying herself as the mother of the child, and publicly expressing endearments to the child. "Sungwon's mother" writes about her baby's photo: "My lovely Sungwon. Twentieth day after birth. He is no longer with me, but, forever, my son."[42] Or consider "Sad Mother," who writes, "Here is my daughter; Yebin was born at 11:53 on December 5th, 2004. ... I miss her dearly. She is my heart."[43] Another birth mother, "*Hanŭl palaki*," released 20 baby photos taken during her visits to the baby ward after the delivery. "These are the photos saved on my phone that I would look at in private. They look all very nice together." She adds, "This photo is taken at the separation. She was smiling; that broke my heart. As of next Monday, it will be a month since the separation. I miss her so much."[44] Thus, the pre-adoption photos capture the period of time preceding the baby's separation from the birth mother.

For birth mothers, post-adoption photographs are among the most precious and desirable objects once the child has been relinquished; these photographs generate the most comments on the website. Why? Particularly for birth mothers who did not or could not see the baby after delivery, the photographs present—for the first time—a visual image of the child lost to adoption, thus substantiating the loss that birth mothers have no visual memory of. The photographs confirm a safe, successful adoption placement, and affirm the sustenance of the baby's future life. Furthermore, the baby's smiling face in the photograph assures the baby's well-being, well-adjustment, and healthy development within the adoptive family.[45]

Yet, a careful examination of these baby photographs, as well as of the birth mothers' postings on the photographs, makes it clear that only birth mothers who chose transnational adoption could be reconnected with their children via photographs. In contrast, birth mothers who opted for domestic adoption were not allowed to have any form of communication with the child, or the child's adoptive parents. Upholding a principle of utmost secrecy, domestic adoptive parents have long hidden the fact of adoption from the child, relatives, and friends. This practice is slowly changing toward a more open policy, whereby adoptive parents publicly acknowledge the adoption; yet, any contact with birth parents is still rare.

In the Internet café, birth mothers with children placed in domestic adoption expressed envy and frustration over the photographs. For example, "Hyuni" posted, "Today, I have been thinking of you a lot. It's been a year since ... I would love to see you, even in photographs, but I can't because of domestic adoption."[46]

Yet, despite their desperate desire to have adoption photographs of the baby after his or her placement, some birth mothers still chose domestic adoption. Why? The following entry from *"Hanŭl palaki,"* who chose domestic adoption, highlights this dilemma, as she laments upon her motherly choice.

> ID: *Hanŭl palaki*   Date: 2003.08.19 01:26
> Subject: From your mother who dreams of you
>
> What if I sent my babe ... farther?
> I could see my babe grow, [then] I would not be worrying,
> if my babe would be hurt, growing up,
> if my babe would forget about the language, so
> then later no language between us, by the time we see each other
> ... In each breath, coexist happiness and unhappiness.
> I am happy to have you as my daughter
> I am unhappy because I miss you too much ...

This entry suggests that the birth mother selected domestic adoption to protect the baby from potential problems that the baby might face growing up in a foreign country, indicating her awareness about the possibilities of racial discrimination, and of linguistic and cultural displacement.

Since the 2000s, the growing presence of Korean adult adoptees in South Korea has testified to the difficulties of growing up in a foreign country, and their testimonies have been incorporated into the transnational adoption discourse. Thus, *"Hanŭl palaki"* writes that she selected domestic adoption for the child to protect him/her from various dangers and losses; and, as a result, gave up the possibility of an ongoing exchange of letters and photos with the child and adoptive parents. Her desire to protect and connect with her child through a shared language and culture is mutually exclusive of her desire to reconnect with her child through photographs, or by some other means. The post underscores how the birth mother's photographic connection with her child is, most likely, only possible on the condition of geographical, cultural, and linguistic displacement, as associated with transnational adoption; thus, cultural and linguistic differences between a child and a birth mother are inevitably produced.

However, not all birth mothers who choose transnational adoption automatically receive post-adoption photographs. Rather, the acquisition of such photographs requires a birth mother's active labor, along with persistence, patience, and resilience. In order to receive photographs from the adoptive parents—or, more precisely, from the adoption agency—a birth mother must express explicit interest in an ongoing exchange of communications with the adoptive family. Often, they must take the initiative of writing letters, and/or sending a gift, in hopes that the adoptive parents will be willing to respond. Furthermore, they must persistently ask for updates from the adoption agencies. Thus, "Byori" writes, "Today, I called the adoption agency, and the staff told me my son's photographs arrived a week ago. I have been waiting for a year to receive the photos."[47] Without her persistent endeavors, her son's photographs would probably have been received much later, if at all.

Not only does the acquisition of a photograph require persistent communication and patience, it also demands overcoming ambivalence and fear that the baby photographs will serve as a reminder of the lost child, potentially leading to emotional despair. For example, "Minee mom" confesses, "I am going to pick up the baby photo tomorrow at the agency. … Though, I am not supposed to feel this way, I fear receiving the photograph because it might cause pain again."[48] In other words, the post-adoption photographs displayed in the café express the birth mothers' labor of care and patience, in spite of their resilience.

The photographs on the site—both pre- and post-adoption— feature only the baby. Except for two images, none shows the face of the birth mother or of the adoptive parents.[49] The absence of the birthmother's face in the pre-adoption photos expresses the birth mothers' self-regulating behavior of maintaining the secrecy of the baby's existence and its life beyond the normative family. Meanwhile, the absence of the adoptive parents' faces in the photos hints at the reluctance and ambivalence of adoptive parents, and/or the protocol of adoption agencies to have an open communication with the birth mothers. Or, it may be the result of conscious editing by the birth mothers, as they are the ones who select the photos to upload; or, it could be an unconscious, orchestrated effort by all involved parties. Whichever, the absence of parents—whether it be the birth parents or the adoptive parents—renders the baby in the photographs as a free-floating child, thus providing the visible underlying condition whereby a birth mother can perform virtual mothering via her engagement with Internet technology.

Before examining the intersecting effects of the photographs, let me briefly discuss photography and its losses. As theorists of photography have argued, photography is entangled with loss. The nature of loss emanates from the disrupted temporality embodied in the photographs, illuminating simultaneously the presence of both life and death.[50] The referent is both present/alive (as implied in the photograph) and absent/dead (it was there, but is not here now). Following the disjunctive existence of the photographic referent—that is, the simultaneity of presence/absence and life/death—the baby photographs are perched onto two disjointed, spatiotemporalities. The photographs present a baby that is absent in the here and now. The baby returned via the photograph is no longer the child, as of now. He or she, is therefore, always already lost in time, and returns as a ghostly child. The child's photograph embodies its multiple losses—by signifying the birth mother's lost mothering and her lost child, lost again in the photograph. Thus, birth mothers are reminded that such losses are impossible, irretrievable. Then, what does it mean to share online the personal photographs of the bygone child, signifying multiple, impossible losses? In what ways does the birth mother's act of showing the child's photograph enable her to reconnect with the child, thus enacting a virtual mothering?

To contemplate the ways in which the baby photographs are presented, mediated, and shared online, thus facilitating the process of virtual mothering, I draw on Roland Barthes' insight about photography's regenerative power to build a connection. He writes:

> The photograph is literally an emanation of the referent. From a real body, which was there, proceed radiations which ultimately touch me, who am here ... A sort of umbilical cord links the body of the photographed thing to my gaze: light, though impalpable, is here a carnal medium, a skin I share with anyone who has been photographed.[51]

Barthes' interpretation of the photograph and its generative power, cutting across time and space, between its creation (the moment the photo was taken) and its reception (the moment the photo was viewed), offers a framework with which to consider the connections that the photograph—the lost referent—could possibly create among visitors to the Internet café. Barthes' somewhat magical treatment of photographs, as possessing an emanating power apart from the camera, in its own right, endows the photograph with a nonhuman, technological agency that generates a connection between the photograph and the viewer. Such a connection, according to Barthes, is made possible only through light. In the field of vision, light draws the viewer and the viewed closer to each other, thus generating a new layer of skin between the photograph and the viewer. As Barthes' light functions as a carnal medium, generating connective tissues or skin between the photograph and the viewer, similarly, the Internet technology illuminates what otherwise would be secret, that is, personal baby photographs, and carves out a capillary communication matrix in which multiple connections between the viewer and the baby photographs are generated, thereby producing a new skin, a skin of connectivity. At and via the new—constantly updating—surface of these intermedial connections emerges a virtual mothering.

In what ways is virtual mothering activated by connections between the viewer and the baby photographs? In *Family Frames*, Marianne Hirsch considers the ways in which the familiar subject is constructed through the act of looking, and describes a "familial look" that enables normative familial relations:

> The familial look, [then], is not the look of a subject looking at an object, but a mutual look of a subject looking at an object who is a subject looking (back) at an object. Within the family, as I look, I am always also looked at, seen, scrutinized, surveyed, monitored. Familial subjectivity is constructed relationally, and in these relations I am always both self and other(ed), both speaking and looking subject and spoken and looked at object."[52]

Applying Hirsch's "familial look" to the act of showing baby photographs, one can see that, as the birth mother uploads the photograph, she presents her look, although it is absent, in a literal sense. Her absent figure calls out her apparent desire for the bygone child's recognition—the recognition from her to the child, and from the child to her. By displaying her desire for this mutual recognition, she invites, or is inevitably exposed to the looks of "others," including those of birth mothers, and all other visitors to the Internet café. In this way, the baby photographs unleash a closed circuit of mutual recognition, extending beyond one of biologically rooted kinship and creating a wider, extended network of looks that recognize a connection between the child and the mother, and looks that acknowledge the birth mother's loss of the child, and her (loss) of mothering, as well as the loss of the familial tie.

Rather than deploying a narrative of "maternal instincts" or a "natural" connection between a mother and a child, I want to narrativize how the fractured connection between a mother and a child is re-sutured by a network of familial looks, as evidenced in the traces of highly viewed Web pages, sometimes more than 100 times, as well as by comments about a child's photograph. For example, "Jaewon" engages with a photograph uploaded by "December 9th," telling her that the photo reminded her of when she sent away her child, and that she should feel free to unload difficult feelings, whenever needed[53]; likewise, "ilmare" acknowledged the child's beautiful face, in response to "I love Jaehwan."[54] In other words, the familial look, revolving around online baby photographs, is not just a mutual recognition between the mother and her bygone child, but rather a composite of non-synchronized, intersecting looks from other birth mothers and visitors to the site. In the café, the birth mothers' mothering is no longer a solitary, imaginary action, for the private act of uploading a child's photograph, or sharing a personal narrative, always involves collaborative efforts from onlookers.

I use the term *virtual intimacy* to describe familial looks that forge a reconnection between a mother and the photographed baby. Virtual intimacy refers to online, affect-driven, public intimacy, based on a mutual recognition over adoption losses, that operates beyond blood-based kinship. Its unique intimacy arises out of the website, in general, and the photo room, in particular; through these intermedial processes, the photo display is reframed as a family album. Seeing these photographs as part of a collective family album enables a "familial look" that sorts the baby photographs, from pre-adoption to post-adoption, thus constructing a developmental narrative structure that creates a space where birth mothers can transpose their loss and anguish over their lost child to relief and hope for the child's immanent happiness. Secondly, such a cooperative familial vision offers a critical perspective through which to see how the children in the photographs are affiliated with one another, based on a shared history rooted in the contempt for the value and labor of the birth mothers, thus leading to the baby's separation from the birth mother, and his or her subsequent displacement into transnational adoption. I argue that the online photo room is a salient example of a new materiality, one which provides affective textures and a narrative structure that constitute a virtual sense of affinities and solidarity.

5.4 Virtual Kinship

With the shared experience of adoption losses, birth mothers relate to the postings and the baby photographs as if it were their own child and their own loss. A shared recognition of adoption losses is the motivation to post for the majority of birth mothers who participate in "Let's Talk"[55] and "Consultation for Concerns," chatrooms where postings are directed toward members, as opposed to the bygone child.

Here, birth mothers express the emotional devastation they are suffering over their lost child, and are consoled by fellow members. Members offer practical advice on dealing with the adoption agency and/or adoptive parents. They also post personal updates on their lives, and support one another in their life struggles. By exploring the site's most popular topics (e.g., a child's birthday, the adoption agency, a gift/letter for the adoptive parents), it becomes clear how the website has (1) performed as a counterpublic, resisting the social stigma and pressing silence around adoption; (2) served as a site of care, support, resistance and empowerment; and (3) cultivated a virtual kinship based on affective affinities over adoption losses.

Not surprisingly, the child's birthday, or the 100th Day[56] celebration, is a day that is invoked by birth mothers, and often the most frequent subject of postings. As might be expected, these birthday invocations and remembrances are not like a typical mother's birthday wish, in that they are often interwoven with painful memories and a lingering sadness over the child's absence. The following string of posts illustrates the collective acknowledgment and appreciation of the bygone child on his or her birthday.

> ID: Real Pooh   Date: 2002.01.29. 13:03
>
>> Today is the third birthday of my son, Se Hoon. Please, let's celebrate! Until last year, I was devastated and drank a lot. I have decided not to do that again. My Se Hoon, born into a difficult situation. However, I believe, he is living happily with adoptive parents now. ... Please, congratulate me!
>
> Reply 1. ID: Jaewon   Date: 2002. 1.30. 00:46
>> I am happy for your son's third birthday.
>> My baby is almost three, too. I can't even imagine how much she must have grown, by now. I hope to see you at some point, in person. Congratulations again!

> Reply 2. ID: Byori   Date 2002.01.29. 18:22
> CONGRATULATIONS
> I am sure he is growing bright and happy, like the snow outside
> I hope you are doing well.
> Cheers, someday you will be able to see your son, Se Hoon
>
> Reply 3. ID: Love for sea   Date: 2002. 01.30. 20:37
> Sorry for my belated congratulations.
> It's already been three years?
> Dear Se Hoon, Happy birthday to you ☺ ☺ ☺
> I hope you grow healthy and brave

In the absence of their baby, birth mothers collectively acknowledge the fact that there was a baby born to, and separated from, his or her mother. This collective recognition for the losses, grounded in the shared experiences of birth mothers, resonates in the birthday wishes for the child's well-being and happiness, and in the wishes for the mother's health and strength. This shared and participatory act of telling and retelling online helps to register the private memory of the child into the collective experience of adoption losses shared by the birth mothers. The mutual recognition of collective losses helps birth mothers to feel legitimate about their right to speak about their lost children, and to exchange their stories and experiences.

Comparing her discovery of the website to finding a secret friend, "With the Sad Heart" posts, "…[F]rom pregnancy to adoption, I didn't have anyone to share my worries with, nor to rely on … I felt much better, after posting my story … glad, as if I found a good friend here."[57] Similarly, "I am sorry," who revealed her adoption story for the first time on the Web almost ten years after it happened, wrote, "After reading (your) stories, I wanted to talk about my adoption experience, which took place in 1994."[58] In such ways, *A Sad Love Story of Mothers* has provided an open forum for the care and support of numerous birth mothers, who have been significantly deprived of such care in their off-line lives.

Often birth mothers offer critical perspectives of the baby's father[59]; the immediate family members; maternity homes[60]; and adoption agencies[61]; and, in general, all those whose involvement pressure them into choosing adoption. In particular, birth mothers are critical of how adoption agencies are dismissive and disrespectful of birth mothers and their inquiries; a widespread frustration toward the adoption agencies resonates in the birth mothers' postings. The following post provides such an example:

ID: Yoo Seung Gyun   Date 2002. 07.25. 12:33
Subject: I am terribly upset

>   Today was the day that I was supposed to see my Seungyun, a picture. I felt so excited from very early in the morning, reciting all the questions, over and over, so as not to forget the questions about the health and the well-being of my Seungyun. I called this morning because they told me to set up the appointment in the morning. For this, I took a day off from my part-time job... I wanted to call really early, but waited so that my call would not interfere with their meeting. At 9:30 am, I called the agency to learn that the agency worker who [handled my case] had something else to take care of and had postponed the meeting to some other time. We had set up today's meeting, according to her schedule a few days ago. I am quite upset at the agency's worker for not keeping her word. I inquired if I could just pick up the baby photograph from another staff member. Then, a response followed that she hadn't picked up the photograph from Seoul yet, because she's been busy, and asked me again to call and set up an appointment next week. I apologized to her for calling too early in the morning, out of my excitement to see the child's photos, and assured her that I would call back next week. Afterward, I became very upset. ... dear Seungyun. I think he is fine, right? Don't get sick. Be well and grow up healthy. Dear God. I will take all the pains, the pains of Seungyun. Please help my baby to grow well and be loved!

Thus, "Yoo Seung Gyun," whose screen name is the name of her relinquished child, tells about her uncontainable excitement to see her child's photograph; about her careful, cautionary preparation for contacting the adoption agency; about the frustration of the canceled meeting; and about the eventual disappointment over the agency's failure to provide the baby's photo. Like so many birth mothers, she was denied the opportunity to see her baby after the delivery. Her second request to see the baby in person, while he was still in the agency's care, was denied again by the adoption agency. The pursuit of the baby's photograph represents her third attempt to check on the baby's wellbeing. After the agency repeatedly ignores her request to see her own child, or to have a photograph of him, and then only reluctantly cooperates, she clearly becomes upset; yet, she maintains a polite, even apologetic, tone for her demands.

Numerous accounts describe similar experiences with adoption agencies.[62] Often birth mothers describe being treated as a cumbersome, if not dangerous or threatening, person, whose continuing contact with—and interest in—the baby could possibly lead to desires to reclaim the baby, or, in some way, undermine the baby's ultimate wellbeing. While it is problematic to suppose that all staff members at all adoptive agencies were unhelpful, and/or mistreated birth mothers, the birth mothers' accounts accumulated at the website suggest that the intention of adoption agencies is to secure the child, as quickly as possible, as soon as the birth mother agrees to transfer the baby's custody to the agency. Yet, many, like "Yoo Seung Gyun," are hesitant to express their complaints directly to the adoption agency, since they are dealing with the institution that takes care of their child, until he or she is placed into an adoptive family, and, also, since it is the only place to which she can return afterward for further information on the baby.

When feeling disrespected by adoption agencies, or discouraged by their arbitrary policies, birth mothers console one another, validating each other's frustrations and anger at the agencies, and encouraging fellow birth mothers to push for further information. In response to a post by "Yoo Seung Gyun," another birth mother "Nickname" counters the agency's claim of why birth mothers are not allowed to see their baby upon delivery: "I don't understand the adoption agency. It is so presumptuous for them to not show the baby to a birth mother, in order to protect birth mothers from additional agony and pains."[63] By sharing her own relief upon seeing her baby, she articulates the positive psychological benefits of such contact, and tells the birth mother to be brave. In a similar vein, a moderator, "Jaewon," posted a supportive and empowering message for birth mothers on the listserv:

> ID:Jaewon   Date 2001.09.09. 00:57
> Subject: Dear mothers who left a child at the agency
>
> > It seems like not many people know this fact.
> > While the baby is at the agency, you can give a gift for the 100th Day and any other significant day. (For example, clothes and toys). Adoption agencies never inform you about this, although policies vary from agency to agency. So, ask first, whether you can buy a gift for your child for the birthday, or take a photograph of your child. Ask, if you have any questions.

In this post, "Jaewon" publicizes the birth mother's right to see the baby at the agency before the adoption placement, as well as the right to ask questions about the adoption and child; she strongly encourages birth mothers to take the initiative in asking what they can do for the child.

As suggested in the entry by "Jaewon," the transnational adoption process can take from a few months to a year or two to complete. The drawn-out process involves matching a baby with adoptive parents; giving the baby a medical examination; and, applying for the emigration documents required for the child's departure from South Korea and entry into a new country. During this transitional period, as expressed in the birth mothers' accounts, some women visited their children, while others did not know this option was possible. There are no set guidelines for adoption agencies regarding the birth mothers' rights to see their children, or to access information about them. The erratic, inconsistent policies are well-documented in the birth mothers' postings. In telling these stories, the website promotes the self-empowerment of birth mothers through the facilitation of knowledge about the rights of birth mothers in seeking out adoption information.

Clearly, in these various ways, the website has functioned as an informal adoption resource center where birth mothers can share their own experiences and adoption information, and thus construct an independent source of adoption knowledge. Challenging the exclusive, uncontested authority of the adoption agencies, especially over their rights to the adoption information, the birth mothers expend much energy on trying to uncover adoption procedures, especially regarding the transfer of the child to the adoptive family.

Other members of the Internet café, such as foster mothers and child-escort volunteers, are crucial to the collective project of learning about the adoption process. For example, "Floss," who escorted a baby from a Korean adoption agency to his adoptive parents in the US, while neither a birth mother nor an adoptive parent, shared extensive ethnographic information. (Escorting a baby is a common practice among adoption agencies since South Korea allows proxy adoptions, thereby saving adoptive parents a trip to Korea to pick up the child.) "Floss" detailed how escort candidates were selected and trained at the adoption agency, before departing with the baby on the plane. She also described the arrival in the US, and the transfer of the child to the adoptive parents.[64]

Meanwhile, "Liz", a foster mother,[65] who worked for an adoption agency, posted that she had raised 13 children between 2002 and 2005. She sought to assure birth mothers of their children's well-being by expressing her loving care for all the children that she had raised prior to their adoption; by sharing her impressions of adoptive parents as kind and responsible; and, finally, by extending her wishes for the well-being of the birth mothers.[66] Empathizing with the birth mothers' losses, such caretakers express their love of adopted children, and refute characterizations of connections between an adopted child and an adoptive mother as "unreal" or "inauthentic." In contrast to the prevailing practice of being secretive about adoption, adoptive parents in the café express their interest in having ongoing communications with birth mothers, as well as wishing for the birth mothers' wellness and happiness.[67]

One of the primary ways that the website serves as an adoption resource center is by offering guidance to birth mothers who want to exchange letters, gifts, and/or photos with their child's adoptive parents. Due to significant cultural differences, as well as a strong desire to maintain an ongoing exchange of information, birth mothers have great apprehension about contacting the adoptive parents, and thus prepare for the occasion with great care and caution.

Birth mothers post drafts of the letters that they are writing to their child's adoptive parents, as well as the letters they receive from them. For example, "Nickname" uploaded ten letters, written by her son's adoptive parents. The letters updated her on his physical development, included a detailed description of his personality, and identified his favorite color and food; other letters described mundane activities, as well as offered updates on the adoptive family. Meanwhile, "Choi Min Joo" not only uploaded the letter from the adoptive parents, she also posted the letter she intended to send her lost child and her adoptive parents.[68] Sharing letters, whether from—or to—the adoptive parents and the child, provides comfort for the birth mothers, reassuring them collectively that their own babies are thriving.

Furthermore, the letters serve as sample letters for other birth mothers who may want to write a letter to their child's adoptive parents. For example, the posted letters may have helped birth mother, "A Real Pooh," who said, with dismay, "I was told to write a letter to adoptive parents, and don't know what to write. If I were to frankly write my mind, it would be way too long."[69] "Byori," another birth mother, who hopes to carry on an exchange of letters and photographs with the adoptive parents, asks for suggestions from the community. Her post ends by asking for feedback from the listserv members: "Please let me know if there is anything odd, or to add, or change."[70] By reading the letters and offering guidance and feedback, birth mothers, who may not have any communication with their child's adoptive parents, also participate in an exchange of letters with the larger adoption community, including adoptive parents.

Along with writing letters, birth mothers send gifts on significant occasions as an expression of their love for the child and their gratitude toward the adoptive parents. These occasions typically included a child's birthday, a child's departure for the adoptive home, or Christmas. Many posters solicit advice on an appropriate gift to get; many also write about wanting to deliver their heart and unsaid love to the child, but also not wanting to offend the adoptive parents. The following post and subsequent replies illustrate the birth mothers' shared concerns about sending a gift or letter to the adoptive parents, and also their considerable trust in the collective knowledge accrued on the website.

> ID: Hyejinee   Date: 2001.10.15. 21:59
> Subject: I want to send a gift to the bygone child …

> My baby left for foreign adoption. Adoptive parents came from afar and picked up the baby. No photo has arrived, but I wanted to send a Christmas card to the adoptive parents, and my baby. I wanted to ask the welfare office [*meaning, adoption agency office*] to see if I could send the letter along with my gift, but I wanted to confirm with you first. Is it possible? I wanted to write a letter, telling the adoptive parents who I am, and how much I miss the baby, even after the adoption, and to show my gratitude and to give a small gift to my baby. I, as a mother, haven't given anything to my baby. So, for this Christmas, I wanted to give a little gift, maybe a Korean *hanbok* (a traditional Korean dress that people wear during a rite of passage) for a kid. If possible, shall I write a letter in Korean, or in their language? Their language is not even English, which we had to learn in school. If there is someone who can translate, then I don't have to worry. Even just once, I want to send something that I have prepared with great care and effort for my baby, hoping my baby can feel some of my traces over those surfaces. Of course, my baby would not know from whom the gift comes. But I would be really happy if my baby touches something that once belonged to me. Is it possible? I need some advice.

> Reply 1. ID: Jaewon   Date: 2001.10.15. 22:53
> Ask a staff member at the department of post-adoption services at the adoption agency. Even in cases of foreign adoption, some do not like the idea of receiving a gift or letters (but, most are okay). As for a gift for the child, a Korean traditional object is fine. You don't have to prepare a gift for the adoptive parents. If you still want to, prepare something simple, not too intimate. Last year, I gave them bookmarks, the ones decorated in the Korean traditional style. But, first most importantly, ask the adoption agency. I also have to prepare something for this year. What shall I do? When I see baby clothes, I want to buy them. But I thought to myself, should I do it again? I should prepare something more memorable.

> Reply 2: ID: Hyoni   Date: 2001.10.15. 22:05
> Foreign adoption allows [a birth mother] to send letters and gifts. Ask the adoption agencies. Each adoption agency has different policies. It is nice to send letters and gifts to the adoptive parents because they raise our children and love them.
>
> Reply 3. ID: Choi Min Joo   Date: 2001.10.16. 05:25
> I prepared a *hanbok* (a Korean traditional dress) and a picture frame for a gift.

Often the birth mothers' concerns about the right kinds of gift to get, as shown in the preceding message thread, result in a present that is ostensibly Korean and usually handmade. Such popular gift items include a tourist momento emblazoned "Korea," Korean teas, Korean traditional baby outfits, traditional dolls, traditional snacks, and cross-stitched baby things. By providing Korean cultural goods that the adoptive parents would not know about, or that they would have difficulty finding, the birth mother delivers her desire to inform the child of his or her cultural roots, and simultaneously takes part in the adoptive family's multicultural family formation.

Providing a gift that features cross-stitching is extremely popular. At *A Sad Love Story of Mothers*, many women in the community do cross-stitching; furthermore, they share patterns of various designs, and even discuss collectively buying needles and threads. "Jaewon," the moderator of this community, said that the act of cross-stitching soothed her pain during the period right after her daughter was sent away for adoption. I observed numerous accounts by birth mothers who voiced similar sentiments. Birth mothers wanted to give something in which their hearts and love were embodied, so they often stitched pillows, baby shoes, and baby portraits. By cross-stitching, the birth mother remembered her lost child. By offering what she has painstakingly made, stitch by stitch, she seeks to embed traces of herself in the gift, so that some aspect of herself will be met, caressed, and loved by her child.

5.5 Conclusion

The mutual recognition of adoption losses, mobilized by the intensities of modulating affects at the website, activates a sense of affinities and affiliations, thereby rendering the performance of anonymous birth mothers as part of larger cultural performances and social practices that I call *virtual mothering*. The café serves as a critical site for birth mothers for multiple reasons. First, it provides self-advocacy for—and—by birth mothers through the sharing of concrete information and emotional support, as evidenced by the birth mothers and other visitors, who give care, empathy, and useful information for those suffering adoption losses. In this way, the Internet café functions as an informal ombudsman, by which birth mothers can express their disapproval and discontent about adoption policies, as well as critique the treatment of single mothers. By challenging the adoption agency's exclusive control over adoption information, the website has empowered birth mothers and validated their rights to know basic adoption facts. In addition, the website has collectively constructed an adoption information resource center, based on the members' collective adoption experiences and knowledge.

By examining the Internet café known as *A Sad Love Story of Mothers*, this chapter argues that this website for contemporary birth mothers activates and materializes a process of virtual mothering. Through this website, a new form of mothering which is highly performative, ephemeral, and collaborative, takes form. Existing outside the disciplinary and discursive framework of "motherhood" in the normative family imaginary, birth mothers "show and tell" about their lost children, whether through letters, photographs, or stories. By featuring, circulating, and rendering legible the birth mothers' performance of mothering, the Internet café makes public the birth mothers' private, stigmatized memories of loss, thereby archiving their adoption losses.

Simultaneously, the website captures the performances of virtual mothering; thereby the ephemeral acts of mothering—short-lived, at times furtively existent—are embodied in the aftermath, even as birth mothers eventually fade away. As a counterpublic, the Internet café counteracts the overwhelming silence of birth mothers who are engaged in transnational adoption, by articulating and recording detailed accounts of their emotional trajectory. Their accounts defiantly contradict the dominant adoption discourse, popular in South Korea since the mid-1990s, that portrays adoption as a shameful relic from the past that was rooted in postwar poverty. Challenging this narrative, the website creates a critical space of mothering that allows for the resurrection of the bygone child who had to be relinquished to maintain normative kinship imperatives.

In the next and final chapter, "I Am a Mother, but Not a Mother," I explore another site of virtual mothering: the oral history collection of birth mothers. In these accounts, birth mothers reflect on their experiences of separating from their child; their involvement in the adoption process; their subsequent life experiences; and, their own reflections upon reuniting with their bygone child. By recapturing the birth mothers' adoption experience via their storytelling, the next chapter explores various paradoxical dimensions of virtual mothering.

Notes

1. Unlike in the US or Western Europe, an Internet café does not refer to a place where people pay for access to use computers. In South Korea, "internet cafe" refers to an online membership community based on shared characteristics or interests, such as hobbies, hometown, or school alumni organization. Yi-jong Suh, *Int'ŏnet K'omyunit'iwa Hankuk Sahoe* [Internet Communities and Korean Society] (Seoul: Hanul Academy, 2003).
2. Jaewon is the screen name she uses on the website. In this chapter, I refer to the listserv participants only by their screen names, within quotation marks.
3. Of 3327 total posts, 97 % were uploaded by birth mothers. To identify the number of birth mothers and their postings, I adopted a method of classification that combines the membership list I retrieved in November 2005, which included self-introductions, wherein a new user must explain their situation and motivation for joining. For entry, applicants must identify their relationship to adoption, from among the following choices: (1) birth parent, (2) adoptive parent, (3) adoptee, or (4) other. After disclosing their relationship to adoption, applicants must write a narrative of why they want to join this particular Internet café. Once the motivation for joining the community has been read and approved by the web master, a participant gains full access to the Internet café.
4. This particular Internet café is composed of the following discrete sections: (1) Let's Talk; (2) Self-introduction; (3) Stories at Your Heart; (4) Unsent Letters; (5) Your Thoughts on Adoption; (6) Photo Rooms.
5. Not all members were birth mothers who had surrendered their children to adoption. The membership included three pregnant women who were considering adoption for their baby, a birth father, Korean adoptive parents or prospective adoptive parents,

foster mothers, adoption agency workers, domestic adoptees, a bereaved mother, and miscellaneous others, such as a documentary filmmaker, and students or researchers who approached adoption as a research topic. Yet, during its active years, the majority of active members at this Internet café were birth mothers.
6. Not all birth mothers were equally active in writing or responding to posts. For example, eight birth mothers of 45 new members in 2001, and nine of 39 new members in 2002, never posted or engaged with other birth mothers. The most active members were "Jaewon", "Nickname", "Hyoni", "Real Pooh", "Junghwan's mom", "Byori", "Choi Min Joo", "Ilmare," "I love Jaehwan", "Unseen Love". About 10–20 % of birth mothers did not participate throughout their entire membership period; this population posted nothing beyond the self-introduction, a requirement for full membership, and remained only readers.
7. According to the profiles, there were some birth mothers in their thirties, and others who once had been married or involved in a common-law marriage. Two women self-identified as being in their forties reported that they had relinquished their babies for adoption about 15 years earlier.
8. I visited the website for the first time in early June 2005 and became a member on June 20, 2005. At the end of November 2005, I downloaded all postings, converted them into Word files, and occasionally read updated postings. During my recent visits during February and March of 2015, I became aware of the changes that the membership has undergone since 2005, as well as the fact that past members had erased their posts. For example, the postings under the screen name of "Cha Seung Won", "Bada", "Little Deul Mae", "qkghfkd" had all been erased, and the user profile had been deleted.
9. The total number of birth mothers who passed through this website during its active years between 2001 and 2005 is estimated to be more than 240.
10. Kristin Langellier, "Personal Narrative, Performance, Performativity: Two or Three Things I Know for Sure", *Text and Performance Quarterly 19*, no. 2 (1999): 136.
11. José Esteban Muñoz, "Ephemera as Evidence: Introductory Notes to Queer Acts," *Women & Performance: a Journal of Feminist Theory 8*, no. 2 (1996): 10.
12. Ibid.

13. This section title is a play on Wendy Chun's article, "The Enduring Ephemeral, or The Future Is Memory," *Critical Inquiry 35*, no. 1 (2008): 148–171.
14. Michel Foucault, "Of Other Spaces," trans. Jay Miskowiec, in *Diacritics 16*, no. 1 (1986): 24.
15. Wendy H. Chun, *Control and Freedom: Power and Paranoia in the Age of Fiber Optics* (Cambridge, MA: MIT Press, 2008), 54.
16. Michel Foucault, "Of Other Spaces," 26.
17. Stacey H. Jones, "(M)othering Loss: Telling Adoption Stories and Telling Performativity," *Text and Performance Quarterly* 25, no. 2 (2005): 113–135.
18. Ibid., 127.
19. Here, telling and listening online can at best be described as a shared experience of telling and retelling stories of pain and loss. Diana Taylor writes that a "shared and participatory act of telling and listening" functions as a venue for "the transmission of traumatic memory," Diana Talyor, *The Archive and Repertoire: Performing Cultural Memory in the Americas* (Durham: Duke University Press, 2004), 167.
20. Other birth mothers, such as "Ilmare", commit themselves to remembering their babies, even if it takes a toll on her own sanity. ("Ilmare", "*Aka Onŭlto Haengpokhani* [My baby, Are you Happy today?]," *A Sad Love Story of Mothers* (Internet café), posted on August 25th, 2003. http://cafe.daum.net/Adopteesmam).
21. Her screen name is a transliterated Korean nickname.
22. A common female name in Korea.
23. In a few exceptions, some birth mothers disclosed their names, including their phone numbers or email address.
24. She writes:
    "Dear Jaehwan, This is mother. I have to say "I am sorry" first of all. You came to me when I was immature and incapable. I didn't have any confidence in myself being able to raise you. I therefore hated, avoided, and turned back against you. I am full of regret now and maybe I am still too selfish. You deserve everyone's love and blessings. Because you were born to me, I sent you far away via adoption in a foreign country. I am feeling really guilty. How could I be pardoned with this short writing? But I dearly love you… I will wait for the day of reunion with you."

(I love you Jaewhan, "Salanghanŭn Nae Atŭl Jaewhana [Dear My Lovely Son, Jaewhan]," *A Sad Love Story of Mothers* (Internet café), May 31, 2005, http://cafe.daum.net/Adopteesmam).
25. Sara Ahmed, *The Promise of Happiness* (Durham: Duke University Press, 2010), 26.
26. Ibid., 81.
27. There is a posting wherein a birth mother expresses her disapproval of the idea of reuniting with the child:
".... What I want the most from you is not to look for me. But to be well and to thank your parents. Although they are adoptive ones they are the one who are raising you. So listen and grow up a good person. That's (your) mother's wish. Even after you grow up, much later, I don't want you to see me. Even after you know my existence, we are not supposed to meet again. It is enough for me to know that you are living, living under the same sky. That makes me really happy and satisfied. And I love you ... forever." (Sŏnhyŏngi, "*Uli Atŭl Sŏnhyŏngieke* [To My Son Sŏnhyŏng]," *A Sad Love Story of Mothers* (Internet café), December 14, 2001, http://cafe.daum. net/Adopteesmam).
28. Kŭlioelo, *A Sad Love Story of Mothers* (Internet café), October 24, 2001, http://cafe.daum.net/Adopteesmam
29. Heebom's Mom, "*Uli Aka Ch'os Saengiline* [It's Your Birthday, My Son]," *A Sad Love Story of Mothers* (Internet café), June 8, 2002, http://cafe.daum.net/Adopteesmam
30. Fashionable Ms. Lee, "*I Sesangesŏ Kachang Salanghanŭn Atŭleke* [To My Dearest Son], *A Sad Love Story of Mothers* (Internet café), November 20, 2002, http://cafe.daum.net/Adopteesmam
31. This is an adaptation of a birth mother's remark. "A mother without shame" is the literal translation, but this does not accurately convey the intent.
32. MazingGa Z, "*Uli Aka Wangchanimkke* [Dear My Baby Price]," *A Sad Love Story of Mothers* (Internet café), November 9, 2002, http://cafe.daum. net/Adopteesmam
33. Hanŭlpalaki, "*Ŏmmaŭi Sikyenŭn Hantalchŏn ˇKunalesŏ Mŏmch'- uŏsstanta* [My Watch Has Stopped on That Day]," *A Sad Love Story of Mothers* (Internet café) May 27, 2003, http://cafe.daum. net/Adopteesmam
34. The equivalent of a GED in the US, in post from 2001.11.27.

35. She writes:
    "... I haven't done much today, it is rapidly flown away. I am wondering what my dear Haemin did today. I spent today thinking of you as well. Did Haemin think of me? Probably not. I understand it because I didn't hug you nor see your face. You are now past two years old. Able to walk and probably beginning to talk, too. I, your mother, will study English and talk a lot on our reunion day. Dear Haemin, I hope you have a bright and smiling day tomorrow." ("Unseen Love", "*Haemini Annyŏng* [Hi Haemin]," *A Sad Love Story of Mothers* (Internet café) May 27, 2005, http://cafe.daum.net/Adopteesmam).
36. She writes:
    "I know I am not supposed to be this way. But it is too difficult to endure. From this time onward, I am going to write you a letter everyday. I will buy a beautiful journal book and write everyday to you. Then, I will give you my journal book to you when you come and look for me." ("Hyuni", "*Nae Ttal Hyŏnchuya* [Dear My Daughter Hyŏnchu]," *A Sad Love Story of Mothers* (Internet café) October 27, 2001, http://cafe.daum.net/Adopteesmam).
37. The following section does not include the baby photographs referred to in the text. At the time of writing this book, many birth mothers who had uploaded baby photographs were either inactive or had withdrawn from the website. I was therefore unable to get their permission to use their photographs in this work. These missing photographs attest to the ephemeral nature of the birth mothers' existence on the Internet.
38. In this online community, the photographs are posted by key, active participants, for instance, "Jaewon", "Byori", "Nickname", "Eunbi's mother", "Choi Mi Sook." Additionally, the photo room displays six baby photographs, three by an adoptive mother, and another three uploaded by foster mothers before the adoption placement.
39. Photos of two domestically adopted children, Eunchong and Eunbyol were uploaded by their adoptive mother under the screen name, "mechu."
40. This person used the screen name, "Liz". She posted two pictures titled "My eleventh son [Hyunso] and my thirteenth son [Woochul]." From her other postings, I learned that she has been working with an adoption agency, taking care of children before

their adoption placement. Hyunso appears to be less than a year old, and Woochul is a toddler, about two years old.
41. Within six months after a child's placement into an adoptive family, a photograph of the child from the adoptive parents is sent to the Korean adoption agency; it is relayed by the partner adoption agency in the receiving country.
42. Sungwon's mother, "*Salanghan ŭn Uli Sungwoni*" [My Lovely Sungwoni], *A Sad Love Story of Mothers* (Internet café), May 5, 2005, http://cafe.daum.net/Adopteesmam.
43. Sad Mother, "Nae Simchang ipnita" [This is My Heart], *A Sad Love Story of Mothers* (Internet café), June 7, 2005, http://café.daum.net/adopteesmam.
44. Hanŭlpalaki, "*Uli Hanŭli P'on Sachintŭl* [My hannŭl's cellphone pictures]," *A Sad Love Story of Mothers* (Internet café), June 11, 2003, http://cafe.daum.net/Adopteesmam
45. At other times, the photographs of children induce a birth mother's posting similar to the following:
"Hi, How are you? I missed my Jaemin so much that I am posting here. I was not going to write anything here but the photos of babies reminded me of Jaemin a lot. Is Jaemin doing all right? I am worried about his health and well-being the most. I wonder if he eats and is doing well. I miss him so much. I believe that his adoptive parents take good care of him, much better than I would. Right? Are you going to raise Jaemin really well? Whenever I think of Jaemin, my eyes are beaded with tears unbeknownst me. [So] I drink a lot. I would get happy once I forget [of him]. But it is not as easy as I thought. I will try hard to forget. Well... I say bye. Please raise well." ("Misuni", *A Sad Love Story of Mothers* [Internet café], October 29, 2001, http://café.daum.net/adopteesmam).
46. Hyuni, "*Hyŏnchuya* [Dear Hyŏnchu]," *A Sad Love Story of Mothers* (Internet café), April 16, 2002, http://cafe.daum.net/Adopteesmam
47. Byori, "*Pankapta* [Greetings]," *A Sad Love Story of Mothers* (Internet café), October 10, 2001, http://cafe.daum.net/Adopteesmam
48. Minee mom, *A Sad Love Story of Mothers* (Internet café), August 31, 2001, http://cafe.daum.net/Adopteesmam
49. Mazinga Z uploaded 10 photographs with a baby taken at an online café. Of those photographs, a child was held by a young woman whom I suspect could be a birth mother. The other

exception is a photo of a white man holding Eunbi during her baptism.
50. Roland Barthes, *Camera Lucida* (New York: Hill & Wang Publisher, 1980); Susan Sontag, *On Photography* (New York: Farrar, Strauss & Giroux, 1977)
51. Barthes, *Camera Lucida*, 80–81.
52. Marianne Hirsch, *Family Frames: Photography, Narrative, and Postmemory* (Cambridge, MA: Harvard University Press, 1997), 9.
53. Jaewon, May 13, 2005, comment on December 9th, "Pomul [My Treasure]," *A Sad Love Story of Mothers* (Internet café), May 13, 2005, http://cafe.daum.net/Adopteesmam
54. Ilmare, June 20, 2005, comment on I Love Jaehwan, "*Uli Jaehwani* [My Jaehwan]," *A Sad Love Story of Mothers* (Internet café), June 16, 2005, http://cafe.daum.net/Adopteesmam
55. 65 % of all postings between 2001 and 2005 were kept in this section.
56. The 100th day is called *Paekil*, the first social event centered around the child. The parents hold a party for family members and friends on the child's 100th day to celebrate the child's birth and to wish his or her well-being and happiness.
57. With the Sad Heart, "*Pimil Ch'inkulŭl Ŏtŭn Kipunieyo*, [I am feeling as if I found a good friend here]," *A Sad Love Story of Mothers* (Internet café), June 26, 2004, http://cafe.daum.net/Adopteesmam
58. I am sorry, "*Nae Kasŭm Kip'ŭn Kose Mutŏtun Iyaki* [A Story Deeply Buried in My Heart]," *A Sad Love Story of Mothers* (Internet café), February 20, 2002, http://cafe.daum.net/Adopteesmam
59. It is noteworthy that birth mothers perceive 'unfair practices' underlying sexual norms in Korean society. A vast majority of birth mothers became pregnant while in a relationship. Often the relationship with the baby's father was derailed by the unplanned pregnancy, with its resulting anxieties, fears, and anticipated responsibilities. Thus, women were forced to bear sole responsibility for the child. Until 2014, fathers were not even expected to provide child support, thereby enforcing the lack of any custodial responsibility. But what infuriated birth mothers more than the lack of support was the father's contempt and accusations of supposed sexual impropriety. The Internet forum occasionally carried birth mothers' responses and sharp words directed against birth fathers. Hamin's

father said to the birth mother, "It is not my child. Just terminate the pregnancy" (Dear love, *A Sad Love Story of Mothers* (Internet café), April 12, 2002, http://cafe.daum.net/Adopteesmam). The birth mother wrote on the site: "...[Y]our father did not like the fact that I carried you even once and blamed me for you. He said that I have all responsibility for you. He did not show any sign of conscience..." (Ibid.). The birth mothers' anger against the baby's father aligned with their own similar experiences with men. However, their anger was often meted out with a motherly compassion. Many said, for example, "If I think about myself, I hated him so badly, but he is still the father of my baby. For that reason, I hope for his well-being."

60. Here, "Nickname" expresses her anger against the counselors at a maternity home facility who imparted adoption information rather than information about public subsidies or shelters for single mothers and their children, despite her clear interest in raising her child (Nickname, "Ihaelŭl Mo Hakessŏyo? [Don't You Understand?]," *A Sad Love Story of Mothers* (Internet café), August 30, 2001, http://cafe.daum.net/Adopteesmam).

61. Jaewon, the webmaster, writes:
"I get really mad when a birth mother misses her baby so much to the point where the heart is bruised. On what earth is each adoption agency and each adoption case worker different. Aren't they all looking for a family for a child? We hear all different sorts of stories upon adoption placement. Who wants to send their children away? If we say that we can raise our baby ourselves, the social worker at the agency defies us. 'How can you take care of a baby without a husband? You don't even have any money. So you should send your child to an affluent and economically stable family. You're young. And later, your baby will resent you. As they enter into adolescence, they will get into trouble. Then, who would like to keep insisting on raising their own children?' ... Another thing that I don't understand is that once a baby is under the adoption agency's custody, they stop us from seeing the baby. Because we signed the relinquishment paper and agreed to adoption. But ... signing the paperwork does not take even five minutes. Single mothers follow an adoption agency worker's instruction. ... How can anyone demand to make such a decision in a few minutes? It seems a business transaction. ... what I want from adoption

agencies [is] the agency should offer better and conscientious consultations with birth mothers." (Jaewon, "*Ipyangkikwane Palanta* [What I want From Adoption Agencies]," *A Sad Love Story of Mothers* (Internet café), November 3, 2001, http://cafe.daum.net/Adopteesmam.

62. Jeonghwan's mom contacted an adoption agency requesting a photo after the adoption placement, and received this email instead. It reads, "Dear Osun, in order for Jeongwhan to grow up in a safe and secure environment, we cannot give the baby's picture that you want. We believe that Jeongwhan will grow well only if you live a healthy life" (Jeonghwan mom, *A Sad Love Story of Mothers* (Internet café), http://cafe.daum.net/Adopteesmam). Fashionable Mrs. Lee posted, "I called the Holt adoption agency yesterday and heard that they had too many children placed overseas and had a hard time finding information on my baby. I was told to leave my contact information and to call back in fall" (Fashionable Mrs. Lee, *A Sad Love Story of Mothers* (Internet café), Feb 22, 2003, http://cafe.daum.net/Adopteesmam).

63. Nickname, "*Seung Kyunŭill Poŏychuchi Anhnŭn KikwanŏSnsaengnim Poseyo* [To the Case Worker Who Doesn't Allow Seung Gyun's Mom's Visit to Her Son]," July 24, 2002, in response to Yoo Seung Gyun, "*Seung Gyunilŭl Ch'ŏŭm Mannanŭn Nal* [It's My First Day to See Seung Gyun]," *A Sad Love Story of Mothers* (Internet café), July 23, 2002, http://cafe.daum.net/Adopteesmam.

64. Floss, "*Haeoe Ipyanga Esŭk'ot'ŭ Huki* [Reflection on My Experience Escorting the Babies for Transnational Adoption]," *A Sad Love Story of Mothers* (Internet café), May 18, 2005, http://cafe.daum.net/Adopteesmam.

65. The foster care system was introduced by Holt Adoption Placement in1965. Eligible foster mothers must be between the ages of 25 to 60; have a child who is older than 7 years; and, have experience with childrearing. In return for their service, foster mothers receive an allowance from the adoption agency. Since 1969, Holt Adoption Agency has given an award for foster mothers who have worked as foster mothers for more than five years. In the mid-2000s, Holt International worked with 530 families in Korea. As of 2014, the number of awardees was 2000. (Yoon, Soo Hui, "*holt'ŭ adong*

pokchihoe, holt'ŭ myŏngyet'oeim, changgigŭnsok wit'angmo suyŏsik" [Honoring Retiring Foster Mothers], *News1*, 2014.12.05).
66. Liz, "*Soy ŏ ngika Mikuk ŭ lo Kako Chunika*... [Soyŏng Has Gone to America and Now Chun Came to Me]," *A Sad Love Story of Mothers* (Internet café), January 9, 2003, http://cafe.daum.net/Adopteesmam
67. All of them are domestic adoptive parents. They show interest in finding and communicating with the child's birth mother and expressed empathy for the birth mothers' losses. Of these adoptive parents, the active screen names include Kŏngchu (2003, 05. 22.), Mechu; Tangsinmanŭl, (2001, 09. 21.), Kim pan suk. Soon after the website was launched, a fully pregnant woman with the screen name yepiŏmma (Expectant Mother) was in dire need of help to cover medical expenses, and received a considerable amount of emotional and financial support from the community, including even residential support from an adoptive family.
68. Choi Min Joo, "*Yangpumonimkkesŏ Ponaeon P'yŏnchi* [A Letter From the Adoptive Parents]," *A Sad Love Story of Mothers* (Internet café), March 11, 2002, http://cafe.daum.net/Adopteesmam.
69. Real Pooh, *A Sad Love Story of Mothers* (Internet café), July 16, 2002, http://cafe.daum.net/Adopteesmam.
70. Byori, "*Byori Yangpumonimkke Ponael P'yŏnchiyeyo. Ŏttaeyo?* [Here is my letter to Byori's adoptive parents. How is it?]," *A Sad Love Story of Mothers* (Internet café), February 18, 2002, http://cafe.daum.net/Adopteesmam.

CHAPTER 6

"I Am a Mother, but Not a Mother": The Paradox of Virtual Mothering

After I discovered an internet café for birth mothers in June 2005, I wrote a post, asking for participants willing to be interviewed. Only one person came forward. The volunteer was Min Yeh Jin, then a 25-year-old birth mother and an active blogger at the internet café. Before heading to our interview, I prepared by reading her postings. We met in person at her two-bedroom, half-basement apartment in Bucheon, Gyeonggi Province, on August 2, 2005. She was living alone with her two dogs. I realized that I had brought my own expectations to this meeting when I met her, and saw that she was different from what I had expected. She seemed to be an ordinary woman in her twenties, like I might see in my own neighborhood. We talked for three or four hours, during which time we ate, listened, cried, laughed and interpreted the letter she received from her daughter's adoptive parents. Finally, it was time to go. It was raining outside and she insisted that I take her umbrella, even though both of us knew that I might not ever be able to return it. Five years passed, during which time I officially began collecting birth mother oral histories. I tried to contact her several times via various means and was not able to reach her.

After meeting with Min Yeh Jin, I met four additional birth mothers in 2005. Each time, I came away with the impression, similar to my first meeting with Min Yeh Jin, that birth mothers were neighbors and fellow citizens, close to us. Despite this sense of proximity and perhaps because of the intensity of emotions provoked from the interviews, it was five years before I finally returned to South Korea to collect more oral histories.

© The Editor(s) (if applicable) and The Author(s) 2016
H. Kim, *Birth Mothers and Transnational Adoption Practice in South Korea*, DOI 10.1057/978-1-137-53852-9_6

When I returned, it was with the desire to search for and realize the "radical potential" of oral history "to document lost histories and histories of loss."[1] Based on my collection of the birthmothers' oral histories, this final chapter examines another ephemeral and performative site of virtual mothering.

This oral history collection emerged slowly, and was finally consolidated into a site of virtual mothering in my research. I had long felt hesitant about collecting and using the oral histories for analytical purposes, despite their potential to shed new light on the marginalized, and to build a foundation for subjugated knowledge. Not only was the nature of oral history collection invasive, there was also an underlying power asymmetry between the researcher and participant, given that the researcher's positivist's approach and manipulative power over the materials can resemble a frontier-like mentality of discovery, as is so often embedded in the knowledge production process. However, despite my ambivalence, I finally decided to engage with the birth mothers' oral histories because of their affective resonance and the potentiality of these encounters. Accordingly, I decided to follow the traces of affects, as well as to produce the affective delivery of virtual mothering, as a part of my affect-driven approach.

Against the largely hidden—or abstract—understanding of the social death of birth mothers, the birth mothers' oral history collection embodies a counterpublic history of the transnational adoption practice that, first and foremost, acknowledges the birth mothers' living existence and their lived experiences, in and of themselves. The oral history collection of birth mothers is a site at which they enact and produce a memory of separation from the child, and a memory of reconnection with the child for others—not for their children or for themselves, but for the immediate, yet distant audience, calling for a recognition of their stories and experiences. Their accounts of losses, saturated with intense emotions, and often incoherent and complex memories of the adoption experience, from separation to reunion, demand us to witness layers of institutional and interpersonal violence structuring their lives, and to recognize their losses in discursive, as well as visceral, ways.

My oral history collection took place in 2005 and during 2010–12; these were critical years for adoptee activism, during which adoptee issues gained public recognition, and led to significant political, cultural, and legal changes in South Korea.[2] One of the key demands by transnational adoptee activists and organizations was for Korean adoptees to be given dual citizenship, and recognized as part of the community of overseas

Koreans.³ The activists also challenged the widespread belief that transnational adoption was the best option for needy children, and advocated the rights of single mothers to raise their children. In 2007, 30 Korean-born transnational adoptees and ten middle-aged Korean birth mothers gathered to pass out leaflets and to ask pedestrians to sign a petition calling for the end of transnational adoption in South Korea.⁴ The event, one of the first collaborative actions carried out by adoptees and birth mothers, fostered a sense of political solidarity between the two groups. It also led to the establishment of the first birth-family organization, *Mindullae* (Dandelion), which was composed of 30 to 50 birth family members, a vast majority of whom were birth mothers.⁵ Members of *Mindullae* volunteer at shelters where young, single mothers temporarily care for their newborn babies, and, since 2010, have participated in advocacy work to defend single motherhood.

Collecting oral history interviews with birth mothers involved a significant community effort. To recruit potential participants, I contacted various organizations working on adoptee and birth-mother issues: G.O.A.'L, TRACK, KoRoot,⁶ and *Mindullae*. Three birth mothers from the Internet café agreed to share their stories. I also contacted two social service organizations for former US camptown sex workers, *Durebang* and *Haessal Sahoepokchihoe* (Sunlit Sisters' Center). Relying on these organizations' working or personal relationships with individual birth mothers, along with help from members of *Mindullae*, I collected 21 oral histories from birth mothers, whose ages ranged from 21 to 70 at the time of our meeting. They represented all strata of birth mothers, including mothers with mixed-race children; poor, working-class, married mothers; and single mothers.

I treat the birth mothers' oral history performances as testimonies of ordinary and normalized injury, or, as Ann Cvetkovich aptly characterized, as "insidious or everyday forms of trauma that are all too often persistent and normalized."⁷ I seek to challenge the erasure and invisibility of birth mothers, and to examine the mechanisms and conditions of those losses that have been erased and covered over in the adoption discourse; and to consider their effects on the birth mothers' lives. Challenging the dominant indifference to birth mothers' lives, this chapter identifies their reflections as a performance of virtual mothering, and commits to rendering them as "affectively rich and discursively paradoxical."⁸ Thus, I aim to offer a memorial site where birth mothers can finally enact their losses and affect others to bring affective recognition for the birth mothers' experiences of losses and their lost lives.

This chapter engages the site of oral history collections in two lights—one, as a critical site of knowledge production, and the other, as a performative site of virtual mothering. Analyzing oral history as a site of knowledge production, as well as of virtual mothering, this chapter attends to the ways in which the platform and technology of oral history transform birth mothers into virtual mothers, and focuses on the birth mothers' "lived paradox" as a prime modality of virtual mothering. My analysis frames three important dimensions of the birth mothers' lives as a "lived paradox," and engages with the losses experienced through adoption, from their involvement in the adoption placement process to their ensuing life experiences to, finally, a reunion with the adopted child. In so doing, I scrutinize the institutionalized neglect and interpersonal violence that perforates many birth mothers' experiences, both during the adoption placement process and in its aftermath.

6.1 Oral History: The Site of Knowledge Production and a Site of Virtual Mothering

These oral histories document the lost history of birth mothers' lived experiences, as well as their experiences of traumatic loss. Loss, as David Eng and David Kazanjian write, is "inseparable from what remains, for what is lost is known only by what remains of it, by how these remains are produced, read and sustained."[9] Eng and Kazanjian poignantly observe that remainders of loss are not constant or fixed, but rather, constantly reordered, revalued, and resignified. By applying this rendition of loss to birth mothers, I cast them as dynamic and variable remainders of loss. I also imagine birth mothers as individuals not just bearing traumatic losses to be engaged, but as having the potential to reproduce, reread, and recreate their own memories of losses. Through this framework, the birth mothers' participation in oral history convenes a site through which they can engage with their losses as creative and crucial lacunae, from which to enter and enact "new interpretations of their persistent and volatile remains."[10] In that sense, this oral history collection sets a new platform via which birth mothers can interrupt their old ways of thinking or not thinking, feeling or not feeling, their losses.

The birth mothers' oral history collection takes place in a format of performance, thus creating a site of performance. Della Pollock, a performance studies scholar, elaborates on the intersection of oral history and performance that establishes a new ground for a counter-narrative, or one might say, a subjugated knowledge through acts of performance. She writes:

> ... performance as promise and practice is at the heart of oral history. ... as oral history is a process of *making history in dialogue*, it is performative. It is co-creative, co-embodied, and specifically framed, contextually and intersubjectively contingent, sensuous, vital, artful in its achievement of narrative form, meaning, and ethics, and insistent on *doing through saying*: on investing the present and future with the past, remaking history with previously excluded subjectivities, and challenging the conventional frameworks of historical knowledge with other ways of knowing. [11]

Pollock's bold, detailed insights into the processes of a performative oral history, and her powerful political conviction for a critical, subjugated knowledge enacted at the intersection of performance and oral history, have oriented my research design, data collection, and analysis. I consider the birth mothers' oral history both as a site of knowledge production and as performances, thus recognizing the birth mothers' lives and experiences.

Theater historian Suk-Young Kim describes interviews as a site of knowledge-producing performance.[12] Staging interviews with such an awareness, Kim identifies interviewees as "living archives," who are capable of producing knowledge.[13] In the book *Archive and Repertoire*, Diana Taylor elaborates on how interview settings act as "the [original] moment of archival creation, knowledge arises out of human bodies and interactions as embodied experience."[14] Following both Kim's and Taylor's insights on embodied knowledge production, I frame my oral history collection as a site of "knowledge-producing performance" in which I engage birth mothers as a living archive with the potential to produce knowledge, and their oral histories as dynamically, spontaneously produced knowledge about losses. At the same time, the knowledge gleaned from each oral history site extends beyond utterances, and includes gestures, body language, variations in a voice's tone and pitch, changing facial expressions, and mood changes.

My oral history collection emphasizes a collaborative enactment of reliving, and releasing the stories from the past and from bodies. It strives to be a spontaneous and performative engagement with the present. Thus, I construct the site of oral history collection as a stage onto which birth mothers can enact the unarticulated and unresolved feelings and affects—at times, traumatic—associated with their lives, thereby allowing them to re-engage with and re-interpret their memories of those moments. Such acts of releasing feelings or words I observe as enactments of virtual mothering. I position myself alongside the narrator, co-performing and co-witnessing heart-wrenching moments of losses fraught with powerlessness, anguish, and deep sadness, and let myself be vulnerable and affected by the losses, too. In so doing, I see the collection of oral history, in and of itself, as a performative site of virtual mothering where the losses of birth mothers are recognized, felt, and registered by the audience, often only by me; in turn, I co-perform for, at, the site of knowledge production.

In the oral histories, virtual mothering is most palpable around losses experienced at three pivotal stages: (1) the adoption decision; (2) her life after the adoption; and, (3) reunion with the child. These narratives embody a particular aspect of the virtual, or "a lived paradox." According to Brian Massumi, a lived paradox is where "what are normally opposite coexist, coalesce, and connect; where what cannot be experienced but be felt."[15] By employing the lived paradox as an explorative lens, my analysis dwells on affectively rich moments of the oral history, and identifies a pattern of incoherent and incompatible thoughts and feelings over various losses, and commits to present such paradoxes in the liveliest format of affective delivery, thereby facilitating other ways of knowing and recognizing their experiences.

My analysis of the oral history collection offers recognition for the lives of birth mothers and their experiences of loss. In that sense, these oral histories are not complete, existing as an a collection of interviews, or as transcripts, or even as part of a final analysis. Rather, oral history is promised and practiced as a site of emergent knowledge, and a site of virtual mothering. Virtual mothering emerges "over there" through the medium of oral history. And, it is not fully actualized unless it is recognized "over here." Thus, the birth mothers' oral history does not fully realize its promise without a collaborative effort to produce a counterpublic history.

6.2   I Abandoned My baby, but I Really Didn't; I Didn't Abandon My Baby, but I Might as Well Have

"*How did you decide on adoption?*" The birth mothers' involvement in the adoption process first manifests through their affects. Often there is a long silence and a bowed head. Then, tears well up, faces redden, voices rise.

Reviewing the responses to this question, there is no single factor, no one single event, that leads to adoption. Rather, the birth mothers' accounts of their adoption are filled with meandering efforts to remember what appears to be a series of violent life events. After reviewing the transcripts and listening to the birth mothers' voices, over and over, I repeated, myself, "*I abandoned my baby but I really didn't; I didn't abandon my baby but I might as well have.*" This incongruent set of statements, repeating throughout the oral histories, manifests the birth mothers' perspective on how they became birth mothers. What follows illustrates key aspects about the birth mothers' accounts of their adoption circumstances.

Exclusion from the Decision-Making Process

"My life turned like this as I followed friends to Ansan in the middle of night...," said Park Hye Sook, 43, as she began telling me her life story. We were in her two-bedroom apartment in Ansan, a heavily working-class city located southwest of Seoul.[16] She was only 17 when she first met the baby's father, who was ten years older. The unexpected first pregnancy led her to start living with him at his father's residence. Not too long after the first child, she had another. For the second child's delivery, she went back to her parents' house in Gwangju, Gyeonggi Province. She delivered a boy, pleasing her father who had only daughters, even though he did not approve of her relationship or the decision to cohabitate with the baby's father. She was waiting for her husband to take her and her newborn baby back to his father's residence; her father-in-law had recently gotten married, and he had a new wife. Days passed, then turned into weeks. Weeks became months.

When the baby was nearly three months old, her husband finally sat down with her to talk about the future and the baby. She told me:

> I asked the baby's father, "What should we do?" He had nothing to say. His stepmother still did not want us back home. He said, "I saw an advertisement–an advertisement from Holt". I asked, "Then are we going to abandon this baby?" No answer. We had no place to go. ... He led me to Seongnam,[17] and I thought we were returning to his family home. I didn't believe that any father could give up his child. So I didn't believe that he would leave the baby there. ... We entered the adoption agency in Seongnam and ... a lady came to take the baby from me. I didn't know what had happened.[18] (Park Hye Sook, her infant child adopted in 1985)

As her husband was counseled on adoption, Park Hye Sook waited with her newborn in the lobby. She was not asked to sign any documents, nor did she receive any information about the adoption from the agency. She merely accompanied her husband to the facility, where he made the decision to give up the baby, without ever involving her. Giving in to the patriarchal authority governing her child, Park Hye Sook implicitly agreed to the baby's father's decision, and became a birth mother in 1985. She was only 20.

That same year, an hour's drive away from Seongnam, Kim Sung Hee, then 26, was a newlywed, middle-class woman, expecting her first child. As soon as I sat down for the interview in her expansive apartment, Sung Hee, in her high-pitched tone, immediately told me, "Unlike unmarried mothers, … everything was normal—after marriage, pregnancy."[19] In January 2011, when I met her for the interview, she had just returned from her second visit to Kansas City, Missouri, where her adopted children lived. She said:

> It was my first pregnancy. One day, I saw bloodletting and immediately went to an emergency unit at a local OBGYN in Bucheon. My babies were born prematurely. Yeah, they were twins. Up until then, I didn't know that I had twins in my belly. It was shocking. What was more devastating was that the babies were born with some complications and would be likely to die or grow up with serious physical impairments. While my newborn twins were in ICU, my husband asked me to sign adoption papers. I was extremely upset, ran outside, and refused to sign the papers, but he insisted. I reluctantly signed the papers. … The decision had been made by my husband and his older brother, my brother-in-law.[20](Kim Sung Hee, separated from twin daughters in 1985)

While cooking lunch for me during the interview, Kim Sung Hee insisted, "I do not blame anyone for the adoption. … It is a shame … and it is done." Then, she murmured that if the twins had been boys, or her brother-in-law's own daughters, they would not have been sent away. Although she said she did not blame anyone, it was clear that she felt that she had been forced to agree to a decision already made by her husband and his brother. She speculated that her brother-in-law, as the oldest son in the family,[21] might have felt compelled to eradicate any seeds of family misfortune that newborn twins' with disabilities might bring.

A few years earlier, in 1982, another set of twin daughters born to Cho Bok Soon, then 31, was relinquished in Cheonan. She is now 60, making a living as a mudang and living with her two daughters in Cheongju.[22] She tells of the circumstances surrounding the adoption decision:

> My husband was a Buddhist monk, the kind of monk who marries a woman and raises a family. With him I had three daughters. Our financial situation was hard when the twins arrived. I carried them upside down for nine months and gave birth to them at the hospital. Everyone said that I would be dead. It was a difficult delivery and I was unconscious for the next few days. When I finally regained consciousness, I learned that my twins had been sent away. It turns out that my husband had consulted with the senior monk at his temple, and had decided to place the newborn twins into adoption because he couldn't help raise them. When I woke up, there were no babies.[23] (Cho Bok Soon, separated from her children in 1982)

Cho Bok Soon never got to see her children's faces until she was finally reunited with them in 2005 via a television show, a variation of the program that I discuss in Chapter 4. During our interview, she kept reassuring me that she understood her husband's difficult decision and said that she did not blame him at all, that it was all due to material conditions. Yet, she also told me that, after she recovered from her delivery, she started searching for the twins. By word of mouth, she finally met an adoption agency worker at the Daejeon branch of Holt International Children's Services, who was familiar with her case. He assured her the twins had gone to a good family; they had been sent to France when they were just 100 days old. Almost 30 years had passed since then, but she still remembers the adoption agency worker's name, Lee Keun Ho.[24]

Meanwhile, Jang Yeon Ja, the most active member of *Mindullae*, never was able to meet her adoption agency worker. She lost her child to adoption after she left her baby at home to go look for work. Prior to leaving, she had been struggling with her husband's addictions, and had finally decided to leave him; she wanted to find work to make a living. Her child's adoption took place without her involvement. She told me:

> Some time passed, maybe about a month passed. But not that long. I heard the baby was gone. [It turns out that] while I was looking for work, the baby's father took the baby back to my mother's. My mother refused to take the baby in, telling him, "That's your seed." Later, I learned his brother and my cousin agreed to give my baby up for adoption at the OBGYN, in Seoul. My mother also accompanied them to the adoption.[25] (Jang Yeon Ja, separated from her child in 1976)

No one in her family would tell her where her baby boy had been sent. She went to Seoul to look for the OBGYN, only to find the clinic closed. She seemed to have a lot of animosity toward those who had orchestrated the adoption, but was unable to express it explicitly because they were family members. She speculated that her mother also must have suffered. After learning of the baby's adoption, she tried to return to her regular routines, but found that she couldn't. She said, "From then on, my life was wrecked, and became aimless."[26] It took 28 years for her to find out where her son was sent, and to see him again.

In the very same year, 1976, Park Mi Hee's first husband filed for divorce and took custody of their child. She was devastated, but consoled herself with the thought that her ex-husband would take good care of her daughter. Years later, she learned that her daughter had been sent to France for adoption; she has been looking for her ever since. As of this writing, Park Mi Hee has not yet found her daughter. She said:

> One day, I ran into that person [ex-husband's relative] at the market. She cried, telling me the adoption story. ... Later I learned that [my ex-husband] tried to return the baby to my mother, saying that he couldn't take care of it. By that time, I had already remarried. So my mother told him, "You should take care of your daughter. My daughter is living well." He said, "If you can't take her in, I am going to give her up for adoption." She never told me ... I guess my mother was thinking about me and my life, and that is why she didn't tell me. ... But, once in a while, I get upset at my mother, who could have taken my daughter in. If I had known [what he would do], I would have worked hard to raise her together with my family [instead].[27]
> (Park Mi Hee, separated from her child in 1976)

In the cases of Jang Yeon Ja and Park Mi Hee, parental obstruction facilitated the adoption; their own mothers refused to take care of their grandchildren. Both women interpreted their mothers' refusal to take in their grandchildren as being rooted in motherly concern for their daughters' well-being. To circumvent a presumably difficult life as a single mother, many birth mothers' family members, especially their own mothers, insist that the primary parental duty lies with the baby's father.

In the younger, post-1990s' cohort of birth mothers, it is more common for parental obstruction to be the primary background or facilitator for the adoption decision. The young birth mothers with whom I spoke experienced levels of coercion and pressure, regarding the decision to relinquish their babies, that were more forceful than what the older birth mothers had experienced. This difference can be attributed to the birth mother's status as a minor and the social stigma of single motherhood. Parents, hoping to secure their daughter's future, often made decisions on behalf of these young birth mothers; and, without financial independence, the birth mothers usually had to acquiesce.

Kim Joo Hee, a divorcée, raising two young children in Busan, whom I met on August 6, 2010, shared such a story.[28] She was 18 when she surrendered her first child to adoption in 2001. Her boyfriend, a college freshman, was three years older. She did not realize that she was pregnant until the day of delivery. That day she had a stomach ache—her mother seemed to suspect something and took her to a local birth assistance center. There, she learned of her pregnancy for the first time, and was transferred to Hyŏntae Hospital to give birth.

> The next morning after delivery, an adoption agency social worker, Hwang Jaepil from Holt, came and asked for my fingerprint for the adoption paperwork. The next morning. I didn't know what it [adoption] was. I told him that I would take the paperwork and think about it first. He told me that I was a minor and that my mother had already agreed to give away my child, so I had to sign the paper. So I did.[29] (Kim Joo Hee, separated from her child in 2001)

Kim Joo Hee did not know what adoption was. No one had explained it to her. Her mother was so upset at her that she did not pick up her when she was discharged from the hospital. Instead, a taxi driver, whom her mother hired, came, paid the medical bills, and took her home. On the way back home from the hospital, she asked the taxi driver, "*What is adoption?*"

Not all birth mothers were as blindly involved in adoption. Yet, for those who did plan for adoption, the decision was often seen as the only alternative to death. Jung Yoon Sook, years before she decided on adoption for her three children (in 1982, 1985, and 1986), tried to commit suicide; she also tried to kill her first son due to the hardship, poverty, battery, and neglect she endured. Well before she became a birth mother, Park Ae Kyung took 70 pills in a motel room, after fleeing from her violent husband. She saw running away from her husband and leaving her home as her only way to survive. During her third pregnancy, she fled again and ended up at a maternity home.[30] This third child was eventually put up for adoption. Park Ae Kyung recounted:

> … Initially, I didn't choose adoption. What I really wanted was not adoption, but, instead, dying together with my baby. Life, for me, was very dif-

ficult. I anticipated a harsh life for my expected child. So I would rather we die together.[31] (Park Ae Kyung, separated from her infant child in 1993)

As a victim of domestic violence, she considered the overwhelmingly difficult life to which she would go back to after giving birth, and she wanted to die with her baby to save them from such torment. Echoing Park Ae Kyung's sense of entrapment, hopelessness, and desire for death, Shin Young Eun, made her adoption decision when she was also near to death and dying.

> One day I went to an inn with my children because we didn't have a place to go. I had been laid off from my job because of my husband. I wanted to die with my kids there. As I was choking my boys, I realized that I should give them an opportunity for life, a life different from mine. So I decided on adoption for them. There was no other choice for me, either we died together, or I sent them away.[32] (Shin Young Eun, two boys adopted in 1987)

The birth mothers' accounts of wishing to die and of being near death before making the decision to place their child into adoption reveal the hopelessness and powerlessness that flooded their lives, and indicate the devastating conditions that led these women to contemplate adoption. In Shin Young Eun's case, adoption and death lay, side by side, as the only possible options, for she had planned to take her own life once the adoption was completed.

The birth mothers' performative narratives of adoption placement detailed above reveal how few birth mothers are able to assert that they made the decision to give up their child. Rather, the adoption decision was initiated, negotiated, and administered, if not coerced, by husbands, relatives, parents, and/or adoption agencies. These accounts illustrate how the decision was made under desperate life circumstances, on the brink of death, and to the point at which many could no longer foresee a life, either with, or without, their children. These birth mothers' enactments suggest what Rickie Solinger might refer to as the choiceless background of the birth mothers' adoption decision in which the term *choice* is irrelevant.[33] The birth mothers' choiceless involvement in adoption, combined with a normative motherhood produces a paradoxical point of view on adoption: *I abandoned my baby, but I really didn't; I didn't abandon my baby, but I might as well have.* Birth mothers experience a sense of alienation from not only the decision-making process, but also the decision itself.

As discussed in Chapter 3, Jodi Kim identifies natal alienation as a structural condition under which a birth mother, due to her marginalized state, may have the right to bear and give birth to a child, but not necessarily the right to parent that child.[34] By juxtaposing these accounts with the concept of natal alienation, I interpret natal alienation not just as a discrete point at which a birth mother's parental rights over a child is relinquished, but rather as a process that is carefully and continuously managed by adoption agencies. To elaborate this point, I take into consideration the following three aspects; (1) the birth mothers' lack of involvement in the adoption decision-process; (2) the almost nonexistent consultations with the birth mothers; and (3) the hostile institutional policies and attitudes toward the birth mothers. Rendering the birth mothers' natal alienation into a technology of exclusion enables us to scrutinize how this common practice provides little to no access to adoption counseling for birth mothers, and how the adoption information it dispenses serves as an institutional mechanism of social death.[35]

Natal Alienation After Adoption

The birth mothers' sense of alienation escalates when they find themselves excluded from all aspects of the adoption process. During the 1970s and the 1980s, adoption counseling for birth mothers was virtually nonexistent. The majority of the birth mothers I interviewed, apart from the three who had planned their adoption over the course of several months, did not know the time or place of their children's departure from Korea, their final destination, or any details about the adoption process (e.g., the immediate foster care provided to the baby, or the selection process for prospective adoptive parents). Almost half of the birth mothers in my oral history collection never even met anyone from the adoption agency, much less received any meaningful information. Meanwhile birth mothers who decided to choose adoption made the decision during the first visit, after just one counseling session. The rest of the birth mothers did not even go to an adoption agency—rather, their adoptions took place at the site of delivery (i.e., hospitals and birthing assistance clinics). In my oral history collection, as illustrated in Chapter 2, only mothers of mixed-race children were aggressively approached with multiple visits from adoption agencies. This deficit of information was a key point voiced by the majority of these birth mothers. This deficit, in addition to the widespread belief that adoption assures a better life for the child, can be interpreted as the procedural background against which the powerful and empty idea of "a better life" is promulgated.

The oral history performances illuminate the misinformation the birth mothers are given about the adoption. Lee Soon Young, who gave away her child at a maternity home in 1983, visited the agency three months after the delivery and was told that the child had already been sent to the US. Later, she found out the child had been in foster care at the time of her visit, and then sent—*after her visit*—to France. In 2000, Kim Joo Hee, then 18, tried to retrieve her baby a day after the adoption paperwork had been completed; she was told that adoptive parents had already been appointed for her child. During our interview, Kim Joo Hee asked me, "Is that possible?"

The oral histories also unveiled the uncooperative, indifferent, and, at times, hostile responses from the adoption agencies, as they told about their experiences of searching for information about their children. Park Mi Hee, whose child was placed for adoption by her ex-husband in 1979, sought information from the adoption agency. She was told that her daughter had been sent to France and that the only thing that she could do was to just wait for her daughter to contact her. In 1982, Soo Yeon, a widow, agreed to give up her child at the birthing center out of fear of being beaten by her father, and finally contacted the adoption agency for information in 2008.[36] Since no one was managing her case, every time she called, she had to repeat her story. During one of the calls, a staff member accused her of having worked at a bar and of delivering the baby at a love motel.[37]

Kim Sung Hee, who learned of her twin daughters' survival and adoption 18 years after having given birth to them, also was ridiculed while actively searching for information about her children. She echoed an agency worker who told her, "You are the one who abandoned your children; why are you looking for them *now?*" Another birth mother, Kim Sun Ae who decided to separate from her child to remarry in 1975, told me of an agency worker who matter-of-factly stated, "An adoption agency is a place for a child to find a home, not a place through which birth mothers get their children back."[38] With these accounts, I do not mean to imply that all adoption agency workers treat birth mothers without respect. Nevertheless, these testimonies of neglect should not simply be interpreted as reflecting the actions of a few unhelpful, isolated, and individual staff workers, but, rather, as reflecting the agencies' official and market priorities. Reflecting the power asymmetry of the adoption triad (i.e., adoptive parents, adopted child, and birth parents), the focus of the adoption agencies' post-adoption services typically prioritizes the needs of the adoptive parents and the adopted children, rather than those of the birth mothers and/or birth families.

What could be the structural motivations behind this foreclosure of information about their child? One way to analyze this lack of access to information is in terms of adoption-market rationality. Adoption, despite its well-publicized humanitarian motivations, is in reality a demand-driven economy that primarily serves prospective adoptive parents, who are its main consumers. The success of the adoption market depends upon the extent to which agencies can cater to the delicate needs and desires of prospective adoptive parents.

Recent studies on adoptive parents and adoptive parents-to-be by Kristi Brian and Christine W. Gailey indicate that one of the most appealing aspects of international adoption is the complete severance of the child from his or her birth family.[39] By restricting the birth mothers' access to information about the adoption, the agencies ensure a complete closure of the child's past, appeasing the adoptive parents' ambivalence and anxiety about their kinship to the adopted child. Put differently, the birth mothers' alienation from any adoption knowledge can be understood as a market strategy that agencies use to promote a baby's adoptability; it functions as a securitizing mechanism, and has become standard practice in the adoption market.

The adoption market, however, as the birth mothers' oral history collection reveals, manages the population of birth mothers via technologies of control carried out by adoption agencies; these include the exclusionary management of information, and a domineering, derogatory attitude toward birth mothers. In other words, the technology of securing the adoptive family is inseparable from the mechanism of social death. Lisa Guenther described social death, thus:

> "the effect of a (social) practice in which a person or group of people is excluded, dominated, or humiliated to the point of becoming dead to the rest of society. ... such people are physically alive, their lives no longer bear a social meaning; they no longer count as lives that matter."[40]

The birth mothers' oral history of their involvement in adoption, as reviewed here, testify to their experiences of being excluded, dominated, and humiliated by two direct forces—one, by patriarchal family practices, and two, by adoption market practices. The birth mothers speak defiantly to and against their state of social death.

6.3 Living Dead: Though I was Alive, It Cannot Really Be Called Living

Among the birth mothers who performed in the collection, the adoption experience was not something that had happened and ended. Many expressed that their adoption experience had fundamentally changed their lives and left long-term effects. Echoing the literature on the long-term effects of relinquishment, they told me about their feelings of shame, guilt, lowered self-esteem, and self-loathing, as well as of depression, an emptiness, and a prolonged sense of unresolved grief.[41] These high levels of unresolved grief are closely tied to the perception of having been coerced into relinquishing the child to adoption. Furthermore, the situation is exacerbated by having no outlet through which to express feelings about their loss; the lack of closure stemming from, but not delimited to, the lack of information about their child's placement; and their resulting guilt and shame over surrendering the child. These intense textures of unresolved grief resonate along and into these oral histories.

Lee Soon Young gave voice to such grief.[42] On January 4, 2011, Lee Soon Young, then 47, and I finally sat down for our interview at around 11:00 pm, after she had been working for 10 hours at her restaurant near Bukhansan National Park in Seoul. Twenty-three years had passed since her adoption placement. Five years had passed since she reunited with her adopted son who had been raised in France. Reflecting upon the impact that adoption had on her life, she offered, in a trembling voice, with a reddened face:

> The fact that I could not and did not raise my child …in fact, abandoned my own child … Even if I try to do my best, to do good for others in my life, I tell myself that I am the biggest sinner, because I couldn't raise, but instead abandoned, my child.[43] (Lee Soon Young, a son adopted in 1983)

Lee Soon Young framed her adoption decision in terms of child abandonment, saying that her failure to fulfill her motherly duties was unjustifiable under any circumstances. She said her sense of failure to mother her child nullified efforts to help people in other parts of her life, and that it had rendered her into "the biggest sinner".

The sense of shame and guilt about not raising one's own child echoes throughout almost all of the birth mothers' accounts, indicating the profound imprint of unresolved grief:

At any rate, it was my fault.... I was too young, and only thought of myself. Over the course of the divorce, I just thought that I [then] could be free from this hellish marriage, so that I would not suffer from beatings. I didn't think about my child.... Had I known better, I could have sought a way to live with my daughter, running away with her, and working at a restaurant or something. But I couldn't think of it then.[44] (Park Mi Hee, separated from her child in 1977, adoption year estimated as 1979)

[The adoption] was an immature thing. As a human being, I think that [truly relinquishing a child] is not possible. It truly isn't. For me, I have carried it in my heart throughout my life... Deep inside me, guilt, the guilt of not being able to raise my child always will be there.[45] (Kim Sung Hee, her twin daughters were adopted in 1985)

Who's going to forgive me? This is a weight that I will have to carry with me until I die. The guilty feelings are something that I can't touch or talk about ... because of my own guilt.[46] (Shin Young Eun, her two children were adopted in 1987)

Park Mi Hee's guilt stems from her feeling that she selfishly thought only of her own life, as well as that she was unable to run away with her child before the daughter's father took her and eventually placed her in adoption. In her words, she blames herself for callously sacrificing her child for her own well-being, even though she was trying to survive by escaping life-threatening beatings from her husband. She felt guilty about not being able to defend her daughter, in a sense, and blamed herself for this failure. Kim Sung Hee echoed Park Mi Hee's guilt, assuming ultimate responsibility for the adoption, despite her lack of active involvement in the decision. She regards the adoption as an indication of her lack of maturity as a mother, and, perhaps, even as an indication that she was deficient as a human being. In this situation, there can be no resolution, no end to her guilt. Shin Young Eun expressed such a sentiment, saying that such harrowing guilt was meant to be permanent, and that her guilt did not deserve to be forgotten or forgiven by anyone, including herself.

The weight of the birth mothers' shame and guilt is often so insurmountable that they cannot speak about the adoption with anyone, even with their own families. If family members were unaware of the adoption placement, the birth mothers typically did not tell them because talking itself is a reminder of an event they desperately wanted to forget. And in situations where family members were either involved in, or knew about, the adoption, they were still unable to speak about the event, and its subsequent effects on them, out of fear of hurting, or reminding, their families and/or themselves of the difficult event:

> I could not tell anyone freely. I did not tell anyone … How dare I cry? I cried underneath my blanket. I can't tell anyone … Who would listen to my story?[47] (Park Mi Hee, her daughter was adopted in 1979)

> Until recently, I hadn't told my daughters. When I finally confided in my daughters, they asked, "Why couldn't you have told us earlier? Wouldn't it have been easier?" But I was so ashamed that I was never able to talk about it to anyone.[48] (Cho Bok Soon, her twin daughters were adopted in 1982)

> My entire family did not know about the adoption except for my youngest sister. What could they do? I don't want my husband to talk about it either. Until Seung Hoon returned, no one knew.[49] (Lee Soon Young, her son was adopted in 1983)

The birth mothers who married after giving up a child to adoption typically did not discuss the event with their newly forged family, especially with their in-laws, but also sometimes with the new husband. This silence was because they feared that the family would block the marriage due to the social stigma associated with single mothers and child abandonment. For example, Kim Sun Ae, whose story appears in Chapter 2 and who gave up her child so she could remarry, has kept the adoption placement, which happened in 1977, and up until the 2007 reunion with her adopted daughter secret from her in-laws, for well over 30 years. Park Hye Sook did not tell her second husband that she had surrendered her child to adoption until she finally reunited with the adopted child in 2010. Jaewon, a webmaster of the Internet café, has never disclosed her child's birth or adoption to her own family. It is quite common for a birth mother's family—both the family of origin and of her own creation—to never know that she had a child who had been adopted. Given this, the topic easily becomes taboo, remaining buried as a secret both from—and in—the family.

The birth mothers' inability to share their losses with either their families or close friends precipitates a sense of loneliness and separation from their loved ones; of all separations, the most profound and devastating kind of severing is a severance from oneself. This devastating psychological state is captured by Lynne Reyman in her memoir, *Musings of a Ghost Mother*, when she writes that she had become "cut off from the girl that she had been, the woman she was becoming, cut off from her own needs, hopes, dreams."[50] Reyman's sense of her own emotional severance consistently emerges in the birth mothers' performative accounts in my oral history collection:

> From the moment I sent my children away, I stopped crying. I just don't anymore. I have lived without shedding tears. ... From the moment when my children were sent away, I haven't cried. ... I neither deserve to cry, nor to pray to God. I cannot ask for forgiveness. ... As soon as I sent my children away, I was gone. Even if I felt happy, I could not smile. I should not be happy. What's most devastating is that I have buried this in my heart for 20 years. I could not express myself. Until today, I could not tell anyone. ... I shouldn't be happy. Do you know what it feels like to have your heart riddled with a big hole? After my children were sent away, my soul was gone. I was not aware of basic life necessities, such as eating and sleeping.[51] (Shin Young Eun, her two children were adopted in 1987)

> As a woman, I didn't have any desire to take care of myself and my appearance. I didn't have any interest in material possessions. ... In my case, I didn't have any thoughts about improving [financially] and getting better. ... I hoped to meet my son who was sent to the US and tell him and my son here that they were brothers, and [then I would] disappear [commit suicide]. ... I had no motivation, no desire, no taste for life ... so I didn't have anything to regret either.[52] (Lee Mi Sun, her child was adopted in 1986)

> I live soullessly. My heart was taken away after the baby was adopted. I really didn't want to live. ... I have lived my life because I could not die. That's most of it. [After] abandoning a child. But life, on the other hand, I could not enjoy anything—even when I ate, I wasn't aware of what I was eating or what it tasted like. My life itself ... I just lived without any joy in life. My heart went out of myself. My soul is gone. I don't know or feel anything. I am just empty, an empty figure.[53] (Park Hye Sook, her son was adopted in 1985)

Following the separation from their children, Shin Young Eun, Lee Mi Sun, and Park Hye Sook became cut off from all feelings of sadness, happiness, and joy. Such dissociation was expressed as an indifference and apathy toward their basic life needs; Lee Mi Sun described it as having "no motivation and no desire in life." These accounts of estrangement from one's life resonate with Reyman's reflection on her own severance from herself[54]: her loss severs her from her past and seeps into her present wherein her feelings, needs, and desires become estranged from her; through this process of estrangement, she becomes cut off from her own future.

The birth mothers' post-adoption accounts are steeped in depression and attempts to run away from life itself. Kim So Jung, who surrendered her first daughter to adoption, spoke of how she sought the comfort of amnesia through work and alcohol:

> After my child was gone, it was so hard. I worked from 6 am to 6 pm, a 12-hour shift at a semi-conductor assembly factory. I lived by myself. Coming home from work, I felt so empty and would drink almost every-day for six months or so, although my tolerance was very low, and I never enjoyed drinking.[55] (Kim So Jung, her daughter was adopted in 2000)

A sense of emptiness and severe depression periodically sweeps over Park Mi Hee since she learned about her daughter's adoption; she said she has been preoccupied with the absent child, sometimes for months during a year. She told me:

> When it turns to late fall. ... when a cold wind rushes into the streets ... Whenever there was a cold wind, depression engulfed me. I felt like my baby was shivering outside. I couldn't eat and just stayed in bed, days after days. It was life, without life. ... Whenever I thought of my child, lost to adoption, I really wanted to die. How can I live without knowing my child's fate or whereabouts?[56] (Park Mi Hee, her daughter was adopted in 1979)

At times, such depression and emotional devastation propel birth mothers toward killing themselves. For Shin Young Eun, while adoption may have seemed the best option other than death, the separation itself still inflicts unbearable suffering:

> It was quite fortunate that I didn't jump off of the second floor as I left my children at the agency. After my children were sent off for adoption, I wanted to terminate my life. So I took pills. That's what I had originally planned. Sending my children for adoption and taking my life. I didn't want to live this life.[57] (Shin Young Eun, her two sons were adopted in 1987)

Cho Bok Soon, who kept assuring me that she understood why her husband made the heart-wrenching decision for adoption placement, ended up seeing a psychiatrist to deal with her depression and suicidal impulses. She told me:

In the years immediately after my twins were placed in adoption and my husband passed away, I saw a psychiatrist. No one knew in my family that I went to see a doctor for depression. One time, I drank a lot and drove into a cliff. A passerby saved my life.[58] (Cho Bok Soon, her twined daughters were adopted in 1982).

The birth mothers' accounts are riddled with the emotional and psychological vestiges of their traumatic severance from their child. The trauma is manifested in their inability to speak about the separation, in their sense of self-effacement, and in the wish for their own death. Often these sentiments are delivered with a cringing face and hunched shoulders, amidst an unstopping stream of tears. At times, their crying would interrupt the oral history collection process; the birth mothers' bodily delivery of their pains and losses imprinted me with a strong sense of injustice and unfairness for a long time. In their explorations of their post-adoption lives, many indirectly or directly indicated that their life was a paradox; often they found it incomprehensible how they sustained their lives and survived, despite all their killing, life-crushing moments. Such a paradox also marks a second feature of their view on adoption, expressed as "*Salato san ke aniŏssŏ*", translated as "*Though I was alive, it cannot really be called living.*"[59]

As discussed earlier, the paradoxical expression "I abandoned my child, but not really; I didn't abandon my child, but might have as well" presents the structural conditions and the process of natal alienation that are integral to implementing the social death of birth mothers, as recounted by the birth mothers. *Though I was alive, it cannot really be called living* reveals the traumatic and tragic effects of social death in their lives.

6.4 Birth Mothers' Reflections on Reunions: I am a Mother, but Not a Mother

Thirteen out of 21 birth mothers I met had reunited with their adult children, and three were actively waiting for their child to contact them.[60] Three of these reunions were facilitated by television search shows.[61] All of these reunions, whether televised or nontelevised, except in the case of Kim Sung Hee and Cho Bok Soon, were made possible only because the child (now an adult) took the initiative to search for his or her birth family.[62] The typical adoptee's search for his or her birth family begins by seeking information at the adoption agency. If successful, an exchange of letters and photos ensues, finally leading to a face-to-face meeting in Korea. The children come from the US, France, the Netherlands, Belgium, and Switzerland, and this unidirectional mode of contact generally indicates the foreclosure of any option for a birth mother to take an active role in searching for her child. Despite this foreclosure, however, the birth mothers' oral histories reveal they did not just passively wait for their children to contact them.

Lee Mi Sun, an unmarried mother involved with the married father, was *actively* waiting for her child to come searching for her. "... [T]he only hope that I had lived with was to live up to the day when I could meet him. That was the only hope and objective in my life," she said.[63] Her waiting began from the moment she was separated from her infant child. After the baby's father divorced his first wife and married Lee Mi Sun, thereby legitimating her relationship to her son, she became more proactive about searching for the child, and regularly updated her contact information with the adoption agency, where she was consistently denied access to any adoption information. Eventually she turned for help to G.O.A.'L, which in 1997 was just being established by a group of adoptees, and met its founder, Amy Inja Nafzer, who contacted the adoption agency in the US, directly on behalf of Lee Mi Sun. At that time, because her son was then only 12 or 13, she was told that her best course of action was to wait for him to contact her. Though her efforts to reunite with her child did not immediately result in a successful reunion, her explicit interests in having contact with the child and her steady calls to the agency might have assisted her adopted son's search and successful reunion six years later. As in Lee Mi Sun's case, many birth mothers, including Shin Young Eun, Soo Yeon, and Lee Soon Young, would diligently update their contact information with adoption agencies, as well as make periodic inquiries about any messages or letters from their adopted child.

The birth mothers' most highlighted and affectively charged accounts revolve around the actual reunion with the child. For many, the reunion was the first time that they saw the child.[64] The typical reunion starts with a phone call from the agency; the reunion might occur in a few hours or many more months later; a physical reunion could be imminent or uncertain. Lee Soon Young vividly recounted the day she was first contacted by her son:

> My son was looking for us first. Because we could not find him. ... It was November 12, 2005. At that time I was running a fish store at Garak

market, and Holt called the store to tell us to pick up a letter from Seung Hoon. At first, I thought it was dream. It felt so unreal as if I were in a dream. My husband went to get the pictures and letters from the agency, and we sent letters. When I saw Seung Hoon's childhood pictures, I was so surprised how similar Seung Hoon was to my two sons here, growing up. It was almost like identical twins. … He [Seung Hoon] finally came … I went to greet him at the airport. As he walked out, I sensed it immediately, that person is my son … When he stayed with us, every morning, I would go and watch him sleep because I was in such disbelief.[65] (Lee Soon Young reunited with her son in 2005).

Another birth mother, Lee Mee Sun expressed the complex feelings sparked by meeting her son. The event took place in November 2004. She was opening her store which sold discounted underwear and socks near a subway station, when she received a phone call from the agency. The caller said, "Your son, Joon Su, has come looking for you. Could we come see you now?" Lee Mi Sun looked at herself in the mirror at her store. Her black overalls were not pleasing, and no one else could keep the store open in her absence. But more than anything, she thought she did not look presentable enough for her son, dressed in her black work overalls. She made an appointment to meet the next day at the agency. She told me:

> … He walked toward me and embraced me. It felt so uncomfortable and awkward. I felt too ashamed and guilty to accept his embrace. I was thinking, "*Umma* [Mother] did so wrong. I could not even look at your face."[66] (Lee Mi Sun, reunited with her son in 2004)

Nonetheless, as affirmed in the oral history collection, the reunion is what birth mothers wanted the most, even as it was accompanied by complex feelings of shame, guilt, and heaviness, as shown in Lee Mi Sun's accounts. Park Hye Sook, whose child was placed into adoption, solely based on her husband's decision, had to greet her returned child alone, due to her ex-husband's premature death. Like Lee Soon Young, Park Hye Sook also immediately recognized her child as hers. She told me:

> As we walked out of the car, I saw three people, pacing back and forth in front of the police station. Instantly, I could recognize her face. I felt heavy. Because I abandoned her. I thought to myself, "How painful and heavy I am feeling is not comparable to her suffering." My desire to meet her was stronger than any other desire. With my bravest heart, I met her. I knew that

there would be a lot of anger and anguish coming toward me. The pains and losses that I have lived outweighed the fear so ...[67] (Park Hye Sook reunited with her child in 2010, after 25 years of separation)

Park Hye Sook's anguish came from her lack of effort in searching for her child. In contrast to Lee Soon Young or Lee Mi Sun, Park Hye Sook did not actively search for her child. She remarried after the child's father died, and consumed herself in her new marriage, and raising a new family. However, she added, "I was going to look for the child, if things got better."

Like Park Hye Sook, five birth mothers who reunited with their child never made an attempt to contact the adoption agency to seek further information once the adoption was completed. Their reasons varied, including a strong belief in the child's better life without her; a new marriage; forgetting; and, an acceptance of the impossibility of reuniting with the child. All these reasons could be subsumed under financial hardships.

Yang Sook Ja, the oldest birth mother whom I met in 2005, reunited in 2002 with her son. Though she wondered whether her child would come looking for her while watching television reunion shows, she did not actively seek out his adoption information. She told me:

> But I thought to myself, "He was too young." So I gave up hopes of a reunion. I would have searched for him if my situation were better, financially. But I am not doing too well so ... [I didn't initiate a search for him].[68] (Yang Sook Ja, reunited with her son in 2002)

Yang Sook Ja had retired after years of arduous physical labor, working as a local vendor for black-market American PX goods, as well as cleaning buildings and doing factory work; when I spoke with her, she was receiving a meager monthly government subsidy. She told me she could not offer anything to the adopted child, and that was why she had not, could not, take the initiative.

Not only does financial hardship demotivate the search, it prohibits the actualization of the reunion, even the possibility of it, as expressed by Im Soon Ja, whom I met in a Pyeongtaek camptown. She received a call from her adopted child several years ago; they have since had occasional phone conversations, but she has not been able to see him in person due to her financial situation. She said:

> One visit would cost at least two to three thousand dollars. I would have to take him sightseeing and stay at hotels. I don't have two to three thousand

dollars at my disposal. So I can't. ... I am not in a position ... If I didn't have to think about money, I would go and see him. ... If my finances allowed, I would love to invite him ... but in my capacity ...[69] (Im Soon Ja, who virtually reunited with her son in 2004)

Throughout the oral history collection, the moment of reunion is pivotal, flooding birth mothers with initially mixed emotions that include disbelief, joy, happiness, ambivalence, apprehension, shame, and guilt; birth mothers express a sense of relief, particularly at finding some resolution to their long-term anguish over lingering questions about their adopted child's life and wellbeing. In October 2006, Shin Young Eun, almost 20 years after her children's adoption, and one year after she had adopted a daughter herself, received a phone call from the adoption agency, relaying an inquiry from her son. A year later, she reunited with him. "What's different after the reunion is that I felt relieved that my children were alive. ... I should just be grateful that they are alive".[70]

Similarly, Cho Bok Soon who went to France with the help of a television show to reunite with her two daughters, with whom she had been separated from upon their birth, recounted:[71]

After the reunion, the feeling that I used to have as if there was something stuck in my heart had disappeared. I used to sigh often out of exasperation. That habit disappeared after meeting with the children.[72] (Cho Bok Soon reunited in 2005 after 23 years of separation)

A profound relief that their child(ren) was/were alive was often expressed as gratitude toward the adoptive parents, particularly the adoptive mothers. Jung Yoon Sook, a birth mother, who met her son's adoptive parents when visiting Long Beach, California, said, "I would have not been able to raise [my child] as well as Liz [the adoptive mother] did."[73] Seung Hoon's mother, Lee Soon Young, wrote several letters of gratitude to his adoptive parents for him to take back to France. The letters were not enough to fully express her gratitude, she said. She hoped to one day meet his adoptive mother and to convey her gratitude in person. Echoing the same hope, Park Hye Sook said she told herself, "I should try hard and harder" to establish herself financially so that she could visit the US and convey in person her gratitude to her child's adoptive parents.[74]

While the reunion is acknowledged as providing a sense of relief, it does not immediately create a sense of intimacy or a familial relationship; rather, it brings out a whole tapestry of emotional, psychological, and practical challenges for adoptees and their birth families. One of the most commonly identified difficulties is the language barrier. The lack of a common language prevents them from communicating what they need to share the most—for the adoptee, details about the mother's life and circumstances, leading up to the adoption—and for the birth mother, an understanding of the adoptee's post-adoption life experiences. Cho Bok Soon illuminated the ongoing difficulties of building a relationship with her daughters due to the language barrier, geographical distance, and cultural differences. Though she often kept her words short, she elaborated at length on this issue:

> First of all, there was a language problem. I wanted to tell them everything, but I couldn't. Though they kept saying that they understood the circumstances that forced me to choose adoption, how could they? So I would like to tell my daughters about everything that has accumulated over the time of separation. ... My daughter calls, and says only a few words in Korean, "*Umma, Gwenchana?* [Hi Mom, are you doing okay?]" I go like, "*Sava sava*". That's it. ... I can't learn French at this age. [My inability to communicate with her] saddens my heart. I have now met my daughters, but I can't speak. And if we were living in the same country, I could go and see them. But I can't. ... They can go back and forth, but there is no real sharing of love. They have become acculturated in the other culture and have another set of family. Korea, they can come visit as a depot or way station, but they are all saturated with "over there".[75] (Cho Bok Soon reunited with her twin daughters living in France in 2005)

The truncated and fragmentary communication that occurs between birth mothers and adoptees can easily turn an already overwhelming emotional and psychologically challenging situation into one of misunderstandings and conflicts. In some cases, the reunion may end abruptly, without plans for another meeting. A few birth mothers recalled that their reunion had been fraught with conflict and that they had felt disappointment afterward. For example, Shin Young Eun's son left Korea when he was eight after he finished the first grade of elementary school, and had since lost his Korean language skills. Since they could only communicate through a translator, she and her son experienced hurtful misunderstandings. She said:

> When I urged him to get out of bed because many people were waiting for him outside, he misunderstood me, thinking I had told him to go back to

France alone. Because of translations… He was terribly upset and didn't speak a word to me afterwards…. After he left Korea, there were no emails or any kind of contact from him. I would check my email everyday. There was no contact from him for almost six months.[76] (Shin Young Eun, reunited with her first son in 2007).

Shin Young Eun is not the only birth mother who has experienced a painful reunion that threatened the potential of a renewed relationship with the child. For example, Lee Mi Sun reflected on how the reunion simply created another scar:

> At the family gathering, his cousin sang an English song for him, which must have offended him badly. [I don't exactly know how and why]… He left Korea, without even saying good-bye to me. I learned of his departure later … [The reunion] must have deeply hurt him, but it also hurt me, as well. The reason why I didn't want foreign adoption placement for my child was that [I already knew] that due to differences in language and culture, we would never be able to reunite with each other … [77](Lee Mi Sun, reunited with her adopted son in 2004).

Given the cultural and linguistic gap between the birth mother and the adopted child, the absence of a common language points to the near impossibility of a relationship developing between them. In this gap, financial situations were cited as the major obstacle to developing a relationship with the child. Elise Prébin, an anthropologist, born in Korea and adopted by a French family, recognized her birth mother's lack of material comfort and its implications for their relationship.[78] Her own birth mother expressed tersely, "I am not a pleasant person because I have no money; when I see you, it puts me in a bad mood because I cannot give you anything."[79] Rather than viewing her as being too materialistic, I interpret these comments—along with those of her fellow birth mothers in my oral history collection—as coming from someone who has few ways to develop a meaningful relationship with her child. The birth mothers' emphasis on their economic circumstances should be contextualized within a limited context wherein gift-giving is one of the few forms of communication that they have to express their sorrow and love, and to even attempt to compensate for the loss of time and intimacy that might have been shared.

Moving the relationship from the initial reunion to a warm, familial relationship remained challenging for even those birth mothers who were able to fund both their adopted child's visits, as well as their own travels to meet the adoptive family. Kim Sun Ae, who remarried after her child's adoption and now lives comfortably, finally met her daughter in 2007. Since then, upon her invitation, her daughter has visited Korea twice with her husband and her adoptive mother. She reflects on their relationship:

> At any rate, even after we reunited, I came to realize that the child is not mine. There is no such connection like a daughter or a mother. She does not seem to have such a feeling for me. ... [Even after I visited my adopted daughter and her husband in Switzerland for about a month and observed their life closely] there was no attachment similar to what I had with the children I raised. ... I realized that she is not my child. There was no point of connection between us as mother and child. I couldn't be her mother. Neither could she be my child.[80]

Kim Sun Ae's frank observations about her feelings and relationship with her child illustrate a lack of a maternal–filial intimacy that cannot be restored either by her ability to pay for the trip, or by giving a gift.

Unlike the popular Korean adoption discourse, so prominently displayed in TV search shows, in which a reunion with the adopted child brings closure to any feelings of loss or sadness that resulted from the separation, the birth mothers' reflective, performative accounts of their own reunions indicate ambivalence, rather than a peaceful resolution; emotional distance, rather than any meaningful connection, thus challenging the idea of a blood-based family tie infused with family feelings that underlie normative kinship affects. In actuality, among the birth mothers I spoke with, the reunion was both a final realization and an acknowledgment of the loss of time, the loss of the child, and the loss of their own mothering:

> I am thankful that they are well, alive, but they are not my sons. ...[She reunited with her older son first.] For two years after the reunion, I had a more difficult time than before the reunion. I finally came to realize that I should just appreciate that he is alive and admit that he is not my son. ... I finally had to give him up as my son.[81] (Shin Young Eun, with two sons who were adopted, she reunited with her older son in 2007)

> Giving birth was not so critical in [building a mother-child relationship]. I am not quite sure how to define my relationship with Phil. I cannot step in, saying I am his mother. The reason why I opposed adoption was that I couldn't claim motherhood over him. I am a mother, but not a mother.[82] (Jung Yoon Sook, reunited with her son in 2008)

> I couldn't be any happier to have met my son. But ... all those years, I was not his mother, he was not my son. There is no way that we can fill the gap of a loss that has spanned the past 30 years.[83] (Jang Yeon Ja, reunited with her son in 2004)

This awareness that she has not been a mother does not mean that she does not imagine or expect any kind of meaningful relationship with her child.[84] Rather, it is an acknowledgment of the magnitude and irretrievability of the loss, and sets the stage for the next phase of her relationship with her adopted child and herself. It is therefore through reuniting with her child that the birth mother finally sees and feels the metaphorical death of her child. In their appraisal of the reunion, a third paradoxical statement emerges: *I am a mother, but I am not really a mother*. In this state of paradoxical motherhood, the birth mother becomes what I identify as a *virtual mother*.

6.5 Paradoxes of Virtual Mothering

Following the birth mothers' lived paradox as a guiding light, this chapter engages the birth mothers' refractory, textured, and complicated interpretations of their own experiences, circumscribing three stages of the birth mothers' life (i.e., the adoption decision, the post-adoption life, and the reunion with the child). The first paradox reads, *I abandoned my baby, but I really didn't; I didn't abandon my baby, but I might as well have*, and manifests the conditions and processes of natal alienation by which birth mothers see their involvement in the adoption decision as a choiceless choice, thus revealing their lack of rights in the adoption process, as well as their lack of access to adoption information. Secondly, by engaging the birth mothers' own reflections on their lives, as in *I was alive, it cannot really be called living*, my analysis fleshes out the birth mothers' unresolved grief, which excises any sense of joy and/or vitality from their lives, thus framing it as a social death. Lastly, the birth mothers' detailed accounts of their reunion experiences, captured in the statement, *I am a mother, but not a mother*, documents the birth mothers' efforts to reunite with the child and their own assessment of the "impossible" reunion; here, the birth mothers finally encounter the permanence of their losses.

Rendering the birth mothers' stories as paradoxical disrupts the dominant narratives of transnational adoption. The birth mothers' recounting of their involvement in the transnational adoption process challenges the simplistic, dominant narrative that depicts the birth mother as a victim of poverty, who, in fulfillment of her maternal duties, chooses adoption to give her child a better life opportunity. The birth mothers' stories cast the reunion as a memorial site, through which they acknowledge and recognize what they have lost in the adoption process, thereby disrupting the popular TV narrative that a reunion resolves all past sufferings and losses. The birth mothers' detailed accounts of their post-reunion experiences complicate the happy ending of the family-reunion narrative, pointing to appalling practical obstacles in their efforts to build a meaningful relationship, such as language and cultural differences, financial difficulties, and bureaucractic barriers geographical and emotional distances.

Standing before the void of information on birth mothers in the transnational adoption practice and discourse, I bear witness to the lived paradoxes that emerge in the birth mothers' knowledge-producing oral histories, fleshing out their often flattened, abstract and hidden lives. By performatively engaging their experiences of losses, the oral history collection suggests that the social death of birth mothers is not merely a state of invisibility; rather, it is the result of violent processes involving a technology of domination and humiliation that devalues the lives of these women. The birth mothers' oral history collection, thereby, demands a new caliber for recognizing the birth mothers' existence and their experiences of loss, in order to attend to the very condition and processes by which the birth mothers' losses are created and erased.

A new frame for recognition would involve affective recognition of their sufferings and their losses in the transformative politics of becoming. Here, Judith Butler's notion of precarity and an ethics of recognition not based on identity or alikeness is useful to consider.[85] Butler proposes a new ground of recognition and transformative politics, based on the awareness of our being in relation to others. She writes, "To ask for recognition, or to offer it, is precisely not to ask for recognition for what one already is. It is to solicit a becoming, to instigate a transformation, to petition the future always in relation to the Other."[86] To recognize the losses of birth mothers, whom many of you may not relate to in terms of alikeness, takes an awareness of our interdependent lives, a commitment to being vulnerable and to being affected by and engaging in a new frame of recognition that challenges the violent normative and exclusionary framework of human values and human life. Through a transformative new becoming, the birth mothers' losses would become legible and their lives would matter.

Notes

1. Ann Cvetkovich, *An Archive of Feelings: Trauma, Sexuality, and Lesbian Public Cultures* (Durham: Duke University Press, 2003), 166.
2. *The Gathering 2004*, the third international conference of overseas Korean adoptees, organized by International Korean Adoptee Associations (IKAA), brought together more than 400 adoptee participants from 14 countries. From this international conference, Adoptee Solidarity Korea (ASK) was formed as an international network of Korean adoptees dedicated to the termination of international adoption. Three years later in 2007, Truth and Reconciliation for the Adoption Community of Korea (TRACK) was founded; it has spearheaded work to promote the rights of adoptees to access their adoption records and has actively advocated family preservation, rather than adoption, as an alternative for single mothers. G.O.A.'L's dual citizenship campaign for Korean adoptees, successfully petitioned to make Korean adoptees eligible for dual citizenship.
3. Although G.O.A.'L spearheaded a petition drive for dual citizenship, not all adoptees or adoptee organizations saw this as priority.
4. This protest rally took place on August 4, 2007, at Dongguk University subway station, the nearest subway station to the hotel where the 2007 Korean international adoptee conference took place. Under the slogan of "Raising our children with our own hands," this group aimed to collect one million signatures.
5. This is important because normally the voices of birth mothers and adoptees are not heard; working together, they made their collective voice much more powerful. Second, it stated that domestic adoption was not the desired alternative to international adoption (South Korean policy currently prioritizes domestic adoption over family preservation) and called for institutional recognition of single-mother families.
6. Established by Reverend Kim Do Hyun in 2002, Koroot (*Ppuriuijip*) offers a cultural and adoption-specific resource center, as well as a guest house, costing $10 per day, for adoptee who visit Korea. As one of the key organizations advocating for adoptees and birth

families, Koroot successfully spearheaded the fight to revise the *Special Adoption Law* in 2012. In addition, Koroot hosts a number of benefit events and holiday parties, as well as publishes academic and nonacademic books about adoption.
7. Cvetkovich, *An Archive of Feelings*, 32.
8. This is a play off David Eng's (2010)'s phrase, "discursive emptiness but affective fullness," that indicates a powerful affect and its intelligibility in the silent history (195). David Eng, *The Feeling of Kinship* (Durham: Duke University Press, 2010), 195.
9. David Eng and David Kazanjian, Introduction to *Loss: The Politics of Mourning*, ed. David Eng and David Kazanjian (Berkeley: University of California Press, 2003), 2.
10. Ibid., 9.
11. Della Pollock, "Introduction", *Remembering: Oral History Performance*, ed. Della Pollock (New York: Palgrave Macmillan, 2003), 9.
12. Suk-Young Kim, "Finding History from the Living Archives: Inscribing Interviews and Interventions," in *Theater Historiography: Critical Interventions*, ed. Henry Bial and Scott Magelssen (Ann Arbor: The University of Michigan Press, 2010).
13. Ibid., 201.
14. Diana Taylor, *Archive and Repertoire: Performing Cultural Memories in Americas* (Durham: Duke University Press, 2003), 201.
15. Brian Massumi, *Parables for the Virtual* (Durham: Duke University Press, 2002), 30.
16. Park Hye Sook (birth mother), in an interview with the author, January 17, 2011.
17. Seongnam is the second largest city in South Korea's Gyeonggi Province, and is a satellite city of Seoul. In 1977, Holt Children Service established the local office as part of its efforts to expand its nationwide network of offices to receive potential adoptees.
18. Park Hye Sook (birth mother), in an interview with the author, January 17, 2011.
19. Kim Sung Hee, in an interview with the author, January 14, 2011.
20. Ibid.
21. Under South Korea's long-standing family registry system (*hojuje*), the eldest son becomes the head of the household in the absence of a father.

22. *Mudang* is a Korean shaman, often female. *Mudang* embodies the powerful spirits from ancestors or inanimate beings and helps to drive away illness, bad fortune, and death, and to strengthen the well-being of the family or the village.
23. Cho Bok Soon, in an interview with the author, July 4, 2010.
24. Throughout the chapter, I use the names of the adoption agency workers supplied by the birth mothers.
25. Jang Yeon Ja, in an interview with the author, August 10, 2010.
26. Ibid.
27. Park Mi Hee, in an interview with the author, June 30, 2010.
28. She was also an active blogger for the Internet café discussed in Chapter 5.
29. Kim Joo Hee, in an interview with the author, August 6, 2010.
30. As a married woman, she was not supposed to be admitted into a maternity home. But, with the director's discretion, she was allowed to reside there for two years.
31. Park Ae Kyung, in an interview with the author, August 17, 2005.
32. Shin Young Eun, in an interview with the author, January 18, 2011. Her account was discussed in Chapter 2.
33. Rickie Solinger, *Beggars and Choosers: How the Politics of Choice Shapes Adoption, Abortion, and Welfare in the United States* (New York: Hill and Wang Publishing Company, 2001).
34. Jodi Kim, "An 'Orphan' with Two Mothers: Transnational and Transracial Adoption, the Cold War, and Contemporary Asian American Cultural Politics," *American Quarterly* 61, no. 4 (2009): 855–880.
35. Lisa Guenther, *Solitary Confinement: Social Death and Its Afterlives* (Minneapolis: University of Minnesota Press, 2013), xx.
36. Soo Yeon did not want to disclose her real name, so she created a pseudonym for herself.
37. "Love motel" refers to a motel for lovemaking. In South Korea, since many adults live with their family until they get married, love motels are used for romantic assignations. The accusation suggests that the birth mother must be sexually promiscuous and that the birth of her child must have been illegitimate.
38. Kim Sun Ae, in an interview with the author, January 17, 2011.
39. Kristi Brian, *Reframing Transnational Adoption* (Philadelphia: Temple University Press, 2012), Christine W. Gailey, *Blue Ribbon Babies* (Austin: University of Texas Press, 2010).

40. Lisa Guenther, *Solitary Confinement*. xx.
41. See, Michael De Simone, "Birth Mother Loss: Contributing Factors to Unresolved Grief," *Clinical Social Work Journal* 24, no. 1 (1996): 65–76, Diana Edwards, "Social Control of Illegitimacy through Adoption," *Human Organizations* 58, no. 4 (1999): 387–396, Patricia D. Farrar, "Abject Mothers: Women Separated from Their Babies Lost to Adoption," in *Unbecoming Mothers: The Social Production of Maternal Absence*, ed. Diana L. Gustafson (Binghamton: Haworth Press, 2005). Ann Fessler, *The Girls Who Went Away: The Hidden History of Women Who Surrender Their Children for Adoption in the Decades Before Roe vs. Wade* (New York: The Penguin Press, 2006).
42. Her adoption experience with the maternity home was discussed in Chapter. 3.
43. Lee Soon Young, in an interview with the author, January 14, 2011.
44. Park Mi Hee, in an interview with the author, June 30, 2010.
45. Kim Sung Hee, in an interview with the author, January 14, 2011.
46. Shin Young Eun, in an interview with the author, January 18, 2011.
47. Park Mi Hee, in an interview with the author, June 30, 2010.
48. Cho Bok Soon, in an interview with the author, July 4, 2010.
49. Lee Soon Young, in an interview with the author, January 14, 2011.
50. Lynne Reyman, *Musings of a Ghost Mother: Losing an Infant to Closed Adoption* (Oroville: I & L Publication, 2001), 37.
51. Shin Young Eun, in an interview with the author, January 18, 2011.
52. Lee Mi Sun, in an interview with the author, August 8, 2010.
53. Park Hye Sook, in an interview with the author, January 17, 2011.
54. Lynne Reyman, *Musings of a Ghost Mother.*
55. Kim So Jung, in an interview with the author, July 20, 2010.
56. Park Mi Hee, in an interview with the author, June 30, 2010.
57. Shin Young Eun, in an interview with the author, January 18, 2011.
58. Cho Bok Soon, in an interview with the author, July 4, 2010.
59. Many birth mothers described their lives as if they were dead, or as living in death, which is similar to what Baek Yeon-Oak (1995) phrases, the "living dead." Baek, Yeon Ok. "A Study on Mental

Health Issues of Birth Mothers who Relinquish their Children (*ah dongul poghee hanun cheenmoh dulee choshin gungahng issue dulee kwanhaun soh goh*)" *Chongshin bohghun kwa sahoe sahyop* 2. (1995). 125.
60. Five of these birth mothers have adopted children who are minors. Because my sampling is not a random sampling, but one recruited through a network of adoptee and birth mother activists, this sample has an unusually high reunion rate, compared to the 2.5 % reunion rate estimated by adoptee activists. Jeannie Hong ed. *Guide to Korea for Korean Adoptee: International Korean Adoptee Resource Book*. (Seoul: Overseas Koreans Foundation, 2006)
61. These three programs, *Happy Sunday* (2005–6); *A Beautiful Forgiveness* (2005); and *KBS Morning Forum* (1997 onward), follow the search-and-reunion narrative format that I examine in Chapter 4. "I am on My Way to Meet Them Now" [*Chikŭm Mannalo Kapnita*] was a 30-minute segment embedded in the Happy Sunday program, between May 2005 to January 2006 on KBS. The show has featured 15 reunions between birth mothers and adoptees. In contrast to an adoptee-initiated search for birth parents, 'I am on My Way to Meet Them Now' stages the figure of the birth mother initiating the search, and follows her journey to a foreign country to reunite with the adopted child. "A Beautiful Forgiveness" [*Alŭmtaun yongsŏ*] was a weekly show and aired only twice, according its website. The second show featured Jang Yeon Ja's reunion with her son, from South Dakota, in the US. (http://www.kbs.co.kr/end_program/1tv/sisa/forgive/index.html).
62. Kim Sung Hee's account of her reunion presents an exception. After her husband told her that her twin daughters were not dead, and that they had been adopted by a family in the US, Sung Hee went to the adoption agency, which agreed to relay a message to the partner agency in the US. Six months after she wrote a letter to her twin daughters, she heard back from them. Soon, her family invited both twins, but only one came to meet Sung Hee's family.
63. Lee Mi Sun, in an interview with the author, August 8, 2010.
64. Cho Bok Soon met her twin daughters for the first time in 2005— the twins had been sent away for adoption while she was still unconscious after delivery. Both Lee Soon Young and Lee Mi Sun did not want to see their babies after delivery, as it was too

heartbreaking to see their children who were already planned for adoption.
65. Lee Soon Young, in an interview with the author, January 14, 2011.
66. Lee Mi Sun, in an interview with the author, August 8, 2010.
67. Park Hye Sook, in an interview with the author, January 17, 2011.
68. Yang Sook Ja, in an interview with the author, August 12, 2005.
69. Im Soon Ja, in an interview with the author, January 3, 2012.
70. Shin Young Eun, in an interview with the author, January 18, 2011.
71. Cho Bok Soon appeared in *Happy Sunday's* "I am on My Way to Meet Them Now" on June 26, 2005 and July 3, 2015. She went to France with TV crews to meet her twin daughters for the first time (Korea Broadcasting Sytems, Inc., 2005, "*Happy Sunday*").
72. Cho Bok Soon, in an interview with the author, July 4, 2010.
73. Jung Yoon Sook, in an interview with the author, January 19, 2011.
74. Park Hye Sook, in an interview with the author, January 17, 2011.
75. Cho Bok Soon, in an interview with the author, July 4, 2010.
76. Shin Young Eun, in an interview with the author, January 18, 2011.
77. Lee Mi Sun, in an interview with the author, August 8, 2010.
78. Elise Prebin, *Meeting Once More: The Korean Side of Transnational Adoption* (New York: New York University Press, 2013).
79. Ibid., 142.
80. Kim Sun Ae, in an interview with the author, January 17, 2011.
81. Shin Young Eun, in an interview with the author, January 18, 2011.
82. Jung Yoon Sook, in an interview with the author, January 19, 2011.
83. Jang Yeon Ja, in an interview with the author, August 10, 2005.
84. Echoing this lack of shared love and a sense of emotional distance, Kim Sung Hee acknowledged that she had limited familial feelings for her twin daughters. She expressed this wish for the future: "When they have their own family and raise children, they could come and visit me, not as a mother but as a friend" (Kim Sung Hee, reunited with her twin daughters in 2006).
85. Judith Butler, *Precarious Life: The Powers of Mourning and Violence* (New York: Verso, 2004).
86. Ibid., 44.

REFERENCES

Ae Ran Won. *Aeranwŏn 50 nyunsa*. Seoul, Korea: Ae Ran Won, 2010.
Agamben, Georgio. *State of Exception*. Translated by Kevin Attell. Chicago: University of Chicago Press, 2005.
Ahmed, Sara. *The Cultural Politics of Emotion*. London and New York: Routledge, 2004.
Ahmed, Sara. *The Promise of Happiness*. Durham: Duke University Press, 2010.
Anagnost, Ann. "Scenes of Misrecognition: Maternal Citizenship in the Age of Transnational Adoption." *Positions* 8, no. 2 (2000): 389–421.
Armstrong, Charles. "Introduction." *Journal of Korean Studies 18*, no. 2 (2013): 177–182.
Bae, Eun Kyung. *Hyŏnda hanguk ŭi ingan chae saeng san* [Human Reproduction in Korean Modernity: Women, Motherhood, and Population Control Policy]. Seoul: Sikanyŏhaeng, 2012.
Bae, Young Mi. "*Ch'ŏngsonyŏn mihonmo palsaeng yoine kwanhan yŏngu.*" [A Study on the Determinants of Unmarried Adolescent Mothers] In *International Women's Research Symposium* 10 (2001): 51–80.
Baek, Yeon Ok. "*Ahdong ŭl p'ogiha nŭn ch'inmo dŭl ŭi jŏngsin kŏngang isyu dŭl ŭi kwanhan sogo.*" [A study on the mental health issues of birthmothers who relinquish their children]. *Chongshin bogunkwa sahoe sahyop* 2 (1995): 121–138.
Bagga-Raoulx, Rupa. "Mothering Across Borders: South Korean Birthmothers' Perspectives." In *Mothering in East Asian Communities: Politics and Practices*, edited by Patti Duncan and Gina Wong, 181–215. Bradford: Demeter Press, 2014.

Bang, Sook. "*Urinara mojapokŏn ŭi hyŏnhwang kwa palchŏn pangyang.*" [The Current Affairs and Directions of Maternal and Child Health in South Korea]. *The Korean Society of Maternal and Child Health* (1996): 21–74.

Barad, Karen. "Posthumanist Performativity: Toward an Understanding of How Matter Comes to Matter." *Signs: Journal of Women in Culture and Society* 28, no. 3 (2003): 801–831.

Barthes, Roland. *Camera Lucida: Reflections on Photography.* Translated by Richard Howard. New York: Hill & Wang, 1980.

Benjamin, Walter. *Illuminations: Essays and Reflections.* Translated by Harry Zohn. New York: Schocken Books, 1969.

Bier, Leslie. "The Family is a Factory: Gender, Citizenship, and the Regulation of Reproduction in Postwar Egypt." *Feminist Studies* 36, no. 2 (2008): 404–32.

Brian, Kristi. *Reframing Transnational Adoption: Adopted Koreans, White Parents, and the Politics of Kinship.* Philadelphia: Temple University Press, 2012.

Briggs, Laura. *Somebody's Children: The Politics of Transracial and Transnational Adoption.* Durham: Duke University Press, 2012.

Butler, Judith. *Precarious Life: The Powers of Mourning and Violence.* New York: Verso, 2004.

Cacho, Lisa M. *Social Death: Racialized Rightlessness and the Criminalization of the Unprotected.* New York: New York University Press, 2012.

Cheon, Hyejung, Sun-Hee Bae, Mal-Hee Song, Hyun-Ae Song, Gil Yang. "Mihonmo poho sisŏl e kŏju hanŭn siptae mihonmo ŭi kyŏnghŏm e taehan yŏngu [A Study on the experiences of institutionalized unmarried teenage mothers: pregnancy and sexual behaviors]." *Journal of Korean Home Management* 20, no. 4 (2002): 1–12.

Cherot, Natalie. "Transnational Adoptees: Global Biopolitical Orphans or an Activist Community?" *Culture Machine* 8 (2008): http://www.culturemachine.net/index.php/cm/search/authors/view?firstName=Natalie&middleName=&lastName=Cherot&affiliation=

Chira, Susan. "Seoul Journal – Babies for Export: and Now the Painful Question," *New York Times,* April 21, 1988.

Cho, Grace M. *Haunting the Korean Diaspora: Shame, Secrecy, and the Forgotten War.* Minneapolis: University of Minnesota Press, 2008.

Cho, Yeon Dong. *Ach'im madang.* Television Broadcasting. Seoul: Korean Broadcasting Systems, Inc. July 20, August 3, and August 17, 2005.

Cho, Sungsook. *Omoni ranŭn idyeollogi* [The ideology of motherhood]. Seoul: Hanool Academy, 2001.

Choe, Sang-Hun. "Group Resists Korean Stigma for Unwed Mothers," *New York Times,* October 7, 2009.

Choe, Won Kyu. "*Oeguk min'gan wŏnjo tanch e hwaltong gwa han'guk sahoe saŏp palch'ŏn e mich'in Yŏnghyang.*" [Activities of foreign voluntary agencies and their influences upon social work development in Korea]. PhD diss., Seoul National University, 1997.

Choi, Chungmoo. "Transnational Capitalism, National Imaginary, the Protest Theater in South Korea." *Boundary 2*, no. 1 (1995): 235–261.
Choi, Seunghee. "Chanŏ lŭl ibyang ponaen mihonmo ŭi sangsil." [Unwed mothers' grief after giving up a child to adoption]. In *Conference proceedings from the mihonmo ŭi hyŏnsil kwa chalip chiwŏn pangan* [Reality of unwed mothers and support for self-reliance]. 26–45, Seoul: Korean Women's Development Institute, 2010.
Chun, Byung Hoon. "Adoption and Korea." *Child Welfare* 68, no. 2 (1989): 255–260.
Chun, Wendy H. *Control and Freedom: Power and Paranoia in the Age of Fiber Optics*. Cambridge, MA: MIT Press, 2006.
———. "The Enduring Ephemeral, or The Future is Memory." *Critical Inquiry* 35, no. 1 (2008):148–171.
Clough, Patricia T. Introduction to *The Affective Turn: Theorizing the Social*, edited by Patricia T. Clough and Jean Halley. Durham: Duke University Press, 2007.
Connerton, Paul. *How Societies Remember*. Cambridge, UK: Cambridge University Press, 1989.
Conquergood, Dwight. "Performance Studies: Interventions and Radical Research." *Theater & Drama Review* 46, no. 2 (2002): 145–156.
Coulter, Myrl. "Birth Mother." In *Encyclopedia of Motherhood*, edited by Andrea O'Reilly. Thousand Oaks: Sage Publications, 2010.
Cummings, Bruce. *The Korean War: A History*. New York: Random House, 2010.
Cvetkovitch, Ann. *An Archive of Feelings: Trauma, Sexuality, and Lesbian Public Cultures*. Durham: Duke University Press, 2003.
De Simone, Michael. "Birth Mother Loss: Contributing Factors to Unresolved Grief." *Clinical Social Work Journal* 24, no. 1 (1996): 65–76.
Deleuze, Gilles and Felix Guattari. *A Thousand Plateaus: Capitalism and Schizophrenia*. Translated by Brian Massumi. Minneapolis: University of Minnesota Press, 1987.
Dorow, Sara, ed., *I Wish You A Beautiful Life: Letters from the Korean Birth Mothers of Ae Ran Won to Their Children*. St. Paul: Yeong & Yeong Book Company, 1999.
Dorow, Sara. *Transnational Adoption: A Cultural Economy of Race, Gender & Kinship*. New York, New York University Press, 2006.
Dwyer, Leslie. "Spectacular Sexuality: Nationalism, Development and the Politics of Family Planning in Indonesia." In *Gender Ironies of Nationalism: Sexing the Nation*, edited by Tamar Mayer, 25–62. New York: Routledge, 2000.
Edwards, Diana. "Social Control of Illegitimacy through Adoption." *Human Organizations* 58, no. 4 (1999): 387–396.
Edwards, Christine E. and Christine L. Williams. "Birth Mothers in Maternity Homes Today." *Gender and Society* 14, no. 1 (2000): 160–183.

Eng, David. *The Feeling of Kinship: Queer Liberalism and the Racialization of Intimacy.* Durham: Duke University Press, 2010.

Eng, David and David Kazanjian. Introduction to *Loss: The Politics of Mourning*, edited by David Eng and David Kazanjian. Berkeley: University of California Press, 2003.

Farrar, Patricia D. "Abject Mothers: Women Separated from Their Babies Lost to Adoption." In *Unbecoming Mothers: The Social Production of Maternal Absence*, edited by Diana L. Gustafson, 51–72. Binghamton: Haworth Press, 2005.

Fessler, Ann. *The Girls Who Went Away: The Hidden History of Women Who Surrendered Their Children for Adoption in the Decades Before Roe V. Wade.* New York: Penguin Press, 2006.

Foucault, Michel. "Of Other Spaces." Translated by Jay Miskowiec. *Diacritics* 16, no. 1 (1986): 22–27.

———. *Society Must Be Defended: Lectures at the Collège de France 1975–1976.* Translated by David Macey. New York: Picador, 2003.

Gailey, Christine W. *Blue Ribbon Babies and Labors of Love: Race, Class, and Gender in U.S. Adoption Practice.* Austin: University of Texas Press, 2010.

———. "Race, Class, and Gender in Intercountry Adoption in the USA." In *Intercountry Adoption: Developments, Trends, and Perspectives*, edited by Peter Selman, 295–314. London: Skyline House Press, 2000.

Glenn, Evelyn N. "Social Construction of Mothering." In *Mothering: Ideology, Experience, and Agency*, edited by Evelyn N. Glenn, Grace Chang, and Linda R. Forcey, 1–31. New York: Routledge, 1994.

Guenther, Lisa. *Solitary Confinement: Social Death and Its Afterlives.* Minneapolis: University of Minnesota Press, 2013.

Han, Hyun Sook. *Many Lives Intertwined.* St. Paul: Yeong & Yeong Book Company, 2004.

Han, Sangsoon. *Dreaming a World.* St. Paul: Yeong & Yeong Book Company, 2010.

Hirsch, Marianne. *Family Frames: Photography, Narrative, and Postmemory.* Cambridge, MA: Harvard University Press, 1997.

Holt International Children's Services. *To My Beloved Baby: Writings of Birth Mothers.* Seoul, Korea: Holt International Children's Services, 2004.

Hong, Jeannie. *Guide to Korea for Korean Adoptee: International Korean Adoptee Resource Book.* Seoul: Overseas Koreans Foundation, 2006.

Hübinette, Tobias. "Comforting an Orphaned Nation: Representations of International Adoption and Adopted Koreans in Korean Popular Culture." PhD diss., Stockholm University, 2005.

Huh, Namsoon. "Services for Out-of-Wedlock Children in Korea." *Early Child Development and Care* 85 (1993): 35–46.

Hwang, Ok Ja and Mi Hyun Yoon. "*Mihonmo tŭksŏng pyŭnhwa e kwanhan yŏngu.*" [The study of the development of the characteristics of unwed moth-

ers in Korea]." *Dongguk Journal: Humanities & Social Sciences* 35 (1996): 219-247.
Im, Seung-Hye. "Korea Passes Law to Change Adoption Policy." *Joong-Ang Daily* (Seoul, Korea), July 1, 2011.
Jones, Stacey H. "(M)othering Loss: Telling Adoption Stories and Telling Performativity." *Text and Performance Quarterly* 25, no. 2 (2005): 113-135.
Kennedy, J. F. Presidential Address to the UN General Assembly, September 25, 1961, U.S. Department of State (accessed on January 15, 2015). [www.state.gov/p/io/potusunga/207241.htm].
Kim, Chang Jo. KBS Sunday Special. "*Who will save Brian SungDuk Bauman?*" Seoul: Korea Broadcasting System, Inc., January 28, 1996.
Kim, Dae Jung. "President Kim Dae Jung's Speech," October 23, 1998 at the Blue House. *Chosen Child* 1, no 5 (1999): 15-16.
Kim, Doyoung. *1972-2002 Dong Bang sahŭi pokchihŭi 30 nyŏnsa* [Thirty-Year history of the Eastern Social Welfare Society]. Seoul: Eastern Social Welfare Society, 2003.
Kim, Dong-choon. *Chônchaengkwa sahŭi* [Korean war and society]. Seoul: Dol Bae Gae. 2000.
Kim, Eleana. *Adopted Territory: Transnational Korean Adoptees and the Politics of Belonging*. Durham: Duke University Press, 2010.
———. "Wedding Citizenship and Culture: Korean Adoptees and the Global Family of Korea." In *Cultures of Transnational Adoption*, edited by Toby A. Volkman, 49-80. Durham: Duke University Press, 2005.
Kim, Eunshil. "*Nakt'ae e kwanhan sahŭi chŏk nonŭi wa yŏsŏng ŭi salm.*" [Abortion discourses and women's lives in Korea] *Hyengsa chŏngch'aek yŏngu* [Criminology research review] 2 (1991): 383-404.
Kim, Hosu and Grace M. Cho. "The Kinship of Violence." *Journal of Korean Adoption Studies* 1, no.3 (2012): 7-25.
Kim, Ji Yeol, "*Mihonmo ŭi kwan han kijojôk yóngu*" [An analytic study of the unmarried mother in Korea]. Master's thesis, Ewha Women's University, 1974.
Kim, Jodi. "An 'Orphan' with Two Mothers: Transnational and Transracial Adoption, the Cold War, and Contemporary Asian American Cultural Politics." *American Quarterly* 61, no. 4 (2009): 855-880.
Kim, Joosun. "*Hanguk mihonmo pokchi sŏbisŭ ŭi kaesŏnbangan e kwanhan yŏngu*" [A study on the social welfare program for Korean unwed mothers and policy implications]. Master's thesis, Inha University, 2004.
Kim, Shin Jung, Soon Ok Yang and Keum Hee Jung. "*Sisŏl e ipsohan mihonmo ŭi silt'ae*" [Reality of unwed mothers at maternity facilities]. *Adong kanho hak hŭi* [Journal of Korean academy child health nursing] 10, no. 4 (2004): 468-478.
Kim, Suk-Young, "Finding History from the Living Archives: Inscribing Interviews and Interventions." In *Theater Historiography: Critical Interventions*, edited by Henry Bial and Scott Magelssen, 197-207. Ann Arbor: The University of Michigan Press, 2010.

Klein, Christina. *Cold War Orientalism*. Berkeley: University of California Press, 2003.
Ko, Jang Suk (director). MBC In'gansidae, *"urinŭn chigŭm – haeoe ibyanga."* Seoul: Munhwa Broadcasting Corporation., 1989.
Korea Women's Development Institute. *Mihonmo silt'ae e kwanhan yŏngu* [Study on the unwed mother with special reference to the analysis of factors relating her occurrence and welfare measure]. Seou: KWDI, 1984.
Korean Women's Hotline. *Hanguk yŏsŏng inkwŏn undongsa* [History of Korean women's rights movements], edited by Korea Women's Hotline. Seoul: Hanul Academy, 1999.
Kwon, Myung Hee. *1984 nyŏn sang pangi salye yŏngu* [The first year report of the Korea Women's Hotline, A case study of the first half of 1984]. Seoul: Korea Women's Hotline.
Langellier, Kristin. "Personal Narrative, Performance, Performativity: Two or Three Things I Know for Sure." In *Text and Performance Quarterly* 19, no. 2 (1999): 125–144.
Lee, Bong Ju. "Recent Trends in Child Welfare and Adoption in Korea: Challenges and Future Directions." In *International Korean Adoption: A Fifty-Year History of Policy and Practice*, edited by Kathleen Ja Sook Berquist, M. Elizabeth Vonk, Dong Soo Kim, and Marvin D. Feit, 189–206. Binghamton: Haworth Press, 2007.
Lee, Hyunsook and Choonsook Jung. *"Anae kut'a ch'ubang untongsa."* [History of Women's movement to abolish wife beating]. In *Hanguk yŏsŏng inkwŏn undongsa* [History of Korean women's rights movements], edited by Korea Women's Hotline, 106–180. Seoul: Hanul Academy, 1999.
Lee, Mijeong. *"Sahŭi chuk p'yŏngyŏn kwa mihonmo kwannyŏn t'unggye"* [Social prejudice against unwed mothers and related statistics]. In *Mihonmo ŭi hyŏnsil kwa charip chiwŏn pangan* [Reality of Unwed Mothers and Support for Self-Reliance], 2–25. Seoul: Korean Women's Development Institute, 2010.
Lee, Soon Hyung. *"Pubugan kut'ahangdonggwa kwallyŏnbyŏnsu"* [Spousal abuse and variables]. *Tŏksŏng yŏja taehakkyo nonmunjip* [Duksong Women's University Journal] 17, 143–158. 1988.
Lee, Young-Mi and Seung-Hee Choi. "The Development and Effectiveness of Group Program to Promote Self-determination for Teen Parents." *Korean Journal of Family Welfare* 16 (2005): 103–126. [In Korean].
Maass, Peter. "Adoptions: Korea's Disquieting Problem; National Embarrassment over Letting Foreigners Take Children." *Washington Post* (Washington, D.C.), December 14, 1988.
Massumi, Brian. *Parables for the Virtual: Movement, Affect, Sensation*. Durham: Duke University Press, 2002.
McClintock, Anne. "Family Feuds: Gender, Nationalism and the Family." *Feminist Review* 44, no. 1 (1993): 61–80.

Min, Kyung Ja. "*Sŏngp'oklyŏk ch'upang untongsa* [History of Women's Movement in the Abolishment of Sexual Violence]." In *Hanguk yŏsŏng inkwŏn undongsa* [History of Korean women's rights movements], edited by Korean Women's Hotline, 17–105. Seoul: Hanul Academy, 1999.

Ministry of Health and Welfare. *Kungnaeoe iby-ang hyonhwang* [Current State of Domestic and International Adoption]. Seoul (http://mohw.go.kr, accessed on June 27, 2014)

Moon, Katharine. *Sex Among Allies*. New York: Columbia University Press, 1997.

Moon, Seungsook. "Begetting the Nation: The Androcentric Discourse of National History and Tradition in South Korea." In *Dangerous Women: Gender and Korean Nationalism*, edited by Elaine H. Kim and Chungmoo Choi, 33–66. London and New York: Routledge. 1998.

Moon, Seungsook. *Militarized Modernity and Gendered Citizenship in South Korea*. Durham: Duke University Press, 2005.

Muñoz, José Esteban. "Ephemera as Evidence: Introductory Notes to Queer Acts." *Women & Performance: A Journal of Feminist Theory* 8, no. 2 (1996): 5–16.

Noh, Jin-A. *Mihonmo ŭi jip: Ae Ran Won* [Maternity homes: *Ae Ran Won*]. *Church Education*, December 1996.

Noh, Choon Rae and Won Hee Kim. "Predictive Factors of Baby Release for Adoption among Unmarried Mothers." *Journal of Korean Studies of Child Welfare* 17 (2004): 49–79.

Oh, Arissa. "A New Kind of Missionary Work: Christians, Christian Americanists, and the Adoption of Korean GI Babies, 1955–1961." *Women's Studies Quarterly* 33, no. 3 (2005): 161–188.

———. "War Waif to Ideal Immigrant: The Cold War Transformation of the Korean Orphans." *Journal of American Ethnic History* 31, no. 4 (2012): 34–55.

Okazawa-Rey, Margo. "Amerasian Children of GI Town: A Legacy of U.S. Militarism in South Korea." *Asia Journal of Women's Studies* 3, no. 1 (2003): 71–102.

Park, Kyeyoung. *The Korean American Dream: Immigrants and Small Business in New York City*. Ithaca: Cornell University Press, 1997.

Park, Kyung Ae. "Teenage Childbirth." *Korean Journal of Obstetrics and Gynecology* 18, no. 11 (1975): 923–928. [In Korean].

Park, Kyung Tae. *Sosuja wa hanguk sahoe* [Minority groups in Korean society]. Seoul: Humanitas, 2006.

Pate, Soojin. *From Orphan to Adoptee: U.S. Empire and Genealogies of Korean Adoption*. Minneapolis: University of Minnesota Press, 2014.

———. "Genealogies of Korean Adoption: American Empire, Militarization, and Yellow Desire." PhD diss., University of Minnesota, 2010.

Patterson, Orlando. *Slavery and Social Death: A Comparative Study.* Cambridge, MA: Harvard University Press, 1982.
Pollock, Della. Introduction to *Remembering: Oral History Performance*, edited by Della Pollock, 1–17. New York: Palgrave Macmillan, 2003.
Prebin, Elise. *Meeting Once More: The Korean Side of Transnational Adoption.* New York: New York University Press, 2013.
Reyman, Lynne. *Musings of a Ghost Mother: Losing an Infant to Closed Adoption.* Oroville: I & L Publication, 2001.
Robinson, Katy. *A Single Square Picture: A Korean Adoptee's Search for Her Roots.* New York: Berkley Books. 2002.
Rothschild, Matthew. "Babies for Sale: South Koreans Make Them, Americans Buy Them." *Progressive* 52, no. 1 (1998): 18–23.
Sarri, Rosemary C., Yenoak Baik, and Marti Bombyk, "Goal Displacement and Dependency in South Korea–United States Intercountry Adoption." *Children and Youth Review* 20, no. 1–2 (1998): 87–114.
Seigworth, Gregory J. and Melissa Gregg. Introduction to *The Affect Theory Reader*, edited by Gregg, Melissa and Gregory J. Seigworth, 1–25. Durham: Duke University Press, 2010.
Selman, Peter. "Intercountry Adoption in the 21st Century: An Examination of the Rise and Fall of Countries of Origin." *Proceedings of the First International Korean Adoption Studies Research Symposium*, edited by Kim Park Nelson, Eleana Kim, and Lene Myong Peterson, 55–75. Seoul: 2007.
Seung. "Ae Ran Welfare Center." *Daily Economics*, Section 9 March 18, 1982.
Shin, Eun Hye. *1983 Nyŏn habangi saryeyŏngu, hanguk yŏsŏng ŭi chunhwa, kaewon il chunyŏn kinyŏm pogosŏ* [The first year report of the Korean Women's Hotline, A case study of the latter half of 1983]. Seoul: Korea Women's Hotline, 1984.
Shin, Eun Hye and Hyun Hee Kim. "Report on Former Kijichon Sex Workers in Gyeonggi Do." *Conference Proceedings.* Seoul: Sunlit Sisters' Center, 2008.
Smelser, Neil. "Psychological Trauma and Cultural Trauma," In *Cultural Trauma and Collective Identity*, edited by Jeffrey C. Alexander, Ron Eyerman, Bernhard Giesen, Neil J. Smelser, Piotr Sztompka, 31–59. Berkeley, University of California Press, 2004.
Social Welfare Society, Inc. *Pitanhyang k'och'mu ŭi k'och' chŏm ch'ŏlŏm* [Like a word of stock]. Seoul: Social Welfare Society, 2001.
Social Welfare Society. *Pyŏl ŭl poneda* [Send Away the Stars]. Seoul, Korea: Social Welfare Society, 2003.
Solinger, Rickie. *Beggars and Choosers: How the Politics of Choice Shapes Adoption, Abortion, and Welfare in the United States.* New York: Hill and Wang Publishing Company, 2001.
Song, Jesook. *South Koreans in the Debt Crisis: The Creation of a Neoliberal Welfare Society.* Durham: Duke University Press, 2009.
Sontag, Susan. *On Photography.* New York: Farrar, Strauss & Giroux, 1977.

Suh, Jae-Jung. "Truth and Reconciliation in South Korea: Confronting War, Colonialism, and Intervention in Asia Pacific." *Critical Asian Studies* 42, no. 4 (2010): 503–524.

Suh, Yi-Jong. *Int'ŏnet k'omyunit'I wa hanguk sahoe* [Internet communities and Korean society]. Seoul: Hanul Academy, 2003.

Taylor, Diana. *The Archive and the Repertoire: Performing Cultural Memory in the Americas*. Durham: Duke University Press, 2003.

Vickery, Martha. "Reunions: The Task of Finding." *Korean Quarterly* 8, no. 2 (2004).

Wegar, Katarina. *Adoption, Identity, and Kinship: The Debate over Sealed Birth Records*. New Haven: Yale University Press, 1997.

Whang, Bum-Ju. *Fifty year History of Holt Children's Services, Inc.* Seoul: Holt International Children's Services, 2005.

Yang, Myung Ji. "The Making of the Urban Middle Class in South Korea (1961 – 1979): Nation-Building, Discipline, and the Birth of the Ideal National Subjects," *Sociological Inquiry* 82, no. 3 (2012): 424–445.

Yngvesson, Barbara. *Belonging in an Adopted World*. Chicago: University of Chicago Press, 2010.

Yoon, Mi Hyun and Jae Yeon Lee. "Characteristics of Teenaged Unwed Mothers in Korea." *Korean Journal of Child Studies* 23, no. 3 (2002): 149–167.

Yoon, Soo Hui. "*Holt'ŭ adong pokchihoe, holt'ŭ myŏngyet'oeim, changgigŭnsok wit'angmo suyŏsik*," (Honoring Retiring Foster Mothers), *News1*, December 5, 2014.

Yuh, Ji-Yeon. *Beyond the Shadow of Camptown: Korean Military Brides in America*. New York: New York University Press, 2002.

Yuval-Davis, Nira. *Gender and Nation*. London: Sage Publications, 1997.

Zamichow, Nora. "Searching for Missing Pieces of a Painful Past." *Los Angeles Times* (Los Angeles, CA), November 28, 2004.

Index

A

abortion. *See also* oral history collection, accounts of
  as self-regulating mechanism, 83
  in camptowns, 50
  laws against, 83
  maternity homes and, 92, 105n31
  rape and, 60
  rate in South Korea, 83

Ach'im Madang (tv show), 115, 119, 121, 126, 131

adoptees
  activism by, 102n3, 190
  as adults, 164
  birth family search, 115
  dual citizenship and, 190, 219n2
  identity formation of, 4
  media coverage of, 116
  names and, 221n24
  neoliberal resignification of, 117
  as orphans, 4, 7, 50

  See also mixed-race children; transnational adoption practice
  domestic, 42, 64, 80, 82, 94, 146, 162–4, 219n5
  interracial, 42
  proxy, 173
  triad, 202

adoption agencies
  birth mothers' experiences with, 171
  loopholes and, 7
  and maternity homes, 25, 84, 85, 98, 99
  orphan production, 97
  picture exchanges, 183n41
  post-adoption services of, 175
  recruitment by, 49
  restriction of information by, 203
  as surrogate child welfare, 43
  technologies of control used by, 203

Note: Page number followed by 'n' refers to endnotes.

adoption decision
American Dream ideology and, 134
"a better life", 15, 95
as best future for child, 156
birth mothers' involvement in, 25, 200, 201, 203, 217
contributing factors, 38, 66. *See also* domestic violence; oral history collection, accounts of; disabilities/special needs, 38, 196; divorce, 205; economic hardship, 15; illegitimacy, 57; racial discrimination, 164; social stigma, 56; survival needs, 199; twins, 74n68, 196
exclusion of birth mother in, 203
long-term effects of, 204
as motherly love, 94
online accounts of, 154
parental obstruction in, 198
reasons for choosing domestic adoption, 163–4
role of adoption agencies in, 49
role of patriarchy in, 203
adoption discourse. *See also* search and reunion narrative
challenges to, 177, 191, 218
DNA and, 121, 123–5
emphasis on poverty, 177
exclusion of excess population in, 138
family separation and, 131, 133
normalizing role of, 116
as a regulatory technology, 157, 160, 161
shame and guilt in, 129
television's role in, 118
US military intervention in, 10
Adoption Special Law (ipyang t'ŭklyepŏp), 96
Ae Ran Won (maternity home), 19, 83, 84, 95, 106n38

affect
adoption loss and, 14
affect-driven analysis, 16
citizenship and, 130
motherhood and, 119
narrative of shame, 129
recognition, 191
technological mediation of, 136, 137
traumatic affect, 118
The Affective Turn (Clough), 12
Agamben, Giorgio, 39
Ahmed, Sara, 129–31, 157
alienation. *See under* birth mothers
American Dream, 44, 134
Anagnost, Ann, 9, 137
apparatuses (term), 17, 18, 119, 137
Archive and Repertoire (Taylor), 193
Armstrong, Charles, 39
Asian Financial Crisis, 39, 141n12
ASK (Adoptee Solidarity Korea), 219n2
assemblage (term), 12, 21, 30n33
Australia, 40
Austria, 40

B
Bae, Eun Kyung, 54, 73n52
Baek, Yeon Ok, 22n59
Bagga-Raoulx, Rupa, 94
Barad, Karen, 17, 18
Barthes, Roland, 166–7
Bauman, Brian Sungduk, 141n12
Belgium, 40, 209
Benjamin, Walter, 21
biopolitics, 11, 14, 80, 85, 86. *See also* Foucault, Michel
birth mothers
absence in critical adoption scholarship, 4
activism by, 5
active labor by, 165

and adoptive parents, 134, 165; gratitude toward, 213
alienation; from adoption knowledge, 203; from informed consent, 6; natal-, 9, 201–4, 209, 217; prenatal, 81, 100; self-, 206–9
categories of, 79; two figures of, 2–3
counterhistory, 26
and class, 58
experiences with adoption agencies, 171
language and, 135
legal erasure of, 8, 9
letter collections, 81, 95
lived paradox of, 192, 217, 218
maternal citizenship of, 125, 126, 129, 130
modalities of becoming, 14
as remainders of loss, 192
reunion with child, 209; impact of financial hardship on, 212; language difficulties in, 214, 215; and loss, 164, 209, 218; as painful, 152, 161; as relief, 98; shame and, 119, 129, 158, 160, 205
sacrifice of own mothering, 134, 137
self-regulation of reproduction, 38, 54, 86
single mothers; agency of, 106n38; as *mihonmo*, 6, 79, 93, 100; social stigma against, 26, 28n7, 67, 83, 88, 93, 145, 149, 151, 154, 199, 206; as source of children in transnational adoption, 55; as subjects of research, 93; two figures of, 3; as widows, 37, 38

on television, 22, 118
terms, 5, 11, 12, 15, 151
in the US, 6
as virtual, 13, 16, 119, 201
as virtuous, 11
younger cohort of, 145
Bohr, Neils, 17
Bombyk, Marti, 103n10
Brian, Kristi, 203
Brink, Susanne, 116, 140n6, 141n12
Butler, Judith, 218

C
Cacho, Lisa M., 9
Cadbury, George, 51
Camp Humphreys, 47
camptown purification movement, 46
camptowns. *See kijich'on*
Child Placement Services (*adongyanghohoe*), 45
Cho, Bok Soon (birth mother), 196, 197, 206, 208, 209, 213, 214, 223n64, 224n71
Cho, Grace M., 70n6, 103n4
Choi, Chungmoo, 133
Choi, Hee Sun (single mother), 88, 89, 91, 92, 94, 97–9, 106n38, 106n39
Cho, Soon Ok, 115, 119–30, 132–4, 136, 137. *See also* de Bruijin, Nina
Christian Adoption Program of Korea (CAPOK), 42
Christian Children's Fund (CCF), 41, 44
Christian Crusader, 42
Christianity, 44, 92, 101
See also foreign aid

Christian Reformed Church of
    Michigan, 42
Christian Reform Korean Mission, 42
Chun, Byung Hoon, 69n4
Chun, Doo-hwan, 39
Chun, Wendy H., 148, 149
Church World Service, 42
Clough, Patricia, 12
Cold War, 10, 14, 44, 45, 51, 66
Concerned United Birthparents
    (CUB), 5
Connerton, Paul, 118, 119
Conquergood, Dwight, 19
contract marriage, 49, 73n44
Coulter, Myrl, 6
CUB (Concerned United
    Birthparents), 5
Cvetkovich, Ann, 191

D
Daily Economics, 84
Dawson, Toby, 141n12
de Bruijin, Nina, 119
    ambivalence of, 15, 91, 145, 151,
        161, 165, 190, 213
    contact with birth mother, 164,
        171, 210
    DNA tests and, 121, 123, 124
    as Lee Jung Soon, 120
    reunion with birth mother, 136
Deleuze, Gilles, 30n33
developmental nationalism,
    role in justifying lack of
    social services, 40
discrimination, against
    mixed-race, 45
divorce, custody law, 8, 38
domestic violence. *See also* oral history
        collection, accounts of
    institutional complicity in, 61
    justice system and, 76n84, 76n88
    rates of, 61

role in transnational adoption, 16,
    38, 60
social acknowledgment of, 139
Dorow, Sara, 75n75
Draper Committee, 51
Durebang, 20, 47, 191
Duri Home, 83

E
Eastern Children's Welfare Society,
    42, 84. *See also* Eastern Social
    Welfare Society
Eastern Social Welfare Society, 72n24,
    105n24
economic development, as
    anticommunism, 51
Edwards, Christine E., 104n20
Eisenhower, Dwight, 51
Eng, David, 10, 192
Esther's Home, 99

F
family
    and excess population, 37
    kinship support and class, 63
    normative, 5, 10, 15, 53,
        54, 60, 68, 83, 125,
        165, 177
    patriarchal family law, 16
    patriarchal kinship, 58, 118
    as self-reliant, 37, 38, 54, 67
    as unreliable, 60
Family Frames (Hirsch), 167
Family Law revision, 62
family planning policy, 37, 38,
    51–68. *See also* family;
    foreign aid
    child welfare, 67
    impact on fertility rate, 52
    maternal duty, 218
    as national defense, 52

as part of economic development, 51–66
as rationale for lack of social services, 63
role in economic marginalization of women, 53
transnational adoption, 25, 37, 66–8
foreign aid
  donor countries, 40
  fundraising, 41, 44
  impact on; adoption law, 42; family planning policy, 25, 37, 66; national welfare budget, 72n25; transnational adoption practice, 67
  and the Korean war, 44
  as missionary work, 40
  missions of, 42
  withdrawal from South Korea, 43, 44
foster care, 42, 43, 50, 98, 201, 202
Foster Parents' Plan, 41
Foucault, Michel, 22, 23, 80, 85, 86, 148, 149
France, 40, 87, 88, 197, 198, 202, 204, 209, 213–15
From Orphan to Adoptee (Pate), 71n16

G
Gailey, Christine W., 8, 9, 29n16, 203
Gender and Nation (Yuval-Davis), 125
Germany, 40
Glenn, Evelyn Nakano, 12, 13
Global Overseas Adoptees' Link (G.O.A.'L.), 210
  campaigns by, 60, 219n2
  English classes, 58
  role in author's research, 58
  services of, 191
Grandmother Kang (birth mother), 46–50
Guattari, Felix, 30n33
Guenther, Lisa, 203

H
Haessal Sahoepokchihoe (Sunlit Sisters' Center), 20, 47, 191
Halley, Jean, 30n34
Han, Hyun Sook, 50
Han, Sang Soon, 105n31, 106n38
heterotopia (definition), 22–3, 148–9
Hirsch, Marianne, 167
hojuk, 58
hojuje, 57, 80, 220n21
Holt Adoption Placement, 42, 49, 186n65
Holt, Bertha, 45
Holt, Harry, 45
Holt International Children's Service, 42, 84, 197
House of Mary (*Maliaŭi Chip*), 83
How Societies Remember (Connerton), 118
Hubinette, Tobias, 69n4, 80, 81, 104n17, 126, 130
Human Reproduction of Korean Modernity (Bae), 54
Hye Rim Won, 85

I
ilmin-jui (ideology), 50
Im Soon Ja (birth mother), 46–50, 212
In Ae Welfare Center, 99
International Korean Adoptee Associations (IKAA), 219n2
International Planned Parenthood Federation (IPPF), 51, 52, 73n55
International Social Services— USA, 42
Internet
  as a site of resistance, 146
  as a site of virtual mothering, 146
  as skin of connectivity, 167
  technologies, 149

internet cafés, 24, 139, 145–7, 149, 150, 153, 162, 164, 167, 178n1, 178n3, 178n4, 189, 191, 206. *See also* A Sad Love Story of Mothers
  as adoption resource center, 173
  for birth mothers, 16, 22, 26
  as self-advocacy, 152, 177
  as self-empowerment, 173
I Want to Meet This Person. *See Ach'im Madang*
I Wish You a Beautiful Life, 95

J
Jang Yeon Ja (birth mother), 20, 62–4, 197, 198
Jones, Stacy H., 150
Jung Yoon Sook (birth mother), 64–6, 199, 213, 216
Jun Hae Rin (birth mother), 98

K
Kazanjian, David, 192
KBS (Korean Broadcasting Systems, Inc), 122, 139n2, 140
Kennedy, John F., 51
kijich'on, 25, 46–50, 60, 101, 102, 138
Kim, Chong Sook, 141n12
Kim, Dae Jung, 128
Kim, Do Hyun, 219n6
Kim, Dong-choon, 39
Kim, Eleana, 50, 80, 124
Kim, Eunshil, 83
Kim, Ji Yeol, 55
Kim, Jodi, 8–9, 29n17, 100, 201, 221n34
Kim Joo Hee (birth mother), 199, 202
Kim So Jung (birth mother), 208
Kim, Soon Hyung, 76n87
Kim, Suk-Young, 193, 220n12
Kim Sun Ae (birth mother), 58–60, 202, 206, 216
Kim Sung Hee (birth mother), 196, 202, 205, 209, 223n62, 224n84
Klein, Christina, 44
Korea Association of Voluntary Agencies (KAVA), 71n13
Korean Broadcasting Systems. *See* KBS
Korean War. *See also* foreign aid
  armistice to, 39, 41
  beginning of, 37
  as excuse for securitization, 25
  as justification for transnational adoption, 39
  orphans, 1, 2, 44
  as a political mechanism, 38
  separated families, 117
Korean Women's Development Institute, 55, 74n71, 93, 108n48
Korea Social Service, 42, 120
Korea Women's Hotline, 61, 75n75
KoRoot (*Ppuriuijip*), 191, 219n6
Kyunghyang Daily, 29n15

L
Langellier, Kristin, 147
Law Against Morally Depraved Behaviors (*yullakhaengwi pangjibŏp*), 46, 90, 91
Lee, Bong Ju, 7, 28n12
Lee, Jung Soon. *See* de Bruijin, Nina
Lee, Keun Ho, 197
Lee, Kyung Ae, 98
Lee, Mi Sun (birth mother), 57, 58, 75n77, 207, 210–12, 215, 223n64
Lee, Soon Hyung, 61
Lee, Soon Young (birth mother), 87–90, 92, 96, 98, 99, 202, 204, 210–13, 223n64

Lee, Won Man, 55–6
Los Angeles Times, 55
love motels, 221n37

M

Massumi, Brian, 12, 194
maternity homes, 16, 22
   background of, 68
   as biopolitical security apparatus, 81
   Christianity and, 92
   conditional admission policy of, 91
   government regulation of, 81, 91
   motherland tours and, 94
   orphan production, 97
   regulation of single mothers in, 100
   relationship with adoption agencies, 84, 90, 94, 97, 99, 170
   role in patriarchy, 22
   as site of population management, 80
   subjectification of birth mothers in, 81
   sex education in, 99
   terms used, 103n8
   in the US, 104n20, 202
McClintock, Anne, 138
methodology, 15, 18, 119. *See also* affect; oral history collection; performance and performativity;
   analysis of nationalism and gender politics, 15
   data collection, 19–21
   methodological dilemmas, 4, 14, 94, 136, 161
   translation and, 21
mihonmo. *See* birth mothers
Militarized Modernity (Moon), 53
Mindullae (Dandelion), 191, 197

Ministry of Gender Equality and Family, 76n84
Ministry of Health and Welfare, 27n1, 41, 72n40
Min, Yeh Jin (birth mother), 189
mixed-race children
   as proportion of all transnational adoptions, 46
   racism against, 50
   as rescue mission, 42
   social treatment of, 46
Moon, Seungsook, 53, 68, 125
Morning Forum. *See* Ach'im Madang
mothering. *See also* virtual mothering
   affective, 119
   biogenetic, 119, 126
   conventions of, 23
   definitions of, 12–13
   developmental, 119
   enactment of, 16
   performance of, 150
   sites of, 149
motherland trips, 11, 109n51
Muñoz, José Esteban, 148, 179n11
Musings of a Ghost Mother (Reyman), 206

N

Nafzger, Amy Inja, 210
Netherlands, 40, 115, 122, 134, 141n16, 209
NGOs, 44, 51, 86. *See also* foreign aid organizations
1988 Summer Olympics, 82

O

Oh, Arissa, 41
OKF. *See* Overseas Koreans Foundation

oral history collection. *See also* methodology; performance and performativity
  accounts of; abortion, 56, 60, 86, 87; active waiting, 209; adoption as child abandonment, 204, 206; attempted suicide, 199; depression, 208; domestic violence, 60–1, 200; grief and shame, 204; guilt, 205; marriage, 196; parental obstruction, 198; rape, 57, 60, 62; reunion with child, 211; silence, 206; stigmas against, 206
  birth mother sample, 69–70n5, 191, 223n60
  as a counterhistory, 26
  as a counterpublic, 26, 146, 152, 169, 190, 194
  as a countersite, 148
  as a counter-narrative, 192
  as knowledge production, 19, 96, 190, 192–4
  "lived paradox" framework, 192
  participants as living archives, 193
  as a site of study, 5, 16, 22
  as a site of virtual mothering, 146, 177, 190, 192–4
Oriental Missionary Society, 41
orphanages
  age and adoption, 7, 41, 71n15
  as temporary childcare, 71n15
Overseas Koreans Foundation (OKF), 109n51, 117
Oxford English Dictionary, 11

P

Park, Ae Kyung (birth mother), 199, 200
Park, Chung-hee, 39, 52
Park, Hye Sook (birth mother), 195, 196, 206, 207, 211–13
Park, Kyeyoung, 133
Park, Mi Hee (birth mother), 60–2, 64, 198, 202, 205, 208
Pate, Soojin, 27n3, 43
Patterson, Orlando, 9, 100
Pearl S. Buck Foundation, 42, 47, 49
Pearl S. Buck Welcome House, 44
Pellerin, Fleur, 141n12
performance and performativity. *See also* methodology
  cultural performance of loss, 147
  expressions of mothering, 148
  oral histories, 20, 22, 24, 189, 190
  performance ethnography, 19
  role in knowledge production, 19, 26, 96, 193
  subjugated knowledge, 193
  testimonies, 191
photography, loss and, 166
Planned Parenthood Federation of Korea (PPFK), 51, 52, 54
Pollock, Della, 192, 193
population control. *See* family planning policy
Population Council, 51
Prébin, Elise, 215
prenatal alienation. *See* birth mothers, alienation
Prevention of Domestic Violence Act, 76n88
The Promise of Happiness (Ahmed), 157
Pyeongtaek, 20, 47, 212

R

reality search shows. *See* television search and reunion shows
reunion. *See under* birth mothers
Reyman, Lynne, 206, 207

Rhee, Syngman, 45
Rhew, Dahl Yeong, 51, 52
Robinson, Katy, 55
Rockefeller, John D., III, 51
Roe v. Wade, 222n41

S
Sad Love Story of Mothers. *See also* internet café
  accounts of adoption decision on, 22
  baby photographs in, 26, 162
  collective experience of loss, 170
  as a counterpublic, 146, 152, 169
  criticism of birth fathers on, 184n59
  as cultural performance, 147
  fantasies of reunion on, 159–60
  foster mother participation, 173
  membership, 147
  photos in, 151; pre-and post- adoption photos, 162, 163, 165; transnational *vs.* domestic adoption, 80, 82, 163; virtual mothering in, 139, 146, 152, 162–8, 177
  screen names, 153
  as site of collective knowledge; adoption process, 173; gifts for adoptive parents, 175
  as a site of resistance, 146
  as a site of virtual mothering, 146
  website sections, 178n4
  virtual intimacy in, 168
  virtual kinship in, 152
Salvation Army Women's Center (*Kusekun Yŏchakwan*), 83
Sarri, Rosemary, 103n10
search and reunion narrative
  apologies in, 126
  and the birth father, 132
  loss as retrievable, 137

normalization of transnational adoption, 138
television technology and, 118, 119, 121, 145
Seo, Chae Rim (birth mother), 91, 99
sex workers. *See* kijich'on women
Shin, Ho Bum, 141
Shin, Young Eun (birth mother), 35, 36, 63, 64, 200, 205, 207, 210, 213–16
Shin, Yu-Suk. *See* Brink, Susanne
single mothers. *See* birth mothers
Single Square Picture (Robinson), 55
Sisters of the Good Shepherd, 83
Smelser, Neil, 118
social death
  concept of, 9
  mechanisms of, 8–10, 201, 203
  misrecognition, 9
  as nonliving, 100
  resistance to, 146
  rightlessness, 9
social governance, institutions involved in, 102
social memory, 118
Social Welfare Society (SWS), 42, 84
Solinger, Rickie, 200
Song, Jesook, 86
Soo Yeon, 202
South Korea
  adoption recruitment by, 49
  child welfare program, 36, 37, 40, 41, 43, 51
  civil liberties in, 40
  class in, 63
  collective amnesia about birth mothers, 4
  collective memory of birth mothers, 3
  development agenda, 10, 131
  developmental state formation, 39

South Korea (*cont.*)
  economic development and
    transnational adoption, 14, 36,
    38, 52, 117, 138
  ethnic nationalism, 3, 26
  Global Korea, 137, 138
  institutions of, 37, 41, 43
  legislation, adoption law, 80
  militarized prostitution in, 50
  national budget of, 43
  national security priorities of,
    37–40, 50, 52, 116
  national shame, 82
  neoliberal state, 10, 14, 15, 39
  orphanages in, 84
  perceptions of United States, 204
  reliance on foreign aid
    organizations, 37, 41
  social welfare; development of, 43;
    policy of, 10, 16, 37, 40;
    stance toward, 136
  stance toward mixed-race children,
    45–6, 50, 55
  stigma against "illegitimate"
    children, 56
  transnational adoption history of,
    36, 82
  US perceptions of, 134
Special Adoption Law, 6, 220n6
*Special Law on Adoption Promotion
  and Procedure (ipyang chokchin
  mich' chŏlch'ae kwanhan
  tŭklyepŏp)*, 96
state of exception (term), 39
Status of Forces Agreement
  (SOFA), 49
Suh, Jae-Jung, 39
Susanne Brink's 'Arirang'
  (documentary), 140n7
Sweden, 40, 116, 162
Swedish International Development
  Agency, 52
SWS. *See* Social Welfare Society

T
Taylor, Diana, 180n19, 193
television search and reunion shows,
  16, 19, 22, 115
  participants as working class, 63, 133
  production of, 121–2, 126–7
television technology, 121
3.3.35 campaign, 52
TRACK. *See* Truth and Reconciliation
  for the Adoptee Community
  in Korea
transnational adoption practice
  as an act of US patriotism, 46
  as baby export business, 82
  the Cold War and, 45
  consent in, 6, 56
  economic development and, 36,
    51, 52
  economic marginalization of
    women, 53
  "excess" children and, 10, 25, 37,
    38, 45–6, 55–60, 66–8, 80, 96,
    98, 102, 117
  as family planning, 37, 52–4, 64,
    66–8, 79
  growth in, 36, 84
  humanitarian market, 37, 43, 44
  market aspects of, 10
  military violence and, 4
  orphan imagery in, 44
  as population control, 79, 80
  as population removal policy,
    50, 66
  role of patriarchy in, 58
  salvation narrative of, 4, 10, 14
  as social governance, 25, 79–81, 89,
    99, 101, 102, 145, 157
  and South Korea's social welfare
    policy, 10, 37, 40, 53, 67, 83,
    101
  sponsorship adoption, 41, 44
  Western colonialism and, 4
Trenka, Jane Jeong, 20

Truth and Reconciliation for the Adoptee Community in Korea (TRACK), 20, 219n2

U
Uijeongbu, 47
UN Family Planning Agency, 73n55
United States
　benevolent image of, 43, 44
　Cold War policies of, 37, 44, 45, 51
　economic and cultural dominance, 10
　foreign policy, 44
　humanitarianism and, 43
　military and foreign aid, 25, 43
　military occupation of Korea, 43, 46, 50
　military relief efforts of, 44
　as receiver of adoptees, 2
US Agency for International Development, 73n55

V
van Lierop, Eleanor Creswell, 83
Vietnam War, 43
virtual (term), 11–13
virtual intimacy, familial look, 168
virtual mothering. *See also* mothering
　acts of, 26
　affect in, 12, 13
　ambivalence of, 161
　concept of, 5
　dimensions of, 16, 151, 152, 178
　emergence of, 16, 19, 25
　mutual recognition, 167, 168, 170, 176
　other mothering, 22–6
　paradoxes of, 24, 192, 194, 217
　as performative, 5, 149, 194
　phenomenon of, 13
　processes of, 5, 13, 14, 17, 135
　radical finitude of, 137
　shame in, 129
　sites of, 23, 139
　technologically enactive form of, 137
　three stages of, 217
　virtual kinship in, 145–87
virtual mothers. *See also* birth mothers
　appropriation by the state, 135
　as heroic figures, 133
　in the search and reunion narrative, 115–43
　three tropes of, 116
virtue, 11

W
Wegar, Katarina, 28n6
Western Europe, as receiver of adoptees, 128
Where Are We Now? (urinŭn chigŭm-haeoe ibyanga) (documentary), 116
Williams, Christine L., 104n20
World Council of Churches, 51
World Vision, 41

Y
yanggongju (term), 46
Yang, Sook Ja (birth mother), 56–8, 212
Yngvesson, Barbara, 11, 80
Yuh, Ji-Yeon, 133
Yuval-Davis, Nira, 125

The manufacturer's authorised representative in the EU is Springer Nature Customer Service Centre GmbH, Europaplatz 3, 69115 Heidelberg, Germany. If you have any concerns regarding our products, please contact ProductSafety@springernature.com

Printed and bound by CPI Group (UK) Ltd, Croydon, CR0 4YY

23/03/2026

02076682-0004